FULL CIRCLE

A MARINE RIFLE COMPANY IN VIETNAM

by

WILLIAM L. BUCHANAN

Full Circle: A Marine Rifle Company in Vietnam
by William L. Buchanan

Copyright 2003 by William L. Buchanan
Cover design and graphics by RSB Consulting
www.rsb-consulting.com
Edited and Typeset by Bob Spear, Heartland Reviews
www.heartlandreviews.com

ISBN: 1-931093-01-6

Library of Congress Control Number 2003096259

Printed in the United States of America

Published by
Baylaurel Press
Mill Valley, California
www.baylaurelpress.com

This book is for Sgt. Wayne Eugene Dawson, an exemplary squad leader whose untimely death on 19 December 1966 at the hamlet of Thon Bon (1) haunts me to this day. It is also for the gallant men and officers of G Company, 2nd Battalion, 5th Marine Regiment who taught me the true meaning of the term "warrior."

CONTENTS

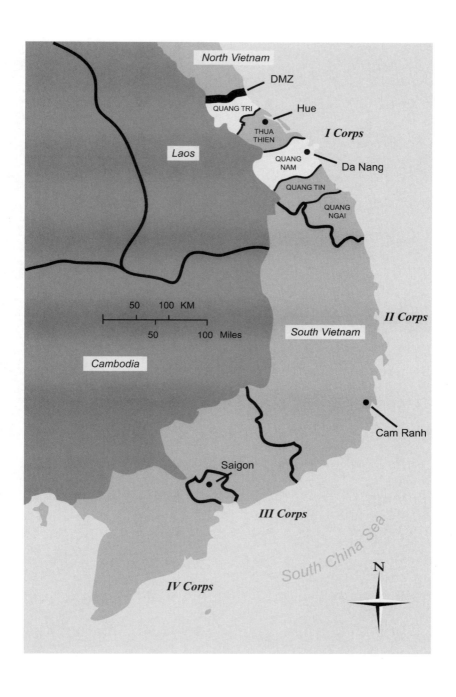

PREFACE

6 April 1967, twelve hours before my departure from the Republic of South Vietnam, I was celebrating at the An Hoa combat base "Club," an olive drab strong-back tent. Halfway through my third Budweiser, I heard a voice chime out through the smoke and noise, "Hey Lieutenant Buchanan. Outside. Someone wants to see you." Well, why the hell don't they come on in, I mused as I stepped out into the thick night air. In the glow of the open door were six or eight enlisted Marines from 2nd Platoon G Company, the unit I commanded before my promotions to company executive officer, then assistant battalion operations officer.

"Good evening, lieutenant," one of them said. "We heard you're leaving tomorrow and we thought we would come on over and just say goodbye and good luck and all that and wish you well."

I took a moment to recover my composure. Then I thanked them for being such a great platoon and encouraged them to continue to develop the fine tactical edge that we had honed so carefully together. We said goodbye and they faded into the night. I left Vietnam the next day. That was over 36 years ago. I've forgotten much about the war and the role I played in it, first as a platoon commander of an anti-tank unit, and then an infantry unit—2nd Platoon G Company, 2nd Battalion, 5th Marine Regiment: radio call sign "Cassandra Golf Two." What I have not forgotten and will carry with me always is the image of those

Marines standing in reflected light outside the Club at An Hoa and the many images this book pulls into sharper focus: a young Marine rifleman apologizing for getting hit; a machine gun team breaking the back of an ambush with a stream of luminous steel from an M-60; a staff sergeant platoon commander charging an enemy position as if it was the end zone at a touch football game; a platoon sergeant leading an assault across a manioc field through heavy fire at my command; a dying squad leader's last words.

And why, you wonder, did it take 36 years to put pen to paper about those experiences? The answer is it took that long to find the words—the right words and the right format. There were catalysts along the way, although I didn't recognize them as such at the time. In March 1987, The San Francisco Chronicle published an op-ed piece of mine called *What's Wrong with "Platoon"?* It took issue with Oliver Stone's portrayal of infantrymen as dope smoking, incompetent, rapacious, homicidal maniacs, and the media's embrace of the movie as "The Truth About Vietnam." Two weeks later the paper forwarded a letter written by Marine Captain John Bates in San Bruno, California, a short drive south of San Francisco. Bates claimed we had served together in Vietnam. Over lunch we confirmed John was the private first class rifleman who inspired an entry scribbled in my platoon commander's notebook dated 17 December 1966:

A fallen warrior lying on still disputed sand stained red from a twice-wounded lung, raised his bloodied face and made apology for his condition and for letting me, his lieutenant, down so miserably in his first battle. Selflessness, sacrifice, courage, are weak words to describe the stuff such men are made of—not very grammatical, but heartfelt and written by candlelight in my command bunker after a very difficult day in the field.

Another subliminal catalyst imprinted itself when my father, Brigadier General William W. Buchanan, veteran of landings at Iwo Jima, Saipan, Tinian and Roi Namur, died of bone cancer at home in Mountain View, California on May 10, 1996. Priceless stories died with him because I had not taken the time to interview him and write them down. It reminded me the river of time flows relentlessly.

In the late fall of 2001 I returned to Vietnam and visited the combat bases that G Company occupied at Con Thien and An Hoa, as well as parts of the country, including Hanoi, I never had seen before. I was struck by the beauty of the country and the optimism, friendliness, and entrepreneurial fervor of the people, even under the heavy hand of a communist regime. I returned with many photographs, a few souvenirs, and a resolve to write a book. What I did not want to do was write another entirely personal narrative about the war. I could not compete with the excellent memoirs already in circulation.

I chose the title *Full Circle* to convey my sense of people, places and events forming a series of circles within circles: my father's deployment to the Pacific islands in World War II; his return to Asian lands during the Korean War; French military operations against the Viet Minh from 1950 to 1954 that ended with the agony of Dien Bien Phu; my combat tour of duty in Vietnam and a return to the United States, where over twenty years later, I reconnected with John Bates; my return to Vietnam in the fall of 2001.

The reader should note that text in italics represents either verbatim interviews, my personal letters home, or excerpts from official Marine Corps records. My efforts to interview Vietnamese communist soldiers for their perspectives on battles with Marine units failed: e-mails to official Vietnamese guides went unanswered; inquiries at the Socialist Republic of Vietnam consulate in San Francisco produced nothing; requests within the Vietnamese communities in San Jose and Los Angeles, California generated only silence. Draw your own conclusions from that. Consequently, I was forced to recreate the communist battle perspective from intelligence reports, post war military studies, and notes I took in the field. For instance you will meet such a recreation in VC Main Force R-20 Battalion company commander Nguyen Lan in the chapter titled *Ambush at Thon Bon (1)*. The cover design reflects core elements of the major opposing forces during the Vietnam War: to the Vietnamese, bamboo is a cherished symbol of life, especially of youthful vitality, endurance, and faithfulness. The Marine Corps eagle, globe and anchor device represents the immutable traditions of an elite fighting force, the reality of cold steel and overwhelming firepower.

The author intends to contribute 10% of profits from sales of the book to The Marine Corps-Law Enforcement Foundation, Inc. (www.mc-lef.org) a non-profit organization created January 2, 1995 to render educational assistance to children of Marines and federal law enforcement personnel who were killed in the line of duty or died under extraordinary circumstances while serving our country at home or abroad.

On that day in March 1987 when John Bates and I became reacquainted, I sat down to dinner with my wife in Mill Valley, California and went on and on about how much it meant to me to be able to retrace memories after two decades with someone who had walked the same ground. My wordiness was so out of character Claire walked around the table and gave me a big hug, pointing out she had never heard me talk about my experiences in Vietnam, nor much else, with such passion and emotion. The reunion with John had awakened within me a desire to retrace the ground we had covered so long ago, to put names with faces, to reaffirm our abiding conviction that despite public antipathy towards the conflict and those who fought it, media misrepresentations, and revisionist history, we had been worthy warriors who fought well, and at the very least, believed in each other. My reaction convinced me there must be thousands of other Marines with stories to tell, and those stories would die with them as they had with my Dad, if no one provided a medium of expression.

Marines whose reluctance to participate springs from a deep inner pain, a smoldering resentfulness over the outcome of the war, a loss of memory, or whatever reason, now will have a permanent record of a remarkable period in their lives. Even the fallen—those whose voices have been stilled forever—will speak to us from these pages.

These then, are the Marines of G Company, Second Battalion, Fifth Marine Regiment.

CON THIEN

"Military force is the (Communist) Party's essential means for the attainment of any political aim." Vo Nguyen Giap, Viet-Minh Commander-in-Chief in a "Voice of Viet-Nam" broadcast October 1, 1951

Cease fire, cease fire! You're hitting friendlies. Cease fire, cease fire!" I screamed into the ANPRC 25 radio handset. Arcing down from a clear blue sky and detonating twenty meters away, 81-millimeter mortar rounds punctuated my commands with concussive explosions that sent razor-sharp fragments ripping through the vegetation. Both my radioman and I were hunkered prone beside the forest trail like two tortoises, hands and arms tucked beneath our flak jackets, wishing our helmets were big enough to crawl into. Every exposed square inch of flesh seemed ripe for puncture by the flying metal. I could hear Marines screaming as the rounds worked their way along the trail towards us with uncanny accuracy. Through smoke, dust and noise, we heard Captain Gruner's radioman, Rick Wilhite, yelling obscenities, trying to stop the deadly missiles. It was October 21st, 1966, my first combat patrol with G Company, 2nd Battalion, 5th Marine Regiment, and I was receiving my baptism of fire, not from the North Vietnamese, but from our very own 81mm mortar men.

Twenty minutes before the "friendly" mortar attack, our

company of Marines had been making its way in column formation cautiously north along a narrow jungle trail just below the Demilitarized Zone (DMZ) when firing broke out ahead. I deployed my platoon for flank security as best I could, then waited for developments. After the firing subsided, Staff Sergeant Mihalcik, my platoon sergeant, sauntered back down the column with a soggy cigar in his mouth, glanced at the mud on my utilities, and said with a chuckle, "Found some cover, did you lieutenant?" A few minutes later someone from Captain Gruner's command group yelled, "Fire mission: eighty-ones inbound." For some reason, the trajectories from the battalion firebase at Con Thien had converged on us rather than the North Vietnamese. Joe Barry, a nineteen-year-old rifleman from Dover, New Hampshire, was soon to become the squad leader of Second Squad. As he tells it…

"I was close enough to the company commander and the radioman that I could hear him yelling on the radio. He was just trying to stop the barrage, and the company commander was not having any success stopping this guy from swearing. He says something about, 'I'll take a stripe away' or something. Finally, you heard a transmission from the hill and, I mean, it was as clear as a bell … out of a 72 round mission, there's 51 in the air, right? And only 6 had hit at the time and Ski was probably one of the first two or three that got hit. Hit a banana tree and killed him. Ripped his face right off. This Lance Corporal Ski; he had a child on the way only in a couple of days. In fact the night before the patrol he had me put my shelter half together with his; he wanted to talk to me. That's when he told me how he claimed he had either more time in grade or was better, you know, suited to be the squad leader and they were giving it to him. He says, 'Are you upset with me?' and I said, 'No.' And he said, 'Well if I need any help, would you… I know your training was better.' Some guys don't have a lot of training before they get over there. I had a Caribbean cruise, the landings down at Vieques; that's all good training, you know?"

"I happened to be one of the people that carried casualties to the landing zone. And I'm there and I've got my head down, I've got a loaded M79 in one hand and a loaded 45 in the other, both of them cocked. I'm just unbelieving. Then somebody walked by and said, 'Who's this?' It was Ski with a poncho thrown over him. And before I

16

could even open my mouth to say, 'Well, that's Ski,' they lifted the poncho off and you saw a faceless body and the tattoos on his two forearms. They just threw him in the helicopter like a sack of cement. It's pretty shocking, you know; one of your first patrols. Really. It was nobody's fault."

Dan Day, a nineteen-year-old private first class rifleman from St. Louis, Missouri, moved with the company from Chu Lai to Con Thien as part of Sgt. Wayne Dawson's First Squad of the Second Platoon. Corporal Crum was his fire team leader. He remembered the name of the first casualty in this unfortunate incident...

"The NVA shot the point, a black kid from Detroit named Danny Riley. He was a small, wiry guy who had a little bit of an attitude. He bled out very quickly; the blood seemed to go down the trail in this little ribbon only about an inch wide, but about 20 feet long or so. I think he got hit right in the head and he just bled for a long ways down this trail as they carried him. So they called for 81s and I don't think they called for marking rounds. They just let fly with HE and it came right down on a squad that was near us. No adjusting round. They just fired a barrage. They were close, but I was unscathed. I remember a corpsman being hit. He had a huge shrapnel wound in his back. I also remember after it was over, when we walked back up to the hill at Con Thien, all the 81 mortar guys felt bad and they were greeting us at the wire and giving us cans of water and stuff."

The sight of wounded and dead Marines being carried past me towards the rear, their flak jackets and packs lacerated by mortar shrapnel, dark blood pooling onto the ponchos and stretchers, was a sobering introduction to the complexities of ground combat in this war without front lines. In addition to Danny Riley, four Marines lost their lives to our own supporting arms that day and three were wounded. From that point forward, I would spend as much time looking over my shoulder for friendly fire as I did looking ahead for enemy fire.

Four days before that engagement, a CH-46 helicopter had flown me, along with several other Marines, two journalists—one of them a French photojournalist named Catherine Leroy,

17

the other possibly Jack Lawrence, a correspondent for CBS—and pallets of C-rations and ammunition, from Chu Lai, a seaside combat base south of Danang, to Dong Ha, then to the top of Con Thien, a brace of low hills facing the so-called Demilitarized Zone (DMZ) on the northern edge of Quang Tri Province. At altitude, the combat base stood out from the meadows and forest below like a suppurating boil, belying the translation of its Vietnamese name as "Place of Angels." Two and a half miles to the north lay the DMZ and beyond it, North Vietnam. Fourteen miles to the east, warships of the U.S. Seventh Fleet studded the South China Sea. To the southeast lay Quang Tri and Dong Ha, outposts along the "Street without Joy" made famous by Bernard T. Fall, noted chronicler of Vietnamese conflicts. To the west, grassy savannahs woven into a patchwork of rice paddies laced together with hedgerows lay close up against the Annam Mountains.

Once we touched down, I staggered through a whirlwind of red dust, C-ration cartons and ponchos whipped up by the idling rotors and hauled my sea bag to G Company headquarters where I found Captain John Gruner dozing on flattened C-ration cartons under a canopy of poncho liners—hardly what I had expected in the way of office space. The captain sat up and extended his hand.

"Welcome aboard, lieutenant. Where you coming in from?" Gruner was in his late twenties, short, with a sandy-colored flat top.

"Chu Lai, Sir. I had an Ontos platoon on perimeter security at the airfield."

"Well, I'm giving you Second Platoon. Staff Sergeant Mihalcik will show you the positions over on the north side of the hill. It's a squared away outfit, and he knows what he's doing."

As dusk enveloped the hill later that day, Staff Sergeant Mihalcik appeared at my CP carrying a pipe. With him were three squad leaders and the platoon guide. I liked "Sergeant Mack," as the Marines called him, instantly for his avuncular manner and lack of condescension, even though I was a "butter bar" second lieutenant with no field experience in an infantry company. After I introduced myself and summarized my assignments to date, he lit up his pipe and briefed me on the condition of the platoon, the company's operations and the routine on the hill. It was thus I became part of Second Platoon G Company, an outfit I had observed from a distance while participating in combat operations as commander of an anti-tank platoon the previous summer. After the darkness of Con Thien had swallowed up Sergeant Mack and the squad leaders, I settled into my shelter half "hootch" and reflected on the sequence of events that had dropped me into the middle of a rifle company after so many months as platoon commander in an anti-tank battalion. Sleep did not come easily, as I pondered the many challenges that lay ahead: getting to know the platoon sergeant, the squad leaders, and Captain Gruner; learning and applying infantry tactics that had evolved "in country" as the result of engagements with fresh North Vietnamese divisions that had been pouring across the DMZ; negotiating the hills, watercourses, meadows, roads, trails, and jungle of Quang Tri Province; using supporting arms effectively (and safely); and prevailing over well-trained and equipped enemy forces.

The next morning I woke up floating on my air mattress in a small pond with the northeast monsoon beating against my shelter half and my canteen cruising by at eye level. After a C-ration breakfast of turkey loaf, applesauce, and lukewarm coffee, I took a stroll around the double hill and found rudimentary defenses: one roll of concertina, backed by fighting positions that were not sufficiently sandbagged, and way too much distance between the holes. Golf Company positions were on the north side of the hill facing the DMZ. Foxtrot and Hotel Companies were deployed on the other sides. A 105 mm howitzer battery, an 81mm mortar platoon, and two platoons of tanks occupied the flat ground near the crest. It was typical for two companies to operate daily in the field at distances of up to 5000 meters, leaving one company on the hill to improve defenses. The monsoon season was upon us and Marines on the perimeter living under shelter halves, with their fighting holes a few yards away from the concertina, complained of the growing cold at night.

Joe Barry, the new Second Squad leader, didn't have the luxury of a helicopter ride. He arrived at Con Thien on "shank's mare"…

"When I arrived in country in September of '66 it was at Chu Lai… and there was some Marines there that greeted me. I guess they thought I was a replacement for the airstrip there and they were telling me, you know, things aren't too bad around here; the worst thing that happens is we get rocketed now and then. You just run out to the hole and you'll be all right. Somebody finally got around to asking me, 'What do your orders say?' And I said Golf Company 2/5 and they just looked at me like there was a white sheet over my face. Like I was already dead."

"I joined Second Platoon at Chu Lai, and we flew up there in C130s, something like that. We landed at Dong Ha and when we got there, we did a forced march from Dong Ha to Con Thien and I think it took about a week, you know, time distorts things. And we were getting action every day and at night we would dig in. In fact, you had to use your entrenching tool, the pick end of it, to get down as best you could because you knew you were going to get mortared every night by 60mm mortars. Every night we dug a hole for three guys. All three of us got in it and the last guy would pull the flak jackets over the top.

"My first firefight happened on the march from Dong Ha to Con Thien. We were advancing and as an unblooded Marine, I didn't even know incoming from outgoing. You just hear when they're getting close to you and then you can hear those zings and see the dirt kicking up around you. I looked up and I saw an enemy soldier hanging from a tree in a net. And here I am, instead of just shooting him, I'm new; I said, 'I see one, I see one,' and somebody else says, 'Don't just say you see one, shoot him!' He was out probably 50 yards and up in the trees and had a good view of all of us. He was picking us off. You could see he just slumped in the net after I shot him and then I wanted to get up close. You know, I just killed somebody. As we advanced, and the shooting slowed down, I guess what had happened; the NVA, they left him. He's dead, and the rest of them are bugging out. And I went under a barbed wire fence and then the order was given to—we were just pulling back. And here I am out quite a ways in front of other people, so I had to rush to get back under that fence, because what if

the enemy pulls right back in and my guys are gone: I'm a prisoner. A week in country, you know?"

While manning his position on the north side of the hill, Corporal Barry was witness to another "friendly fire" incident...

"My squad was facing a listening post (LP) on Con Thien near where we would leave on these big patrols. There was an opening there in the concertina and we would unfasten a wire and go out. By then the concertina was three rows high. We were probed one night and the guy on the tank got nervous and fired a beehive canister with the barrel level and shot the LP. The LP was a black kid, and his leg was just swollen right up two, three times the size. The medic was working on him, you know, trying to... I don't remember if he died or not."

"We ate C rats all the time, which I really don't remember complaining about. In fact, whenever we did have a hot meal, and I don't know if we did there at all—we may have—when you did, it messed with your insides. Your body gets used to the C rats, then you're given a hot meal. Now you got the runs, you know. Another thing is what little water we had on the hill—one canteen per day. It was almost a relief to go on patrol so we could drink out of the rivers and streams."

One morning Joe and another Marine decided to "police up" the Second Platoon sector of the line in accordance with Marine housekeeping doctrine.

"At Con Thien we were being probed and we'd throw grenades. We had quite a few duds. I think there was eight duds out of 13 or something. One of the guys I was friendly with says, 'Come on outside.' So I went outside the wire with him. He would grab each grenade with no spoon on it like it was an egg. He'd shake it and then hand it back to me. I had eight of them and I brought them to Lieutenant Buchanan's CP. Well, we didn't know what to do with them and I'm new, and he's been there for a while. Unbelievable."

Dan Day, the First Squad rifleman, had a similar experience with uncooperative ordnance...

"One night, they probed us and an NVA soldier tripped a flare. It

*scared the shit out of him and he started yelling in Vietnamese. We
didn't want to give away our whole firing position, so we threw
grenades. All 11 grenades that we threw at that guy were duds. The
one good thing that came out of it was that they took all of our old
ammo and we got a resupply. I think it was from walking through so
many streams up there at the 'Z'. Somehow, either it was bad ammo
from World War II or bad grenades. It was really unbelievable, eleven
grenades that were duds."*

On a combat patrol one day, Sergeant Arthur Morrill, the
Third Platoon right guide, and Corporal Charles Mohney were
stunned by an even more bizarre approach to disposal of dud
ordinance. A 250-pound bomb, or a 16 inch shell fired by one of
the U.S. warships off the coast had failed to detonate on impact
and was lying in the middle of the trail. The platoon commander,
a lieutenant whose name has been obliterated mercifully by the
mists of time, ordered the Marines of Third Platoon to hoist the
ordinance on their shoulders and hump it back to the hill.
According to Corporal Mohney, the platoon sergeant slipped
away with the radioman and reported the situation to Captain
Gruner, the company commander. Gruner ordered the lieutenant
to leave the shell alone and prepare for helicopter extraction.
The helicopter arrived, but the only person to board it was the
lieutenant, who subsequently was assigned to battalion
headquarters.

Marc Glasgow, a solidly built 25 year-old Lieutenant from
Pittsburgh, Pennsylvania, with A Company, Ninth Engineers,
responded to a call for volunteers to replace junior officers who
had become casualties in the summer battles of 1966—
Operations Hastings and Prairie near the DMZ—by reporting
in to 2/5 at Chu Lai along with three other lieutenants. They
arrived at Con Thien by helicopter in late October or early
November. Captain Gruner assigned Glasgow to the Third
Platoon, which had been without an officer platoon commander
since its lieutenant had been hit by "friendly mortar fire."
Glasgow's first patrol was instructive. As he tells it...

*"On the first patrol we were to go up along the road that ran
northeast. So I just kind of sat back and let the sergeant who I just met
organize the patrol. We went out the east gate. Little did I know, we*

were not going north. I kept looking at the sun and saying, 'Jeez, we're going the wrong way.' Well, then I found out midway in the patrol that the sergeant couldn't read a goddamned map. Boy, I had to take charge real quick and get swung up around to the north side of the hill and complete the patrol route. I could tell, you know, just from training and compasses we were going the wrong way. I kept asking him, 'Why are we going this way?' And then I realized he couldn't read a map. So there was a long time before I radioed in checkpoints to Captain Gruner and that was on purpose because we were trying to get back on the right track. But we finally made it back and that was my first patrol. Nothing happened, fortunately."

In no time, Lieutenant Glasgow and his new platoon became an effective combat team…

"We used to patrol constantly, come off the hill going north, and then there was a road that paralleled the Ben Hai River back by the DMZ line and went northeast. It goes out to the coast to Cua Viet or someplace. We pulled many patrols up that way, either company patrols or platoon patrols. We'd go up that way and I remember finding remnants of 1/26, I believe, from the SLF, one of the regular battalions of the 26th Marines. There was pieces of 782 gear, helmets. There were tremendous bomb craters with pieces of an NVA buckle and 782 gear down in the holes, big holes. You know, it must have been heavy bombs. I don't think they were Arc Lights, there weren't that many, but they were big bombs they dropped." [Operation Arc Light was a tactical bombing campaign carried out by B-52 bombers against enemy troop concentrations and positions.]

"The first time I personally saw the NVA, we were out there on a platoon patrol going up that road. It was early in the morning and I saw them through the jungle on another trail. It must have been maybe twenty yards through the jungle; I saw troops going the other way. And my thought was, 'Man, somebody screwed up. They got two patrols within 20 yards going the other way and nobody knows the other's here.' And my thought process wasn't finished when I heard a bolt go home. They were NVA with gear hanging on them. They did a right face, we did a right face. Everybody blew up a magazine and nobody got hit on either side. It was a squad, because I was right behind my first squad and they were from the point all the way back to my platoon command group. And when the shooting was all over, nobody

got hit. I was just amazed, but more or less in shock. I thought they were Marines."

Dan Day's baptism by fire occurred during one of the frequent patrols around the combat base...

"We were on one of those long patrols all day. We hadn't had much contact at all, but that night we were digging in and it was kind of rocky and hilly there. It was real hard to dig in, because we were so exhausted. Madruca and Crum told me, 'You gotta dig in. You gotta dig in.' I finally dug out a little foxhole and got myself into it. Then that night somebody, maybe a Marine in H &S, or 81s says, 'Oh, look! A shooting star.' Then I said, 'That's not a shooting star. It's incoming.' So sure enough, it was North Vietnamese 82s and they were walking them in toward us. That was my first experience with enemy fire and I'll tell you, it was very unnerving. I was in that hole and they kept getting so loud, you know, as the fins swished through the air, and boom! Boom! It's getting louder. They're walking them toward us. It seemed like about ten of them. Then all of a sudden it stopped; but I was so nervous because that was my first experience being mortared— I was shaking. Madruca says to me, 'Hey, Day! Quit shaking. You're making me nervous.' So then I quit. Somebody called for counter battery fire with 81s but Gunny Mayberry, who was a Korean War vet, said, 'No, use 60s not 81s.' He thought the 81s would give our exact position away, because of the bigger flash and the louder report. So they did. They fired 60's at where they thought the 82s were coming from and then things quieted down."

On another combat patrol, Day learned something about the rules of engagement...

"On 1 November I was on point. We started into a ville and I saw a man with a gray uniform on. Now I'm brand new. I'm not very experienced. This guy started running away from me and I drew down on him with my M14 on full automatic with bipods on. But my team leader stopped me because he was surrounded by women and children, so he got away. Since he was surrounded by civilians, it really was the right thing to do."

Compared to the battalion and regimental dust-ups that started in July with Operation Hastings and rolled on into

September with Operation Prairie, the area was ominously quiet. Had we mauled the NVA battalions that badly then, or were they using the western mountains to skirt Con Thien, doing an end run to the Central Highlands where they could marshal their troops for attacks on the allied forces? Our daily patrols typically resulted in encounters with small bands of enemy soldiers. As I sat on an ammo box near my CP one afternoon watching the setting sun paint the coastline with pastel hues, I realized the bitterly contested terrain I was surveying was not exactly unfamiliar to me...

My first visit to the area had been in July as part of Battalion Landing Team (BLT) 3/5 (Third Battalion Fifth Marine Regiment) that had been designated part of a Special Landing Force (SLF). Then I had been platoon commander of an Ontos anti-tank platoon on board the Landing Ship Dock (LSD) U.S.S. Alamo. The Ontos was a light tracked vehicle carrying six 106mm recoilless rifles. Since the NVA rarely used tanks, its deployment in Vietnam proved to be mainly defensive. Although there were instances where the terrain permitted integration into infantry operations, most commanders were not inclined to risk being bogged down by broken tracks or other mechanical uncertainties. Therefore, most of our assignments were perimeter defense and convoy security.

What triggered our thrust into this vulnerable area was in May 1966, infrared films taken by Marine photoreconnaissance aircraft flying over the DMZ at first produced black film plates, then later, film plates with little white dots. Photo interpreters identified the dots as NVA cook fires and estimated each dot represented ten soldiers. When the dots multiplied on subsequent plates, the conclusion was the jungle south of the DMZ was swarming with NVA troops; so much for North Vietnamese adherence to provisions of the 1954 Geneva Convention.

By late June, reconnaissance Marines from the 4th Marine Regiment operating in Quang Tri Province around Cam Lo and Dong Ha encountered...

Armed, uniformed groups and no patrol was able to stay in

25

the field for more than a few hours, many for only a few minutes. Reports of this activity brought a skeptical Third Marine Amphibious Force Commander (III MAF) General Lew Walt to the scene. But after talking to the reconnaissance teams, one of which was still in its jungle garb, having been extracted under fire minutes before General Walt's arrival, he apparently decided there was something to the rumor that the NVA was crossing the DMZ.[1]

A fortuitous break occurred On 9 July 1966 when a South Vietnamese paratroop battalion operating near a cone-shaped terrain feature along the Cam Lo River nicknamed the "Rockpile", surprised elements of a platoon-sized reconnaissance team from the 812th Regiment of the NVA 324B Division. When the smoke cleared, an NVA lieutenant walked out of the jungle with his hands over his head. The South Vietnamese turned him over to U.S. intelligence officers who learned the mission of his division was to "liberate Quang Tri Province" and block any reinforcing ARVN units from moving north.

This intelligence nugget convinced the Marine high command as well as General Westmoreland a major effort was needed to find, fix, and destroy the infiltrating units. Westmoreland launched B-52 raids on the DMZ and directed Third Marine Amphibious Force (III MAF) commander General Lewis Walt to move up to a division of Marines supported by the Seventh Fleet Special Landing Force (SLF) into Quang Tri Province to lock horns with and destroy the NVA. Ultimately arrayed against the NVA 324B Division was Task Force Delta: four Marine infantry battalions, an artillery battalion and other supporting units. The First Marine Aircraft Wing would provide fixed-wing and helicopter support.

On 16 July, BLT 3/5 commanded by Lt. Colonel Bronars disembarked from the squadron of ships offshore and landed over Red Beach some five miles south of the DMZ, calling the amphibious landing "Deckhouse Two." After the landing, my Ontos platoon served as perimeter security for the beach support

---

[1] U.S. Marines in Vietnam: An Expanding War 1966

area. Because of unsuitable terrain and the probable need to be relocated quickly by helicopter, we left the Ontos aboard ship and carried 30 caliber machine guns ashore so we could be integrated into the battalion command post defensive perimeter. Soon after landing, the line companies reached their objectives against light resistance. On the beach, we ran a few recon patrols around the perimeter, discovering a couple of fighting bunkers in the process.

The area we were operating in was flat, sandy, and broken by dense groves of pines identical to the ones we had seen on Operation Deckhouse One, another amphibious landing we had conducted in mid June 20 miles south of Qui Nhon. The dunes flowed inland for about eight miles then merged with the typical Vietnamese coastal lowlands of rice paddies and cane fields, which eventually led up to the foothills of the Annam Mountains.

On the evening before helicopters lifted us further inland from the beach to join Operation Hastings, we saw orange flames erupting from the coastline of North Vietnam and columns of black smoke pillaring out over the water. Later we learned two F-4 Phantoms had been hit while returning from a strike over North Vietnam. The two pilots had crashed some nine miles from the Landing Platform Helicopter (LPH) Princeton and had been fished out along with their radar intercept officers. The pyrotechnic display was a retaliatory run against the offending NVA antiaircraft batteries.

The next day helicopters lifted the entire battalion 14 miles inland to join Operation Hastings, which had begun two days earlier and already involved four infantry battalions. Beating our way inland at 500 feet over flat rice paddies and villages half-hidden by palm trees and thick hedgerows, we could look down and see fighting trenches zigzagging around the perimeters of towns held by ARVN (South Vietnamese) troops. Thirty choppers descending on the landing zone in sequence resembled a swarm of voracious locusts.

Mike Company sprinted out into a hot landing zone and lost five Marines killed and 12 wounded right off the bat. Seizing the initiative, they overran the NVA troops opposing them and

27

captured grenades, anti-tank weapons, 1000 rounds of ammunition, automatic weapons and a 12.7 mm machine gun on wheels. The enemy dead wore khaki uniforms and belonged to a North Vietnamese battalion. The surrendering NVA lieutenant's information had been right on the mark.

After things had quieted down to sporadic firefights, we ran reconnaissance and combat patrols along the valley, searching for any sizeable units of NVA that might have been maneuvering for an attack on the command post. One evening, one of the patrols brought in a load of propaganda material: banners, flags, and identification packets they found in a receiving and indoctrination center up in the hills. Our S-2 (Battalion Intelligence Officer) explained that this center briefed infiltrating NVA soldiers about the National Liberation Front program, issued their identification cards, and assigned them to units. They never attacked our battalion command post, except for a few volleys of badly aimed mortar rounds that never hit anyone. NVA Patrols in the area avoided contact for some reason.

On Sunday, July 24th an NVA unit attacked India Company on Hill 362 with mortars, recoilless rifles, automatic weapons, and machine guns, inflicting significant casualties within a few minutes. At the battalion command post, I heard the beleaguered India Company commander radio back that he had, "A lot of dead Marines and wounded up here." The tide of battle swung in favor of India Company when one man—Lance Corporal Richard A. Pittman from First Platoon—grabbed an M-60 machine gun and several belts of ammo and rushed forward, wiping out several enemy positions at close range. Then he destroyed two NVA automatic weapons positions. Moving forward through a storm of small arms and mortar fire, Pittman looked up to see 30 to 40 NVA soldiers assaulting towards several wounded Marines. Calmly setting his M-60 in the middle of a trail, Lance Corporal Pittman unleashed a stream of 7.62mm fire that cut down the soldiers like threshed wheat. Trading his damaged M-60 for a submachine gun, a pistol and a grenade, he continued to pour fire into the hapless NVA soldiers until they withdrew. Only then did Pittman rejoin his platoon. As a result of his astonishing bravery, Lance Corporal Pittman received the nation's highest award for valor—the Medal of

Honor.

Lieutenant Joe Mingo (an embarkation officer whom I had befriended while on the SLF) took over a platoon in Mike Company after the platoon commander had been hit. The next day, Joe's platoon went up against a labyrinth of bunkers and trenches and he took four rounds over the heart while trying to throw a grenade, which flipped behind him and exploded, wounding him in the back with shrapnel. Although the doctors gave him a less than 50-50 chance to live, he survived, albeit paralyzed from the waist down. His company went on to do a masterful job in reducing the trench/bunker system, engendering General Ryan's compliments for losing only one man during the engagement.

On 29 July, the day before we terminated Hastings, General Westmoreland flew in by helicopter accompanied by a Major General and Lieutenant Generals from the ARVN. He complimented Lt. Col. Bronars on a fine operation: the Marines and the ARVN had inflicted about 700 casualties on the NVA and captured 17, suffering 147 killed and almost 500 wounded in the process. The BLT itself lost about 50 Marines killed and 200 wounded. Over 200 weapons and in excess of 300,000 rounds of ammunition fell into allied hands. This battle for domination of Quang Tri Province had been decisive in favor of Task Force Delta and the ARVN.

Back on Con Thien, a helicopter beating its way down through the ashen sky and landing in a maelstrom of C-ration boxes, shelter halves and dust, dissipated my reverie about last summer's operations. After the chopper settled on its landing gear, out popped comedienne Martha Raye wearing olive drab fatigues, spit-shined boots, a green beret, and the honorary rank of lieutenant colonel in the U.S. Army Special Forces. She shook hands and talked briefly with the Marines, signed a few autographs, ribbed us a little bit, *"Oh boooy! Do you guys have it soft here. Great view, interesting neighbors, and three 'squares' a day."* Once again, "Colonel Maggie of the Boondocks," was risking her life on the front lines to assure the Marines that despite news reports to the contrary, the American people were solidly behind

29

them.

Martha Raye's morale-building tours began during World War II and continued through the Vietnam War, where she spent as many as six months of the year for nine years straight. Before the war ended, many a mud-smeared soldier or Marine manning a far-flung combat post would experience a glow of gratitude and admiration for her cavalier disregard of the danger such front line appearances presented. Too soon she was gone from our lonely outpost, leaving a tightly packed group of two dozen Marines, many of them teenagers, listening for the ominous "thoop" of North Vietnamese mortarmen taking advantage of a dream target.

Marc Glasgow also remembers this feeling of "incoming anxiety"...

"She stood up on that dead tank that was in my part of the perimeter and I didn't think it was a good idea. The tank was part of a platoon of tanks that came up from Cam Lo. When they were crossing the Cam Lo River, the NVA were hiding in the stream, popped up, knocked out one or two tanks, killed the platoon leader. So the able tanks, when the shooting was all over, dragged the dead tank up there, the one they killed with an RPG. Its gun still worked, but its motor wouldn't work, and they set it in the perimeter. I was grateful that it was there because they had some canister rounds. They weren't bunkered in or anything. They were just above ground: no hull defilade, they were just sittin' up.

I believe it was the general who was with her. They got up on the back of the tank and when he was pointing, he was very, very obvious. I've got a picture of them standing on the tank. They were just dead ducks had there been any snipers out there. But little did they realize there was only one foxhole between them and all of North Vietnam. The foxholes weren't very close because Golf Company was way under strength. There was only one band of concertina, you know. From an engineer's standpoint, if the NVA had wanted to overrun us, they could have real easy."

Captain Gruner wasted no time in getting me "snapped in"

with the platoon. Aggressive patrols and ambushes were designed to keep the NVA off balance and detect any further build-ups such as had occurred during the summer. The first few patrols with Second Platoon found me sprinting to keep up with the point and wondering whether the previous platoon commander had been a college 880 man. Every time the point fire team spotted an enemy soldier, they took off after him, running pell mell along the muddy trails until they caught him or shot him.

On one patrol, they flushed a small group of VC or NVA out of a cluster of bamboo "hootches" at the bend in a trail, knocked one of them in the head and took off after the rest, chugging along the winding trail until they got a clear shot. The prisoner scampering alongside us with his hands tied behind his back jabbered such rapid fire Vietnamese he immediately overloaded my rudimentary language skills; but at least he was smiling. A burst of M-14 fire up ahead signaled one of his communist buddies had been sacrificed for the fatherland; rarely did these Marines miss. However, this time we found only a profuse blood trail leading off towards the DMZ.

On another patrol, we came upon six villagers living in houses that should have been abandoned long before. After searching the area thoroughly for enemy soldiers and weapons, we moved out in patrol formation, trailed by an ancient Vietnamese man who was wailing and waving his arms. He kept repeating, "Doi giay! Doi giay!" over and over until I realized one of my Marines had strapped the old man's sandals to the top of his pack as souvenirs. I berated the Marine, handed the gentleman his sandals, and we continued up the trail. So much for "hearts and minds." Since pitched battles during the summer of 1966 had pretty well cleared out the civilians, only occasionally did we encounter small clusters of diehards or outright communist supporters.

Half an hour later, my point fire team rushed two thatched bamboo structures while firing from the hip at several black-clad figures who were sprinting into low shrubbery. The Marines hit the deck firing just as an enemy machine gun cut the grasses and low-hanging tree limbs a foot above their heads, neat as a gardener's scythe, dropping instant camouflage onto their helmets. Then the enemy soldiers melted into the half-light of the jungle canopy.

On one memorable foray, the farther we ranged from Con Thien, the darker and wetter the night became. A light mist turned to drizzle, then to steady rain that glistened on the leaves, giving them a polished look and turning our soaked utilities from green to black. Wind gusts buffeting bamboo groves produced a metallic *clack-click, click clack,* that sounded for all the world like a rifle bolt chambering a round. Golf Company was setting in a night ambush.

A string of automatic fire at the head of the column sent us into the flanking shrubbery. Since our intended site was a quarter mile away, I thought we had become ambush victims ourselves; but the column soon resumed its steady, serpentine windings along the narrow trail, past a clearing where the steaming body of a North Vietnamese soldier lay staring sightless at the pewter sky, covered with cooked rice, his ankle torn open like a broken chicken leg, his rain poncho fluttering in the wind.

I stopped the platoon just shy of a trail intersection, allowing Sergeant Dawson to move his squad forward and deploy in an L-shaped ambush with an M-60 machine gun trained down the long leg. Soon the only sound was the constant wash of the storm pouring down through the jungle canopy. About an hour and a half after the platoon settled in, I heard a Marine in Dawson's squad yell, "Halt!" followed by bursts of automatic weapons fire, then silence. The rain fell harder. No one moved. I left my position beside the radioman and did a low crawl towards two Marines on the far side of the clearing who were pointing their weapons in the direction of the firing. As I approached, one of them swung the muzzle of his M-14 towards me and the other Marine grabbed it, whispering, "Hold it. It's the lieutenant!" Another close call with "friendly" fire. Word filtered back two enemy soldiers had sprung the ambush. One was down on the trail; the other had escaped into a marsh.

Sergeant Joe Barry, Second Squad leader, heard the commotion and learned later from Sergeant Wayne Dawson, that… *"Everybody was so tired, most fell asleep. Then he heard two men talking; one's eating and he's got that submachine gun across the front of him. He's eating out of that rice bag and walked right past Dawson. Dawson jumped to his feet right on the trail and shot him. I guess he shot 'em both and one dropped dead right there and the other one escaped into the marsh. Well, what happened, all of a sudden, Dawson realizes, 'Oh my God. I'm right in my own kill zone.' So he told me he dove to his face and as soon as he hit the ground, the machine gun opened up and fired right over his head. He's yelling out 'Cease fire, cease fire.' I could hear when he yelled, 'Halt,' and then the shots fired, and the machine gun opening up and all that."*

After a cold, wet night, a brightening eastern sky revealed a Vietnamese soldier sprawled in the middle of the trail where he had fallen. Wearing black pajamas, a clear plastic rain tarp and "Ho Chi Minh" sandals made out of automobile tires, he carried a short-barreled sub-machine gun with a straight magazine. A cylindrical bag of rice lay near the body. We never located his companion.

In November, a patrol took us well beyond the usual radius around Con Thien. Bright morning sunlight streamed out of a cobalt sky as we searched an abandoned North Vietnamese base camp well inside the DMZ. It sat next to a stream flanked by close-cropped meadows. The condition of the bamboo "hootch" and other artifacts suggested it had not been used in a long time. The quiet and lack of contact was almost unnerving. I stuffed a tattered NVA knapsack into my own pack and directed the platoon to continue searching the area. About a half-mile away to the north, beyond a ridge, we heard the rhythmic hammering of an NVA antiaircraft battery emplaced squarely in the DMZ. Suddenly the deep roar of a piston engine spinning a four-bladed propeller heralded a South Vietnamese A-1 Skyraider fighter soaring into view over the treetops several hundred meters away. It was headed straight for us.

I thought we were all dead. Surely the pilot had pegged my platoon as a North Vietnamese unit; at that very moment his gloved finger probably was squeezing the firing button that would unleash four 20 mm cannons firing 2000 rounds per minute, scattering our body parts in a smear of fresh hamburger across the clearing. Seeing smoke streaming off the fuselage, I braced for the impact.

"Hit the deck now!" I yelled, and we all dove for what little wrinkles there were in the ground.

As I watched the aircraft hurtle towards us, it rolled well to port and something fell off of it, then plummeted towards the forest canopy. It was the pilot. Just above the crown of the forest, his chute blossomed. Then he was in the trees. Instantly I knew what had happened. The NVA antiaircraft battery we had heard earlier had hit their target, igniting an engine fire, the smoke from which I had mistaken for gun smoke. The abandoned fighter flipped upside down, then slammed into the ground nose first at full speed carrying a load of 500-pound bombs, napalm, and 20 mm cannon ammunition with it. The impact, punctuated by a grotesque orange and black fireball, was apocalyptic.

In the silence that ensued, I looked at my platoon deployed in defensive positions, stunned by the spectacle. The pilot, who must have survived the jump, was perilously close to the NVA positions. We would have to move fast. Marc Glasgow was near the company command group when the plane appeared.

"I was standing by Gruner for some reason and I thought the plane was shooting. Then I saw it roll and the chute came out. Well, I kind of had a bad feeling what was going to come over the radio. I knew the squelch was going to break. That somebody would tell the Captain that we got to go get that plane."

The radio command from Captain Gruner was not long in coming. "Alright, move out in that direction," I said, pointing towards the crash site. "Third Squad takes the point. Let's get that pilot the hell out of there!"

We took off running across what looked like Soldier's Field in Chicago: carpenter level flat, with close-cropped grass. A narrow stream soaked us to the armpits, then we were running full tilt again towards the dark tree line on the far edge of the clearing, muddy water squirting out of our boots. Just before the jungle foliage swallowed us up, we heard the unmistakable concussive rhythm of a large helicopter: a very large helicopter, bigger than a Huey or a CH-46. Sure enough, from the south appeared a "Jolly Green Giant," a CH-53 Sea Stallion used for air/sea rescues. Barreling in behind us at two hundred feet, it disappeared overhead. Soon we heard it hover, pull power, and climb into the sky; in five minutes it had appeared, picked up the pilot and was heading back to Dong Ha. Silence descended once again. Even the antiaircraft battery was quiet. In my mind's eye I pictured the NVA platoon that had been dispatched to find the pilot moving stealthily towards us through the twilight of the undergrowth, deploying for a violent assault.

"Retrace now," I whispered. "First Squad on point. Move out."

Soon we had rejoined the company and were briefing Captain Gruner on our adventure.

The terrain of Quang Tri Province severely tested the navigation expertise I had acquired at Oregon State College School of Forestry and on extended backpacking and mountain climbing excursions into the Swiss Alps, the Cascade Mountains and the High Sierras. Keeping track of our position at all times was vital for calling in artillery or mortars, close air support, or helicopter medevacs during an engagement with the enemy. However, unlike open country at home, the terrain of Quang Tri Province had no trail signs or Forest Service section markers nailed to the trees.

Nui (mountain) Con Thien, rising over five hundred feet above sea level was one of many useful landmarks within our operating area. Its flanks were open savannah traversed here and there by low hedgerows. However, after traveling less than a thousand meters from the perimeter wire on combat patrol, trees and bushes often swallowed us up, obscuring the summit and leaving us to navigate by dead reckoning—using time traveled in a certain direction—to keep tracking. Once in a blue moon a glimpse of Con Thien from a clearing or through the clouds and mist afforded an opportunity for a "resection" or compass shot to fix our position along a certain azimuth. The 1:50,000 scale topographic maps the Marine Corps issued were

35

adequate, although not as exquisitely detailed as the 1:25,000 "orthophotoquads"—larger scale maps combined with aerial photographs—that I was able to acquire later in my tour.

A few ass-chewings from Captain Gruner about drifting off course while on combat patrol, taught me quickly delegation has its limits; I began taking more personal responsibility for navigation. I soon realized part of the difficulty was the Marine Corps issue compass. Our navigation improved after I made available to all three squad leaders the type of Swedish compass that had served me so well in the forests of the Cascades Mountains: the liquid-filled Silva Ranger. Constructed of plastic and aluminum, the Ranger model had a hinged cover with a mirror inside that doubled as sighting bezel. You could literally plot a course while walking down the trail by using the housing and base plate as a protractor. A shortcoming was it was not as battle proof as the lensatic compass. After practicing with these compasses on short patrols across the slopes of Con Thien, our navigation skills improved. Second Squad Leader Joe Barry remembers...

"Lieutenant Buchanan insisted that all three squad leaders track our position on their maps so they could take over if necessary. He got us compasses that were so much easier to use than the issue ones. I still have mine. It's got a little air bubble in it, but it works fine."

On one sojourn into the eerily quiet countryside, the battalion command group joined us on a rare walk in the sun along what we called, "The Yellow Brick Road," a secondary road that ranged east of Con Thien, eventually linking up with Route One. We traveled five kilometers east to some high ground near a lake, established a defensive perimeter, and sent out patrols. I remember watching Dave Moore, the company First Sergeant and a unique character, drop a wild duck with a few shots from a shotgun, then wade out bare-chested into the middle of the lake to retrieve the pathetic carcass. That was the only gunfire we heard all day. One of the patrols came back with a Vietnamese gentleman who must have been in his sixties. For some reason, the Marines suspected him of contact with the enemy so we handcuffed him and hauled him back towards Con Thien that afternoon. After S-2 questioned and released him, we watched him disappear down the road with his poncho flapping, pummeled by sheets of cold rain, shivering violently, his arms full of C-rations we had given him just for the inconvenience.

Marc Glasgow remembers a combat patrol with a sort of zoological theme...

"One day we were ordered to go out to try to find elephants...to find this elephant supply trail. And we did see tracks and some dead NVA soldiers...two of them were down there in this ditch. That stunk so bad. They had brand new uniforms, but they were well-rotten bodies. That was the trail where, I believe, we found they were using these elephants."

I soon learned being inside the concertina wire at Con Thien was no guarantee against "friendly" fire. One soggy night in November I had assembled my squad leaders, right guide, and platoon sergeant in my tent for a chat about some administrative or operational issue when we heard an increasingly shrill whistling sound hurtling towards us out of the sodden sky. I had seen enough Roadrunner cartoons to know what was coming next. Anticipating a strobe-like flash of light followed by an ear-splitting explosion, and metal ripping through the air, all of us except the platoon guide went sprawling on the dirt. Instead of an explosion, all we heard was a soggy, "sbloop." Sergeant Dale Farnham, a cool 23 year old professional, looked down at us calmly and declared, "Bomb, Sir." We learned later an A-6 Intruder had dropped a 250 pounder by mistake just inside the wire. Since it was a dud, no one was killed, injured, or rendered deaf by the unprovoked aerial attack.

Sometimes when dusk rose upwards from the flatlands and enveloped fighting holes of the 2nd Battalion Fifth Marines like the shroud of death itself, you could imagine ghosts of a French Foreign Legion battalion smoking Gauloise Troupe cigarettes and muttering over a card game in the flickering shadows of the battered and stained concrete blockhouse that sat on the east side of our hill. Other sounds at Con Thien were more comforting. For instance, the night H & I (harassing and interdicting) fires from U.S. warships off the coast sounded like Volkswagen Beetles hurtling through the sky from 20 miles away,

37

followed by a cosmic explosion. Woe be to the NVA unit that was anywhere near the point of impact.

Rick Wilhite, Captain Gruner's radioman, was eighteen and a half years old, five feet, seven inches tall, and weighed 137 pounds when he joined Golf Company during the summer of 1966. As he tells it, the assignment was not exactly a reward for sterling performance...

"One day they told me to get a radio and get on a chopper and go to an outpost with a squad of Marines not far from Chu Lai. Hill 69 I believe. The second night there, Capt. Cooper, the CO of Echo Company, called and said his company was at the foot of the hill and they had spotted a company of NVA coming up the hill. He told us to get our heads down and he would call in arty. Well, he did. At least three 105 batteries, a 155 battery, and naval gunfire pounded the hill most of the night. We were totally worn out, and around daylight I fell asleep. Radio operators do not fall asleep on watch. Well, I did. That morning, since they had lost radio contact, they sent two choppers over to see if we were all dead. Far from it; we did not even have a WIA much less a KIA. What is even stranger, not one NVA or blood trail was to be found. They took me off the hill and the communications officer ate on my ass for what seemed an hour and then put me on shit details. The communications chief hated me for making him look bad, so he sent me to Golf Company, hoping I would catch a bullet. It was June 1966. I was eighteen years, eight months old and going to join up with Golf Company and meet Captain Gruner for the first time."

Like most of us, Wilhite remembers Captain Gruner as a low-key, but very competent leader...

"I found him to be short, built like me, and had a blond flattop. He was quiet and seemed easygoing. However, when he wanted you to do something, well, you just did it. He was a take control Marine and most always made the right decisions. He cared for his Marines and knew how to keep them alive. He was cautious and deliberate in his actions. He kept to himself and never talked about home or personal problems. He made decisions quick and without hesitation. His main concern was to achieve his objective and not lose any of his Marines: my kind of leader. We spent 24 hours a day, 7 days a week eating, humping, sleeping, living together, and I learned nothing about his

family, likes and dislikes. It was always business as usual."

As I discovered early on at Con Thien, Captain Gruner generally admonished his troops in a low-key manner. When it was over, you knew exactly what he wanted you to do. His instructions were clear, without the usual static of yelling and cursing. Wilhite has a similar memory...

"As a leader is expected to do, he rarely badmouthed his troops. He never talked bad about anyone, well, with one exception. One morning while we were getting ready to go on patrol during the rainy season, a Marine was wearing his poncho and I thought the captain was going to have a heart attack he got so mad. 'You don't wear ponchos on patrol!' he yelled. Never happened again.

"One night when we were moving to a new base camp location, we stopped to rest and then moved on. When we arrived at the new camp and took a head count, we were short a corpsman. Captain Gruner had us saddle up and go back down the trail to find him. We did. He was fast asleep along the trail. That was another time the captain was not too happy. But he took care of his troops.

"Another time Captain Gruner got mad was when we were coming in from a patrol near An Hoa. A sniper fired at me but did not have the correct elevation and the round landed at my right foot. Instead of running or taking cover, I bent down and tried to dig the round out of the mud. Captain Gruner was not impressed and told me so."

We celebrated 10 November, the 191st Marine Corps birthday, as best we could, given our limited resources. By some logistical miracle, each Marine had two beers and two soda pops that day. Taunting NVA gunners, I dressed my platoon into close interval formation for the cake cutting ceremony by the colonel while jets from the First Marine Air Wing screamed over the hill at treetop level then corkscrewed up into an unusually azure sky, barrel rolling and performing other spirited aerial maneuvers. An Army 175mm battery was supposed to fire a 191 round salute into the DMZ from around Dong Ha, but for some reason never came through.

Captain Gruner assigned Catherine Leroy, the attractive

French photojournalist who accompanied me on the chopper from Dong Ha, to my platoon because I was the only one in the battalion who could speak some French. A diminutive lady with her hair pulled back in a ponytail, she was very intense about her work and without hesitation would go off on patrol with any unit that was going through the wire. My rusty French being what it was, our conversations were pretty much limited to the basics of life on the hill: where to sleep, eat and go to the bathroom.

The responsibility for Ms. Leroy's personal comfort fell on the stalwart shoulders of platoon guide Dale Farnham...

"When she came over to join us it was raining cats and dogs. She insisted on having her own little latrine and all because she was a woman and she was a pain in the butt. I took the top of a 60mm mortar round box and cut it up and shaved it down so it would be smooth for her, then we took the lid and put it on backwards so it would cover the seat that she sit on and then we put it over the hole. For privacy, we put a poncho around it She didn't want to share with anyone else, of course."

One time she went out on patrol with us. It was a whole company patrol. But we didn't see much of her because she stayed with Hotel Company most of the time. Captain Gruner gave her to us because of lieutenant's ability to speak French."

After the war, I learned Leroy was twenty-one years old when she joined us at Con Thien. A native of Paris, she traveled to Vietnam in the spring of 1966 and started working for Associated Press photographer Horst Faas who paid her $15 a photograph. No shrinking violet, she made a combat jump with the 173rd Airborne in February 1967 during Operation Junction City. On May 19, 1967 she was with a Marine combat patrol crossing a rice paddy near the DMZ when enemy mortar men targeted them. 35 pieces of shrapnel ripped into her body, breaking her jaw and inflicting other wounds that required evacuation to Con Thien by tank, since the volume of enemy fire precluded helicopter extraction. Six weeks later she was back in the field.

In 1968, Leroy was taking a short vacation with Francois

Mazure, a correspondent for Agence France Presse at China Beach near Danang when the communist Tet Offensive exploded across the country. When they heard about heavy action at Hue, she and Mazure made their way to the besieged city on a rented bicycle and settled in for the night among refugees in a cathedral. The next morning the refugees, fearful of being found with foreigners by the communists, asked them to leave. They had walked only a short distance before NVA soldiers captured them, tied them up, and took them to a French colonial villa. To her surprise, a potentially deadly incident reversed itself when the commanding officer, a North Vietnamese Army colonel about their age, allowed the two journalists to interview him and take photographs. The resulting essay ended up in the February 16, 1968 issue of Life Magazine with a Catherine Leroy byline. The cover shows two young NVA soldiers armed with Chinese AK–47 rifles holding a captured strongpoint.

Dan Day, the rifleman in Sergeant Dawson's squad, had an encounter with another celebrity of sorts while preparing for a combat patrol in the boonies...

"We were going on a night ambush. We're all looking pretty scruffy, you know, mud caked on, some guys had not shaved in a while. We looked like shit! Then a Huey helicopter landed and out popped General Walt. He came walking over and he's got on starched herringbone utilities. He was an imposing figure: three stars and all. He says, 'I want you Marines to know that I was with 2/5 in World War Two. Go out and get some tonight and don't worry. You'll be able to call for support on the coast. You got artillery, mortars, air if you need it. If anything comes up, anything you Marines need, I'll get for you.' It was like a morale booster speech he gave us. We all liked it. We felt kind of pumped up after a visit like that from a three star general."

PFC Day's morale got wrenched the other direction a few days later when he heard from a Marine whose unit had engaged the enemy in a short firefight. On the body of a dead NVA medic, they found a medical kit with better supplies than the Navy corpsmen carried. Sewn inside the bag was a label bearing the words *Friends of the Vietnamese Peace and Freedom Party, Berkeley, California.*

Early November, word circulated across the hill 3rd Marine Division would move from Danang to Thua Thien and Quang Tri provinces. 1st Marine Division (our parent unit) would assume responsibility for the tactical area of responsibility (TAOR) around Danang and Chu Lai. The 9th Marine Regiment would remain at Danang under the operational control of 1st Marine Division. On 22 November, we saddled up and boarded CH-46 helicopters bidding a fond "adieu" to Con Thien in a driving rainstorm. As we lifted off, I watched the rotor wash and monsoon gale hurl some of the goodies my parents recently had sent—cookies, writing pads, a paperback book—away across the landing zone and into the bushes. We struggled for altitude, then followed the other choppers on a vector towards Dong Ha. Through rain-streaked Plexiglas, I could just make out the Yellow Brick Road, the inflamed-looking hills of the combat base, the trace of the Ben Hai River separating North and South Vietnam. I looked across the aisle at Marines of Third Squad—all of them soaked to the skin and some already drifting off in spite of the miserable conditions—and reflected on how much we had accomplished in a little over a month. I had begun to feel almost comfortable with the hand fate had dealt me. A lot of things had become second nature: briefing the platoon before sallying forth on patrols; checking their weapons and equipment; noting health and morale problems. Light contact with enemy forces had been a golden opportunity for me to get to know the platoon and vice versa. The smooth integration of replacements into the ranks, as well as the extraordinary professional competence of my platoon sergeant, right guide and squad leaders bolstered my conviction we would prevail in more intense engagements that probably lay up the road. As for Marc Glasgow, he remembered a rumor that proved almost diabolical in its capacity to disappoint...

"When we got orders we were originally going to walk out south to Cam Lo. My map already had grease pencil checkmarks I made when we were going to walk to Cam Lo. And that was the original plan to get us out of there. I thought it was quite foolish because so many guys had emersion foot so bad and we were in pretty ragtag condition. And fortunately they cancelled it, and we didn't have to walk. I think we went down to Dong Ha in CH-46s and spent a night on the airstrip: layin' there waiting to pick up in the Caribous to go. We were promised

something, like going to China Beach."

After the soggy, mist-shrouded hills of Con Thien, it was hard to imagine China Beach: wide sandy beaches, warm turquoise water so shallow you could wade out 200 yards and not be over your waist; puffy little clouds drifting past Monkey Mountain—a peninsula jutting out into the South China Sea; pitchers of chilled draft beer with rivulets of condensation running down their sides in the tropical breeze; T-bone steaks sizzling on a charcoal grill; real food like fruits and salads and baked breads, pasta even; volley ball and touch football on the powder sand beach; parties lit by tiki torches on the lanai; and nurses and pretty Vietnamese hostesses exuding a fragrance like exotic tropical flowers.

When the fantasy about rest and recuperation on the beach evaporated like so much ground fog, Marc Glasgow was devastated...

"Then the Caribous showed up in the morning. They grabbed the colonel and the sergeant major and there was a big huddle around one of the Caribous and all of a sudden we weren't going to China Beach, even though we were scheduled for some liberty because the troops were in such bad shape. They needed to dry out. Then the word came down that we were going to some place called An Hoa."

AN HOA

My darling, this war is tiresome and dull. The enemy attacks us in small groups, then melts into the darkness or the countryside. Rarely can we bring our superior weapons to bear. Our Captain does his best, but our food is always bad and water not at all plentiful. We march long hours in the dust and sun only to learn the enemy has eluded us once again. Three years will be an eternity before I return to your loving arms.

Greek Soldier to his wife: Peloponnesian Wars circa 500 B.C.

Our flight of Caribous dropped us onto a dirt airstrip that had the color and consistency of butterscotch pudding. After we hauled our gear away from the racket and prop wash, we faced a complex of industrial buildings and a cluster of olive drab strong-back tents. We soon learned An Hoa was a nascent industrialized area located in Quang Nam Province approximately 20 miles southwest of the coastal city of Danang. A patchwork of cultivated rice fields and an archipelago of hamlets clustered together into villages and linked by a network of trails and dirt roads extended as far as the eye could see to the north and east of us. To the south and west of us, the green-clad Que Son Mountains dominated by 675 meter high Nui Hon Chau rose up to meet the monsoon clouds. Rivers and streams pouring out of the mountains included a major waterway called the Song (Vietnamese for river) Tinh Yen, becoming the Song Thu Bon that meandered east-west through the region. The Song Vu Gia, a major tributary to this river, flowed from the northwest into the Song Thu Bon six kilometers north northeast of An Hoa, forming the Song Ky Lam, which eventually became the Song Dien Binh, the Song Cau Lau, and further east, the Song Cua Dai, flowing into the sea at the coastal town of Hoi An. Minor tributaries, some perennial, others seasonal, joined with these two major watercourses to complicate troop movements, especially during the monsoons. A railroad generally following the north-south trace of Highway 1, branched west, skirted the south side of An Hoa, and terminated on the banks of the Song Tinh Yen after curving around the west side of a small peak.

A good-sized water reservoir lay at the foot of the mountains two kilometers south of the base. Another one, six kilometers long, lay east of An Hoa, its shape on the tactical maps prompting Marines to call it "Alligator Lake." A smaller companion lay in a small valley south of "Alligator Lake." Thus we concluded there would be no shortage of water, either from the earth or the sky. Although other roads existed, the only militarily functional one was "Liberty Road" a virtual lifeline that snaked its way south from Hill 55 near Danang to the Song Thu Bon where Mike boats provided ferry service to the south bank. From there, convoys rolled the last ten kilometers into An Hoa combat base. Before he joined G Company as Third Platoon commander, Marc Glasgow, the former engineer officer, was in charge of building Route 5—the road from Danang—down through the valley to Dai-Loc, then to the banks of the Song Thu Bon. From there, Mike boats ferried men and material south to Phu Lac (6), a company patrol base, that was the southern anchor to the crossing. Some time after Glasgow returned to the United States, the Marines built Liberty Bridge. As Glasgow later recalled...

"When I was there we crossed the river in Mike boats. There wasn't any bridge. The reason I'm fairly familiar with that is when we got down to Dai Loc, we were pretty much out of gear due to mines and all this stuff, and that's when I transferred to the infantry. There was nothing left to build. We never did finish the road to Phu Lac (6) from the north side of the river. And the Vietnamese, their job was to finish the road from An Hoa to Phu Lac (6). That was the engineering plan

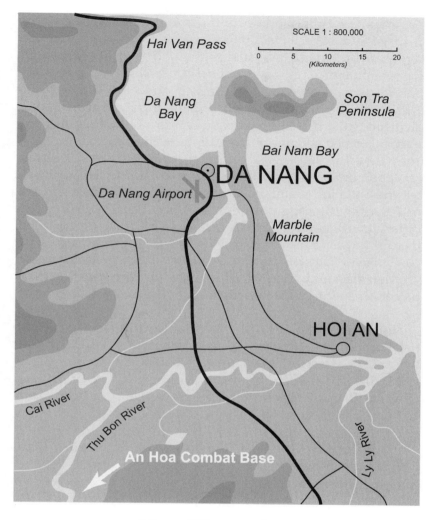

Map of Danang Area

for the main supply route to An Hoa. That's why I was very surprised that I went back with the infantry on the same damn road that I was building."

South Vietnamese government planners saw the area's bountiful water resources represented significant hydroelectric and water purification potential. Nong Son, South Vietnam's only coalmine, sat on the banks of the Song Tinh Yen 11 kilometers southwest of An Hoa. Construction already had begun on a fertilizer production plant. But the Viet Cong had plans of their own. By late 1964 and early 1965, they had cut the main roads leading to Danang, the only logical market and transshipment point. They stopped the railroad spur to Nong Son in its tracks. Foreign investment dried up. Although the ARVN 51st Regiment maintained an infantry company and an artillery battery in the nearby hills, the VC R-20 Main Force Battalion ruled the area surrounding the site.

Upon our arrival at An Hoa Combat Base from Con Thien, Second Battalion commanders were appalled to find no network of defensive fighting positions and bunkers. There was little cover against mortar or infantry attacks. From that time forward, the dirt flew and the concertina unrolled; 2/5 had accepted the challenge of "squaring away" An Hoa. That meant improving the defenses and conducting aggressive search and destroy patrols deep into what became known as "Arizona Territory.[2]"

Every morning a detail of Marines would slide 55 gallon half barrels out of the privies, soak them in diesel fuel and light them off, producing thick columns of malodorous smoke. A daily ritual, it was an efficient method of incinerating excrement. However it hadn't been so when we first arrived from Con Thien, as Marc Glasgow recalled...

"When we landed in those Caribous at An Hoa, I think it was getting dark. That was 3/9 we were replacing down there. I remember I had to go to the shitter so I asked some trooper, 'Where's the four-holer?' And I was sitting on the four-holer and somebody was sitting behind me and he started squirming then jumped up yelling, then ran out. I turned around and turned on a flashlight, and there was just bugs all over. There was a moving mass of maggots. They hadn't burned shitters or anything."

---

[2] Official records refer to "Arizona Territory" as the peninsula formed by the confluence of the Song Thu Bon and Song Vu Gia rivers beginning 2 kilometers west northwest of the patrol base at Phu Lac (6). To the Marines of 2/5, it was the area east of Phu Lac (6) and areas of the TAOR that remained like its wild west namesake; lawless and untamed.

On Thursday 24 November, Thanksgiving Day, I had taken my platoon sergeant and platoon guide out to reconnoiter the Phu Lac (6) company patrol base and plan defensive positions for Second Platoon. We returned late in the day to find a feast laid out before us in the mess hall. We couldn't believe our eyes. Famished Marines were digging in to roast turkey with cornbread stuffing and cream gravy, spicy Virginia baked ham with raisin sauce, snowflake Irish potatoes, buttered mixed vegetables, tossed green salad, chilled cranberry sauce, and if there was any room left after that load, fruit cake, ice cream, mincemeat pie and pumpkin pie. After a steady diet of C-rations, it was delicious fare; but we all paid a heavy price by having the runs for two days afterwards.

G Company spent the first days at An Hoa digging trenches, laying concertina and mines, sandbagging bunkers and conducting local patrols and ambushes. We ate our meals at the mess hall, a large strong-back tent structure, plodding back and forth along roads that were slowly becoming rust-colored quagmires in the steady monsoon rains. The sticky mud sucked at our boots and turned uniforms from olive drab to ochre—in effect converting us involuntarily from "green side out" to "brown side out." Tracked vehicles and six by six trucks churned the butterscotch mess into creamier consistency, then got stuck. Squalls of the northeast monsoon swept in from the sea, drifting across rice paddies in grey curtains, playing a steady tattoo on the galvanized roofs of the huts. Our gear was constantly wet. To the south, the summit of Nui Hon Chau appeared and disappeared mysteriously in the moving clouds. We were all expecting a much-needed period of rejuvenation there, since we were relieving 3/9, the battalion that had occupied the area for seven months. It wasn't much but after the DMZ it looked like New York City.

Action was light those first few days, with few casualties. This interim period gave the Marines of G Company a chance to learn the terrain around An Hoa, to restock stores after Con Thien, to refit, and to enjoy if only briefly, small comforts afforded by life in the battalion headquarters compound. Lieutenant Marc Glasgow, the engineer, saw a lot of possibilities for improvement...

"We actually built the bunker line ourselves. Because I was an engineer officer I was assigned to build the first one as a demo and then for the rest of it, I was to supervise the whole thing. Golf Company, we were on the line. But then we kept going out to Phu Lac (6) or on some operation. So battalion ordered a defensive fire plan for the whole thing. There were no bunkers on the perimeter when we arrived. Then I built the first demo one out of sandbags and a few sheets of corrugated stuff. That's all the construction material we had, so I built an example so everybody could bring their crew over and see how it was built. Every bunker had two rifle pits, and they were built in depth, so each bunker could cover the two bunkers on either side with interlocking fire. What we didn't have in those bunkers was any sheeting against the monsoon season. I knew they were going to have a water problem. We had some Marston Matting from the airstrip and some of the corrugated sheeting that came off of hootch roofs. But other than that, they should have had a water impermeable cover in those layers of sandbags. That would have kept them dry in the monsoon. They filled with water is what happened. We also had to dig fighting holes alongside the hootches."

While filling and stacking sandbags on the perimeter defenses, Ron Carbone witnessed an example of Marine air wing teamwork...

"While we were on the working party I saw four of our jets flying by in the distance. Since they usually flew in pairs, I figured they were headed for a strike somewhere. About three or four minutes later they circled back, flying low. Then I could see that the lead jet, probably an F-8 Crusader, was on fire and the other three were close behind. Helicopters on the airstrip took off and we all watched as they flew around to the south of us. The jet that was on fire started coming down, then the pilot ejected. His chute opened and the choppers went straight for him, arriving before he hit the deck. I'm sure he was OK. Two seconds later the stricken jet banked and exploded in a big ball of red flame and black smoke. The way those aviators gave him cover and assistance impressed the heck out of me."

This unaccustomed luxury was too good to last. Our little sojourn was soon to be interrupted.

MISSISSIPPI

In late November, intelligence units reported the 3rd NVA Regiment and elements of the 1st VC Main Force Regiment had infiltrated into "Antenna Valley," a notorious lair deep in the mountains ten kilometers south-southeast of An Hoa. In response, the new Battalion Commander, Lt. Col. Airheart, ordered Companies F, G, and H to prepare for a helicopter assault in an effort to trap and destroy these units.

The plan was for Company F to land by helicopter in a landing zone in Que Son District located a few hundred meters north of the hamlet of Thon Hai (1) followed by the Command Group, Company H and Company G in that order. The battalion then would proceed west along Route 536, walk over a 250-meter high pass, and make their way into the valley.

After an interminable wait at the An Hoa airstrip, we began boarding CH-46 Sea Knight helicopters at around 1015 on the morning of 29 November and flew southeastward towards the LZ. Strapped into my seat, I peered through the round Plexiglas window down on rice paddies that reflected the sun like pieces of stained glass. The emerald-clad slopes of 675 meter high Nui Hon Chau rose up to meet us. While I was absorbing the beauty of the scene, the radio reported a Marine had been severely wounded in a chopper that was settling into the hot LZ. Faces across the aisle reflected the rising pucker factor.

Air strikes around the LZ took so long, we ran low on fuel and had to fly back to Marble Mountain airfield near Danang. On the way there, my chopper and the one behind us developed some sort of engine fluctuation; so after gassing up, the lift took off without our two 15 man teams, leaving us to sit for two hours in the sand near the runway, watching the fly boys walk past in fresh starched utilities, cameras in hand, headed for the PX or the mess hall. Mess hall? It wasn't long before our recon party was at the mess hall checking it out. They unloaded such a story on the mess sergeant he gave them 100 cups of stateside ice cream, apples and cold-cut sandwiches. We gorged ourselves with this exotic fare until the choppers arrived. Then we stuffed the rest in our pockets and packs, reboarded the choppers, and flew back towards the mountains and the real war.

Only light sniper fire greeted us at the LZ, allowing us quickly to join the rest of Company G and to follow in trace as they began to move west up a narrow road, leaving Third Platoon as the rear element. It didn't take long for the word to spread Second Platoon had been eating sandwiches, apples, and ice cream at Marble Mountain for the last two hours.

We hadn't progressed two hundred meters when a firefight broke out behind us. Third Platoon was in trouble. For Marc Glasgow, Third Platoon commander, the cautionary preamble to the operation was coming true...

"When we mounted out for Mississippi, I had no idea what Antenna Valley was. But Golf was the last unit in. And because I was the last platoon in, I was going to be the last one out of the LZ. Colonel

Airheart came over with Gruner, and said, 'Look; no matter what happens, we expect them to try to cut you off, being the last ones out of this LZ. You cannot get engaged. You've got to depart. We can't come back and get you. You will have no support.' It was the tactics that the enemy was using. And as I recall, it was the Third NVA Regiment that was over there.

I was the last platoon in; it took so long to get us in the LZ because we didn't have enough helicopters. It just took forever. Whichever part of the perimeter I had, I knew I was going to be the last one. Had to wait for Gruner to call the other platoons to go out, the other companies go out, battalion CP goes out, and I would be called last to depart. But we waited for hours. And the enemy? By that time, there was no surprise for him.

We were there a couple of hours, very quiet, troops were deployed. Then I heard the first bang, the first gunshot. What had happened was a guy who turned out to be NVA got up out of a hole. He thought we'd gone. You know, he hadn't heard any helicopters. He came up out of a hole that you had to stand right over to find. There was a ladder going down into it. He came out and started walking away so my trooper shot him right in the back, blew his heart out. The guy didn't have a weapon, but he was a great big guy. When I got there, I rolled him over and his heart fell out. He had a red star on the buckle. I asked, 'What happened?' and the Marine said, 'The guy came out of that hole.' And I went and looked and we threw grenades down the hole and I thought, 'Oh, shit. We're sitting right on top of a goddamned CP. This guy's an officer.' He looked too big to be a Vietnamese. I suspected he was a Chinese."

Glasgow followed orders, holding his exposed position on the west side of the landing zone and becoming increasingly uncomfortable as the rest of the battalion moved out in column formation towards the pass. The battalion commander's admonition to just keep moving because nobody would be coming back for them even if they got hit echoed in his mind. Far across rice paddies that lay simmering in the sun, jungle mountain slopes rose towards the mottled sky. It was quiet. Lieutenant Glasgow ordered his first squad to move out, and the remaining squads to provide cover. The first fire team had gone a few yards when machine gun fire raked their position.

Glasgow was not surprised…

"Just as we got up to go, the NVA opened fire on us with a couple of 12.7mm machine guns from way the hell across the rice paddies, maybe 800 meters. Way up on the side of a hill. Gruner had pre-planned artillery fires, but the artillery couldn't hit the target, because of the trajectory, so he switched to air. But it never showed. Except the helicopter showed, and I don't know where they came from. It was an H-34. And without communications with him, because I didn't have a FAC with me, we couldn't talk to him. We waved him off and then it was so long before the jets showed up. It was a long time. But there was a clearing we had to get over: a hump and a hill we had to get over to rejoin G Company. Well, what happened is, the NVA, they had hours to get ready to go. They had those .50 calibers up there. We couldn't reach them."

Glasgow called up his machine gun teams, and they both got taken out with explosive bullets. He was convinced they were explosive bullets because one impact would cause two or three casualties. He called for replacements. They became casualties as soon as they manned the guns. When new teams finally were able to put out sporadic bursts toward the enemy positions, the fire was not effective. Glasgow became increasingly frustrated.

"I saw the NVA guns. They could have been 1000, meters away. Our guns would chatter and I could see where the tracers were hitting. We'd try to move them but then they'd get whacked. I realized that there wasn't a lot we could do but get the hell out of the way. We couldn't reach them. We couldn't get supporting fire. We had to cross the open. So we more or less hunkered down waiting for Gruner to get the air in. It took so long."

While all this was going on, my platoon was deployed on the west side of a knoll. We kept waiting for Third Platoon to get unstuck from the NVA unit that was trying to cut them out of the herd. As soon as they broke free and joined us, the battalion could start humping over the pass into Antenna Valley. But the situation did not seem to be improving. The volume of NVA machine gun fire into Third Platoon's position was not diminishing. Although we could not see them because of the hill, it sounded as if Marc Glasgow's platoon was responding vigorously. Yet he was not able to move. My radioman gave me the handset.

"Lieutenant Buchanan, this is Cassandra Golf Six Actual." It was Captain Gruner. "I want you to prepare to go to the assistance of Third Platoon if necessary. We may need you to take the pressure off of him so he can join up. An air strike is pending. I'll let you know."

"Aye, aye, Sir," I responded. Then I briefed my squad leaders. Ten minutes later, a Bird Dog flew over accompanied by the sibilant whine of an attack aircraft circling overhead. The Bird Dog must have asked Gruner to mark the NVA position, because a Marine appeared on our side of the knoll shouldering a 3.5-inch rocket launcher. He aimed carefully at a high angle—what appeared to be maximum range—and let fly with a "whoosh!" of backblast and a projectile arcing out to the north. A few seconds later, a white cloud blossomed on the far hillside. To our right rear, we heard the angry whine of a Marine Corps A-4 Skyhawk boring in on the target; then he screamed into view over the trees, zigging and zagging violently, then settling in to arrow-straight flight for the last few seconds before he pickled a 250-pound bomb. The dark cauliflower shaped cloud of smoke, dirt and trees that erupted from the side of the hill was a beautiful sight. He pulled up and to the right and came around again. We heard later the pilot's aerobatics had not been sufficiently radical to avoid a 12.7 mm bullet through his canopy. Marc Glasgow, the beleaguered Third Platoon Commander, saw his opportunity...

"One of those strikes—he hit right on the money. I don't know how he knew where it was. We were trying to mark the goddamned target, but that was the end of it from that hillside, with those 50's. And I sent out one squad at a time while we provided the base of fire, but we couldn't touch those 50's that were wracking the shit out of us. Then it was down to the last squad. Sent them out and it was just my radioman, PFC Oaks and I. I took Oaks' rifle and sent him out. And then it was time for me. When I expended the magazine, I was done. After all that time of adrenaline rushing, I had nothing left: zero in the

tank. I couldn't run over the hill. Oaks took his radio and left his packboard. I said I'd take it out, but I couldn't carry it. I threw it away. Not very proud of that, but I was totally out of gas."

Charles "Chip" Mohney, a twenty year old Marine from McKeesport, Pennsylvania, had a bad feeling about being "Tail End Charlie" for the battalion...

"Third Platoon was the last platoon out of the ville. We had just crossed a little rice paddy into what might have been a cemetery when an enemy 50-caliber machine gun opened up from way across the rice paddy. I deployed my squad on a little knoll facing back across the rice paddy into the village. Almost immediately, a man in 3.5 rocket launchers named Payne took one through the neck. Shortly after Payne got hit, PFC James Carroll Hebert took one in the head. So one of the other Marines, a big ole' college boy, we both ran over and grabbed Hebert: him under one armpit and me under the other. 'Course Hebert was already dead and we're, you know, keeping low and carrying Hebert as best we can by half -carrying, half-dragging him. Then Hebert's flak jacket just pulled right off his body. When he hit the ground, he gave out a death groan, so the guy with me thought Hebert was still alive and started giving him mouth-to-mouth resuscitation. I told him, 'He's dead. Let's grab him and get out of here.' By this time, helicopters were coming in. And it was getting dark. So we dropped Hebert off."

Dusk was creeping up from the low places like ebony fog by the time Third Platoon finally joined us, carrying two dead Marines in ponchos and guiding the walking wounded down the narrow road. Marc Glasgow walked slowly past me like a man in a dream, his hollow stare reflecting the tremendous strain he had been under most of the afternoon. As I helped a young Marine carry one of the dead rifleman—a young shirtless Marine with light colored hair—towards the side of the hill, the only clear spot for loading the casualties, he told me that after one of the 12.7 mm machine guns drilled the man in the stomach, he rose up yelling incoherently and would have run across the clearing to attack the enemy if they had not held him down. Then he died in their arms. An H-34 chopper hovering overhead buffeted us with prop wash and sweet-smelling exhaust, dust and grass, then maintained a high rate of engine revolutions while settling precariously on one wheel against the hill. It was a masterful piece of airmanship. I realized one lost revolution, one cough from the engine and we would be crushed. The crew chief was understandably agitated.

"Get those casualties aboard now, Marines," he screamed. "Hustle it!"

As the bird struggled into the darkening sky loaded with the dead and wounded, a feeling of gratitude and admiration welled up in me. What was it, I pondered, that drove the pilots and their crews to perform such extraordinary feats? Monsoon storms, enemy small arms fire, landing zones tucked into hillsides and surrounded by trees reaching up to rip off a rotor, or entangle the landing gear enormously compounded the basic act of flying one of the ungainly machines. Yet they kept flying in to help out their ground-pounder bretheren.

Exhausted from their ordeal, Third Platoon formed up with the company and we began climbing towards the pass. Darkness enveloped us. We spent the night shivering in our ponchos bivouacked at the crest of the 250-meter high pass. The rest of the battalion stretched out 5000 meters to the west of us. The next morning we resumed our march. As the road dropped down the side of the ridge, Antenna Valley revealed itself to be somewhat of a Shangri-La. Sharply sculpted jungle-clad mountains furrowed with mysterious ravines rose against a sky full of cumulus clouds. A watercourse called Khe Le flowed west-northwest. Like emerald fiords, lush rice paddies lapped up against the base of the mountains. If ever there was a likely base camp for the NVA 3rd Regiment, this was it.

Like an enormous green centipede, the battalion followed the serpentine road from the pass down into a fecund, yet strangely silent community of scattered villages. Near the village of Dai Phong, the battalion command group co-located its command post with Golf Company. Hotel and Foxtrot Companies were deployed within the radius of a kilometer or so.

We settled into a routine of platoon and company-sized patrols along the edges of rice paddies, through villages, and back into the mountains themselves. Sodden days with ceilings measured in the tens of meters allowed only two helicopter resupply runs. Hunger stalked us as relentlessly as we stalked the elusive VC and NVA units. After several days without food, we sent fire teams and squads foraging through the hamlets for anything that was edible. They brought back chickens, rice, potatoes and small peanuts they found stored in caches by the wayside. When I saw a group of Marines chasing down and stabbing a small pig, I demanded they at least shoot it to end its suffering quickly. A squad from another platoon that was foraging beyond the hamlet we were in narrowly escaped disaster when a small VC unit opened fire on them through the trees and shot a chicken out of one Marine's hand, thus saving him the effort of wringing its neck and perhaps of gutting it. At one point we resorted to grinding rough rice into palatable grain by using the wood and stone implements left by the VC. The process was not exactly like pouring Uncle Ben's from a box.

First we had to grind most of the husk off with an implement designed for that purpose. After we had removed most of the chaff, we threw the kernels into a big stone mortar and pestle and pounded it until the remainder of the husk came off. Then we poured the mixture of chaff and rice onto a large wicker disk, fanning like mad until all the chaff blew away, leaving clean rice. Three hours of grinding and blowing produced handfuls of fairly clean rice which we boiled then wolfed down voraciously just in time to start all over for the next meal. Vietnamese women did the grinding, blowing and cooking in about 45 minutes after carrying the stalked rice in from the field.

We gained a healthy respect for the physical endurance and sheer grit of these women when we packed loose rice in sandbags and hauled them to the landing zone with carrying poles. Without the energy-efficient, hip-swaying gait necessary for carrying loads with such equipment, even husky Marines were tripping all over themselves. Ninety-pound farmer's wives would sail along the road to market as if they were contestants in a Central Park walk race.

Constant exposure to wet conditions: rain, streams, rivers and flooded rice paddies created textbook conditions for immersion foot. The bottoms of our feet turned as white as flounder filets: dimpled and sort of de-laminating. It was a nasty sight. Before the operation ended, 49 Marines (most of them immersion foot casualties) had to be evacuated. Thus thinned by the elements, I referred to the five men in my Third Squad as the Third Fire Team. Marc Glasgow observed a curious experiment by higher echelons...

"Headquarters Marine Corps sent in two guys from the research center out there with some kind of goo for our feet. It was like a Vaseline gel to cover our feet and supposedly, that would make your feet impermeable to the water. You wouldn't get trench foot. It was a trial, but obviously didn't work worth a damn."

Ron Carbone, a nineteen-year-old rifleman in Third Platoon who hailed from Somerville, Massachusetts, used his ingenuity to stay relatively dry...

"Talk about soggy. We actually found a plank and were able to raise the plank off the ground and we slept on it. That's only way we could get up off the ground. On one occasion we were balanced on—I don't know what it was—maybe 12 inches, but whatever the width of that plank was, that got us off the ground, it was better than sleeping flat on the ground in your poncho. From then on it was continuous rain that we had."

After midnight, shortly before the operation ended, a frantic NCO from the weapons platoon burst into my CP hootch and reported a terrible accident had occurred; in the darkness, one of his Marines at a listening post had shot another, thinking he was an enemy soldier. When they laid the young man on the hard packed dirt of the floor, I could see a gaping grayish-red crease in the side of his head. He was unconscious. Realizing I could not do anything for him, I ordered the NCO to take the casualty to the G Company CP so a corpsman could look at him. The next day, our Gunny informed me the man had died. He questioned, in a diplomatic way, my decision to send a 3.5 inch rocket team out as a LP. My response was they were an intact team, as good at field tactics as anyone in the platoon. If the enemy approached, they would fall back into the perimeter and man their weapons like any other LP.

Marc Glasgow was appalled at how communist forces treated the refugees in Antenna Valley...

"The only other thing of significance on that operation was—I don't think we had any major contact—but I do remember we were on the hillside, on the southern hillside walking out when the VC/NVA machine-gunned the refugee column. I could hear them. I was told that the villagers formed up a column when they flew the ARVN guys and the Popular Force guys in to escort them down in the valley. Because we were up there on the mountain, we couldn't see the road. But we heard that thumpin', and that's what I was told; they were thumpin' at the refugee column, killing their own people. That became a free fire zone after we got out of there. We went back in there a couple of times."

Ron Carbone, the Third Platoon rifleman, recalled running the gauntlet on the last day of the operation...

"On the march out of the valley, Third Platoon had point and I was point man. We were on the road and on my left flank I spotted two VC coming down a path towards me, say 300 meters away. The order at that time was not to fire without permission, so I called for permission to fire. While this chatter was being relayed, the VC noticed me getting ready to fire. When they made an about face, I was ordered to challenge them to stop. "Lie Day," I called out. They weren't stopping. I fired a half dozen rounds into the bushes they ran to. With civilians in our column, there was no interest in pursuing these two. I never knew if I got lucky with my shots. Then we came under continuous sniper fire. We were directed to a knoll over the road to return fire on our flank. A fire mission was called, so we double-timed it off the knoll and over dikes down to the road to escape the impact area. It was a muddy, slippery, hilarious run. Marines couldn't and wouldn't move fast enough to keep up because they were stuck in the paddy mud. Word was that the gooks were hiding among water buffalo across the paddy. The fire mission was right on and one or two water buffaloes went flying. I never saw any gooks."

On 7 December the battalion traversed the road leading west through the valley through sporadic sniper fire, and emerged at the Song Thinh Yen, a beautiful river with languorous sandy banks, and a backdrop of jungle mountains that rivaled the set from "South Pacific." In fifteen minutes flight time we were back at An Hoa.

Although we never tangled with the main body of either the 3rd NVA Regiment or the 1st VC Main Force Regiment, we felt we had accomplished something by evacuating 2300 citizens (most of them by helicopter), who had rejected NVA dominance over their lives. The final tally of enemy forces at the end of Operation Mississippi was not very impressive for the effort expended: one confirmed VC killed, 3 probables, four wounded, 14 captured, 3 suspected VC taken into custody and 11 surrendered. Documents, clothing, and 50 tons of cached rice, as well as miscellaneous equipment and 4 weapons completed the haul. In the process, we lost four Marines (one to "friendly" fire) and suffered 6 wounded.

In the post-mortem, Colonel Airheart acknowledged the 72-hour delay prior to D-Day had allowed the enemy to catch wind of the operation and scatter. That villagers in Antenna Valley anticipated our arrival and were preparing to leave confirmed this notion. As the Colonel emphasized in the After Action Report ...

"Upon emerging into the eastern end of antenna valley, this Battalion was greeted by villagers as having come to deliver them from bondage. They were frantic in their desire to be evacuated from Viet Cong control and some requested to be put to death by the Marines rather than to be left in their present situation. These people were expecting the Marines and obviously had made some prior preparations to leave the area."

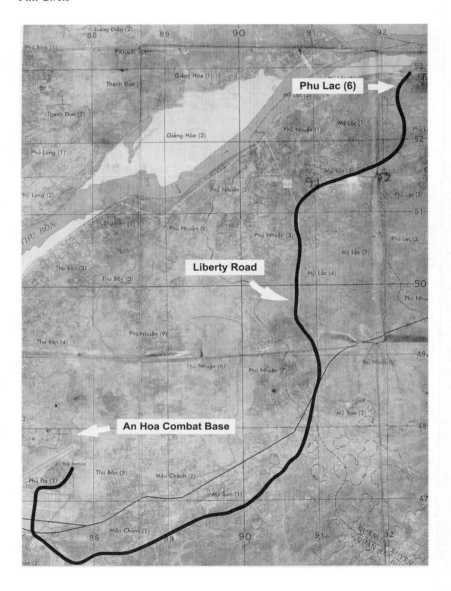

Photomap of An Hoa

PHU LAC (6)

On 8 December, the day following our return from Operation Mississippi, Company G marched 12 kilometers north along Liberty Road to Phu Lac (6), a pork chop-shaped hill about 40 meters high sitting on the south bank of the Song Thu Bon River just east of its confluence with the Song Vu Gia River. As a company patrol base, it protected the Mike boat landing for convoys traveling south across the river from Danang and provided some security for the road to An Hoa Combat Base. It also was a natural launching pad for combat patrols into what 3/9 had come to call "Arizona Territory," and for good reason.

The first significant intrusion into the region by III MAF (Third Marine Amphibious Force) had occurred almost a year earlier in January 1966 when two battalions, 1/3 and 3/7, reacted to intelligence reports about the R-20 Main Force "Doc Lap" VC

Battalion by launching "Operation Mallard": a search and destroy operation in "Arizona Territory" that resulted in little contact. On 21 April, 2/9 and 3/9 further scoured the "Arizona Territory" as well as terrain east and north of the base, using the Song Thu Bon as the northern border of the operation area.

We soon began to realize the VC were not the feckless rabble some had made them out to be. For instance in early spring of 1966 The VC R-20 Battalion sprang a huge ambush on a Ninth Marines platoon, annihilating it with the exception of two Marines who feigned death as the VC stripped the bodies of valuables and weapons. An inquiry revealed the platoon had established an identifiable patrol pattern the VC exploited to their advantage. Several weeks after that ambush, helicopters dropped Third Platoon C Company, Ninth Marines into a landing zone near the Song Yen River northwest of Hill 55. The landing zone had not been prepped by air or artillery and a nearby unit of the R-20 Main Force Battalion cut the Marines to pieces before they were able to leave the landing zone. Another company assaulting north later in the day rescued surviving remnants of Third Platoon which had ceased to function as a fighting unit. On 12 May, the R-20 Battalion mauled a 14-man patrol from B Company, 1st Battalion 9th Marines two kilometers north of Phu Lac (6). Only two badly wounded Marines escaped the encounter. We concluded the VC main force units in that region definitely were not to be trifled with, and we conducted our combat operations accordingly.

Such reverses notwithstanding, by 4 July 1966 3/9 had pushed the Viet Cong R-20 Battalion south of the Ky Lam and Thu Bon rivers. After intelligence reported the VC would contest any Marine movement south of the Ky Lam-Thu Bon line, they made good on that promise by engaging 3/9 throughout the summer and into late October, when Operation Macon ended.

Although few of us were aware of the "big picture" at the time, peering through the looking glass of history reveals the Marine Corps and the Army had some major strategic differences. General Lewis Walt, Third Marine Amphibious Force (III MAF) Commander felt the key to success was eradicating Viet Cong infrastructures from the villages and hamlets first, thus affording the population an opportunity to carry on their livelihoods and develop confidence in the South Vietnamese government. General Charles "Brute" Krulak, commander of Fleet Marine Force Pacific (FMFPAC) concurred when he tried to convince higher ups...

"...that there was no virtue at all in seeking out the NVA in the mountains and jungles: that so long as they stayed there, they were a threat to nobody, that our efforts should be addressed to the rich, populous lowlands. It is our conviction that if we can destroy the guerilla fabric among the people, we will automatically deny the larger units the food and the intelligence and the taxes and the other support they need. At the same time, if the big units want to sortie out of the mountains and come down where they can be cut up by our supporting arms, the Marines are glad to take them on, but the real war is among the people and not among these mountains."[3]

General William Westmoreland, Military Assistance Command Vietnam (MACV) commander, saw the build-up of regular North Vietnamese units and intelligence reports about their plans to mount major offensives around Saigon and the Central Highlands as a major threat that had to be neutralized by taking the fight to the enemy on his home ground: the triple canopy jungles of the Annamite Cordillera—the geographic backbone of Vietnam. By thus locking horns with and destroying sizeable enemy units—companies, battalions and regiments— he would protect the vital infrastructure comprising supply centers, ports and airfields and keep the enemy off balance. Westmoreland's operations officer perceived the Marine effort at their enclaves, Chu Lai, Danang and Phu Bai, as "stalled." He encouraged multi-battalion-sized operations against VC main force units two to three weeks out of every month. As Westmoreland wrote later...

"...I chose to issue orders for specific projects that as time passed would gradually get the Marines out of their beachheads."

General Walt envisioned expanding his coastal enclaves north and south until they linked up then, as increased

---

[3] *U.S. Marines in Vietnam: An Expanding War 1966*

manpower allowed, moving inland until most of the Vietnamese littoral or coastline region was under allied control. Working within broad MACV guidelines, the General developed a comprehensive strategy that committed resources to three directions: pacification, search and destroy and counter guerilla operations.

Thus we found ourselves right in the middle of an area 3/9 had scoured numerous times, provoking spirited engagements. Predictably, the VC main force units hotly contested our first few combat patrols along the road east of Phu Lac (6) by engaging us at close quarters.

On 9 December, we conducted our first search and destroy mission east of the hill. About 1500 meters out, the VC hit the entire company from the right flank with automatic weapons fire. Being on point, my Second Platoon was under heavy fire from close quarters. I was right behind the lead squad but couldn't tell exactly where the rounds, which were kicking up sand uncomfortably close to my boots, were coming from. During one such firefight, Sgt. Wayne Dawson, First Squad Leader, was maneuvering a fire team forward when an enemy bullet smacked into the left side of his chest. After the enemy fire slacked off, Dawson crawled over to me and said, "Lieutenant, look at this! I just got hit but it didn't go through." Sure enough, his body armor was ripped right over his left nipple. Using my pocketknife, I dug out of the fabric what appeared to be a carbine slug and gave it to him. Then our Corpsman patched up the reddening and slightly bruised pectoral muscle beneath the flak jacket. "You're livin' right, Sergeant Dawson,' I told him as we moved out again to the east. " Keep it up."

Sgt. Dale Farnham remembered the incident a little differently...

"Dawson liked to joke around a lot. We had gotten hit and Lieutenant Buchanan called for the squad leaders. We had a squad leader's meeting and Dawson got up from the squad leader's meeting because the lieutenant said, 'Go back and brief your squads.' And he got up; then he fell down and says, 'I've been hit! I've been hit!' We

thought he was joking around, because we didn't hear no rounds or anything. And he says, 'Lookee here!' and he opens up his flak jacket and there was a little bruise. An AK47 round went through his flak jacket and stopped. He had a bruise right by his left nipple. We never heard the shot at all and that's why we thought he was just goofing around. And he says, 'No, I'm hit. I'm hit. Got it right here.' After Lieutenant Buchanan dug the bullet out, Dawson said, 'That one had my name on it. I know I'm going home now.'"

Fate would prove those words eerily prophetic.

After the VC backed off, the company got on line and started moving east, guiding on a road. Within a few hundred meters, a small VC unit opened up on our left flank and really threw some rounds at us. A 57mm recoilless rifle round sailed over our heads and detonated on our right rear flank into an area that had been producing sniper fire. The sudden cessation of sniper fire led me to believe they had blown away one of their own men. They also lobbed about four 82mm mortar rounds at us and a couple of 60mm rounds that fell short. We moved out again and engaged them in a running battle that lasted for about six more hours. We were a bunch of beat Marines when we returned to the hill at Phu Lac (6) that evening.

With each successive patrol we mounted out from Phu Lac (6), enemy units engaged us at ever lengthening distances, opting to harass and delay us with sniper fire and booby traps rather than stand and fight. I had no doubt the aggressiveness, marksmanship, and tactical audacity of the Marines in G Company had everything to do with that reaction. As the days passed, rules of the game became clearer: through direct observation or information from villagers, the VC/NVA unit commanders would determine the direction of each day's combat patrol. Then they would attempt to engage us along the way from prepared positions—trenches and bunkers—that gave them maximum protection from our supporting arms. A favorite enemy tactic was to wait until a Marine unit had left the protection of cover and concealment (for example, moving across a rice paddy) and was fully exposed before opening up. I vowed to myself my platoon would not fall victim to such tactics. We could beat the enemy at his own game, I reminded my squad leaders, by using camouflage more effectively and using the terrain to our advantage—expanding and contracting the platoon formation as we moved from jungle to meadow to rice paddy. We would use flank security as much as possible and cover each other's movement across open areas.

On the way back in from one such patrol in December, we were passing through an abandoned village when I heard faint whining behind a thatched hut. I looked around the corner of the hootch and next to a ceramic water jar spotted an emaciated four-week-old puppy wobbling along the hard packed dirt in front of a rooster that looked as if he wanted to make a meal of him. From the pattern of its fishbone ribs, the puppy was on the verge of starvation. It was buff colored, had a tail curled over its back like a watch spring and was about the size of a squirrel. That it resembled every other dog I had ever seen in Vietnam confirmed my theory the original progenitor of all these animals must have been some stud muffin. Without a clue about what I eventually would do with it, I scooped up the fuzz ball and stuffed it into the front of my flak jacket. It was a cool day and as the platoon moved along the trail, I could feel the little character fidgeting, his needle-like claws scoring the skin of my chest and the cold, moist nose snuffling around. Then his head popped up over the zippered opening. Since dogs had been a part of our family as far back as I could remember, I thought this one might soften the edges around the patrol base at Phu Lac (6). It would remind me of home, give the troops something else to talk about and provide some extra diversion. Sure enough, along the way I took a few barbs.

"Hey. Lieutenant's got a bodacious flea inside his flak jacket. Check it out, man." And from further down the column, "Lieutenant! That pup would taste mighty fine with some ham and limas. Gooks eat them things, you know."

A diet of C-rations put some fat on the pup. It was particularly fond of "turkey loaf." A week later, Doc arranged for rabies shots and dog tags that said, "Magnolia Butt Plate-Second Platoon." The name, coined by one of my riflemen, reflected his admiration for mortars. Since "he" turned out to be a "she", we called her Maggie. Soon the Marines accepted her as the official platoon mascot, and she went everywhere we did—except on patrol.

Sergeant Farnham has fond memories of Maggie…

"She just ran around the area. I have a Polaroid picture of her somewhere if I could just find it. Gunny Hinojosa, the Supply Sergeant and Club Manager, was back at An Hoa. He watched her all the time while we were gone out on patrol and made sure she got fed and everything."

Early on 10 December, the company moved out into our familiar hunting grounds east of Phu Lac (6), making contact by mid morning. A VC unit fired two 60mm mortar rounds at us, causing only light, non-evacuation wounds. After Second Platoon assumed the point again, about a squad opened up on us with heavy automatic and semi-auto fire. We returned fire with an M60 machine gun and M-14s on semi and automatic. They hit us twice more before we finally chased them into a village. At one point during this running gun battle, I had moved one squad to the left flank to cover us across an open area. There they encountered a young woman who told them that she had seen many armed men running down the trail. Moving on, we caught two of them in the open wearing what appeared to be flak jackets and helmets, thus validating an intelligence report we had received two days earlier about a VC platoon equipped with this type of gear. We opened up on them, but they crawled over into a tree line 500 meters away apparently hurt, but still able to move.

After we had advanced 200 meters I had the left flank security squad fall in behind the platoon. Shortly after they executed that maneuver, we came under fire from the direct front and a slight rise off our left flank. One Marine was hit through the legs, but we got him out by chopper relatively quickly. I realized immediately I should have left the covering force in place longer. Had they been there, they might have provided crossfire, thus neutralizing the enemy unit on the left. However, the terrain in that direction was so open, I doubted they would hit us from there. After I called in artillery on the enemy position, an F-4 Phantom leveled a village 500 meters down the trail. Any doubts about enemy presence in the ville evaporated when the Bird Dog AO drew fire as he over flew it. The setting sun cast long shadows as we marched back to the hill. We were learning.

The following two days dawned bright and warm. We took the time off to repair gear, clean weapons and play with Maggie. From the top of our hill, you could see the mountains rising up to meet the base of solid-looking cumulus. The Song Thu Bon curled lazily around the bend, heading for Hoi An and eventually the South China Sea. I took the opportunity to become more acquainted with Nguyen Dau, a Chieu Hoi battalion had assigned to my platoon, because I was the only one in the company who spoke Vietnamese. With little direction from company headquarters, I billeted Dau in our platoon CP bunker. We set him up with a bed made out of 105mm howitzer boxes, collapsed C-ration boxes for a mattress, and a poncho. Battalion had issued him a flak jacket and a helmet that made him resemble a box turtle when he wore them both at the same time. An important detail battalion had neglected to tell us was Dau spoke little English.

He was a pleasant enough looking fellow in his mid twenties, about 5' 4" tall, fit looking, with jet-black hair cut short on the sides. A square face with honest-looking features suggested ethnic Vietnamese (lowland) origins. For the first few minutes after Captain Gruner brought him over, we stumbled around using a mix of Vietnamese, English, and sign language until I thought he knew who was who and understood the basics of the Second Platoon routine on Phu Lac (6). I sensed from body language and a few rumblings the platoon sergeant and the right guide were not happy about the arrangement. After all, he had been a VC soldier not all that long ago. I could imagine what was bugging them: would he turn on us or spy for his buddies? Would he lead us astray in the field? Could he be trusted at all? Sgt. Farnham was skeptical of the whole concept…

"Dau and Mr. Bai were the Chieu Hois in the company. Dau had an M14 with the stock cut off of it so it would fit him. I didn't' trust him. In the platoon bunker at Phu Lac (6) we had the lieutenant, me, Mack, Dau, Shipley and Magnolia Buttplate. I told Dau at night, 'Let me tell you, Mr. Dau, this here's the line. You cross it and I'll shoot

you.' I just didn't trust him. You get that gut feeling. Not that he didn't do good translating out there and feeding us good information. And there was a couple times he forcefully grabbed a hold of VC out there to get some information out of them. I don't know whether he was trying to impress us or not, but I didn't trust him. We had to do our hand and arm signals to get him to understand what we wanted him to do. But he did understand some of the lieutenant's French. But he had to say it over and over. He didn't pick up on it the first time. I just didn't trust him."

Dau's presence was made possible by a Vietnamese government program called "Chieu Hoi" (open arms) that encouraged Viet Cong and North Vietnamese soldiers to defect. General Nickerson, Commanding General of the 1st Marine Division, who was part Native American and quite a history buff, saw some potential for the Marine Corps in the program and coined the term "Kit Carson Scouts" after the 19th Century frontiersman who was renowned for his tracking, hunting and fighting skills. Marine units started accepting Kit Carson Scouts during the spring of 1966. By September of that year, 12,106 VC had surrendered under the Chieu Hoi program, 1000 more than in 1965. By October, the Marine high command had officially accepted the program.

One evening after a B-1 dinner of ham and lima beans, fruit cocktail and crackers, I sat down with Dau in my CP bunker in order to get to know him a little better and perhaps allay the fears of my NCOs. Next to one of the bunks, Maggie was chewing on the corner of Sgt. Farnham's flak jacket. You could hear the frogs singing down by the Mike Boat landing and the H and I fires booming at An Hoa. Over a can of steaming instant coffee brewed over my field expedient stove, I learned to my surprise, Dau knew more English words than I thought. I asked him why he had become a "Chieu Hoi." With my tape recorder running, he reeled off a story in a mixture of Vietnamese and English that had a familiar element in it...

"I have 24 years now. Second month, ninth day, I will have 25 years.[4] It is good omen that we are both same day, year and month—

---

[4] The fact that we shared the same birth date was of great cosmic significance to Dau, who presumably was a Buddhist.

71

both ancients. Tet festival also is on ninth day. This is good omen. The fifth day I will go to Danang and have holiday feast. There will be much beer and I know of a pretty young lady. The French killed my mother when I was eleven. My father is still alive, but I have very little to do with him. He has since remarried. There are no brothers or sisters.

VC come to my village one day in November 1965 and demand I go with them. To refuse would have meant instant shooting. I was ordered to a supply detail that carried ammunition and equipment down the Ho Chi Minh Trail. We met the trucks a short distance below the DMZ. They made us carry very heavy loads. The hills were steep. Many died of hunger and exhaustion. I saw six soldiers die from disease, wounds or the heavy work. It was impossible to carry food because of the very heavy loads. We were to be fed at way stations along the trail. This happened not often enough. I carried 60mm mortar ammunition, often as many as twelve rounds, plus my rifle and the ammunition for it. American planes could not see us. Dense trees covered the trail.

A trip going and coming was very long—sixty days. A month going, a month returning. Once after a very hard trip, I told the captain, who lived east of this place, that I was very angry about the short rations and the difficult, extremely heavy loads we carried. All he did was lecture me on how the Vietnamese should fight the Americans and South Vietnamese traitors. The VC were full of lies. My unit was the D-26 Main Force Company. We engaged the Marines many times, and the ARVN as well. We managed reasonably well in these battles until air and artillery arrived and we were forced to withdraw more often. Once we mortared the airfield at Danang. It was a dark night and I carried 60mm mortar rounds within striking distance. Then we fired them very quickly, withdrawing to the south across the Song Thu Bon afterwards. The withdrawal was exhausting. We attacked the ARVN on Hill 65 one night, causing a good many casualties.

Dau paused and sipped the lukewarm coffee in his can. Smiling, he gestured at Maggie. I reached over and pulled her off Sgt. Farnham's flak jacket. The corner was frayed and gummed up with puppy saliva. He would not be happy. Dau's declaration seemed genuine. He continued his story in the flickering candlelight...

72

"For these operations we carried light machine guns, Thompsons, rifles, carbines, grenades and 60mm mortars. For assault rations we carried a mixture of rice and sugar cane. For our gear we had light packs or small sack-like affairs. Each of us carried a camouflaged cape made of nylon. This we could throw over us when planes were overhead. We hid ourselves further by attaching branches and grasses to a wire device formed in concentric circles with a star design within. It was then tied to the top of the pack and gave excellent concealment. Some soldiers appeared to be bushes! Our bunkers were deep and narrow. Most were simple one-man fighting holes with an undercut portion covered with banana tree logs and dirt. The spoil was camouflaged with fresh cuttings. When possible, these fighting holes were linked by a continuous trench. This helped our safe withdrawal.

When we were not on the move, some of us stayed in a village to the east of here. I was not married, but there was a young lady seamstress — Sau. She had much money and took good care of me. But she did not practice communism. One night a Marine artillery shell killed her. That was not a common thing, but one night a shell caught us in the open, killing our unit leader and four others. At times the night fires were a worrisome thing.

I left the VC because I found the life extremely difficult and unrewarding. One night in the mountains south and west of here I argued and fought with a member of the unit. Then I came to the lowlands, traveling cross-country to the Song Thu Bon. There I found a canoe and with three civilians, set out for my village of Hoa Dong. We tried to pass a Marine position one night, but they saw us and killed the other three. I escaped by swimming some distance downstream. I then proceeded to my village where I ate and slept to regain my strength. A few days later I walked to Danang. In August of this year after many months as VC, I rallied to South Vietnam government under Chieu Hoi (open arms) program. I then was selected to work for Third Battalion Ninth Marine Regiment as "Kit Carson Scout". When Third Battalion went away, they assigned me to Second Battalion, Fifth Marines.

I think the VC will be defeated by the methods you use now but it will take some time, perhaps twelve years. In the meantime I will continue working for the Marines for the agreed four-year period. However, I do not want to be a professional soldier. Now there is no

73

money—but perhaps in four years, I could go to school somewhere. I would like to see the communists defeated so that the country could once again build, educate and be free of war."

With each successive patrol, Dau's stock rose among the Marines as he interrogated captives, alerted us to possible fortifications and ambushes, and helped us try to understand enemy tactics. One disconcerting habit he never got over was non-stop talking in Vietnamese as we approached Phu Lac (6) on the way home from patrols, leading me to conclude he thought my language skills were at a higher level than they really were. His patter was so rapid-fire I caught only one word out of ten, so I just nodded my head most of the time and grunted. It was not uncommon for him to step off the trail and rip some herb or root out of the ground, which he then would cook in a pot of water at the company compound. With a little rice, his vegetable potpourris were downright tasty. One night after the evening meal, he broke out into song called *Ve De Anh*—a nice smooth melody in a clear tenor about patriotic love for the Ben Hai River, a symbol of the North Vietnam-South Vietnam partition. I couldn't catch all the words, but it sounded almost like a national anthem that extolled virtues of life in the south. As far as Sgt. Farnham and Sgt. Mihalcik were concerned, he was no threat to Pat Boone.

During one of our sojourns to Phu Lac (6), we drew the long straw of patrol base defense while a platoon from another company raided the far shore at the confluence of the Song Thu Bon and the Song Vu Gia, 1000 meters west of the ferry crossing. We watched as amphibian tractors (amtracks) hauled the heavily armed Marines across the river. The ensuing sweep, which took several hours, was a bust, turning up nothing of interest. As a matter of fact, even though we had a bird's eye view of the operation from our perch atop Phu Lac (6), most of us had found better things to do. My old Ontos anti-tank platoon was deployed in tactical positions on the military crest facing the river, so I sauntered down to shoot the shit with them while the platoon across the river began to load up on the amtracks for a return trip to our side. One of the Ontos Marines then yelled, "Heads up! They're moving out." It was then I realized the Ontos had the mission of providing supporting fires for the withdrawal from the area of operations, so I eased back up the hill, well away from the lethal backblast of the 106s. I'll never forget the scene that unfolded during the next 10 minutes.

From our vantage point we watched half a dozen amtracks slowly swimming away from the shoreline festooned with Marines perched like roosting pigeons—or, more appropriately—ducks.

You could see some Marines lounging haphazardly on the amtracks watching the scenery flow past. I thought to myself, what a delectable target for an enterprising VC sniper or B-40 rocket unit. Sure enough, the amtracks weren't 100 meters offshore when a superbly concealed VC unit opened fire with automatic weapons from the waterline they had just left, turning the water around the amtracks to froth. Little geysers were erupting all around the amtracks, which accelerated forward, pushing good-sized bow waves. You could see Marines scrambling to get their weapons into firing positions without shooting each other. I was horrified, thinking I was about to witness wholesale slaughter. Then the first fifty-caliber spotting round streaked towards the shoreline from an Ontos on the left flank of our hill. It traced a fiery parabolic arc towards the island and buried itself into the mud at the waterline. Not a second later a concussion and an earth shattering roar signaled the launch of a major round. A HEAT projectile as long as your arm screamed down towards the river like an avenging banshee, detonating near the water, throwing low brush, driftwood and sand high into the air along with a nice ball of gray smoke. The noise of the detonation hadn't reached us yet before another round followed that one, then another and another until the Ontos had fired all six major rounds. Then silence fell. We all cheered and yelled, "Right on! Get some, Ontos." The enemy fire from the shattered shoreline stopped as suddenly as it had started and the amtracks continued their deliberate swimming, pushing V-shaped wakes towards the near shore of the Song Thu Bon.

Late one afternoon, I found myself climbing up a steep part of the pork chop-shaped hill. Ahead of me, Dinh Mien, my young Vietnamese guide, yelled, "We can do this; we are Marines!" Soon there was no more hill to climb and a familiar panorama unfolded beyond the crest: emerald rice paddies, groves of banana trees, and the still mysterious mountains to the south, stacked like fading panels of blue. It was October 2001. The rest of my tour group from the United States was back at the Green Bamboo Hotel in Danang, or shopping for silk clothing or wood carvings in the town of Hoi An. With the encouragement of our tour leader Jim Rosenthal, a former U.S. Ambassador and Consul at Hue, I had chosen to spend the last hours of light chasing old ghosts across the landscape of memory.

At my feet, rust colored clay mixed with quartzite rock was cratered here and there, not by incoming artillery or mortars, but by locals digging for construction materials. Grasses and low bushes had invaded the site of my old platoon CP and the rest of the hill I remembered from 1966 as a dome of raw earth riddled with fighting holes and trenches: a veritable prairie dog warren surrounded by thickets of concertina wire. At the southern base of the hill, where we often placed our listening post, a Vietnamese cattle herder whistled a shrill greeting. To the north, light blue ribbons of the Thu Bon River still flowed between sandy channels. Where Liberty Bridge once stood, there remained only a concrete footing encrusted with asphalt, giving way to shallow water and sand. As Mien stood a respectful distance away, pretending to examine some oddity in the soil, I struggled to match mental images of the shattered terrain in 1966 with the pastoral scene before me. It seemed almost impossible we had ever been that young, and had survived so much death and destruction. Where, I wondered, was Dau? What had happened to Magnolia Buttplate after I left? Most importantly, what had become of the G Company Marines, scattered by now like autumn leaves across the twisting paths of time?

Mien and I walked back down the hill towards the rented Honda that was waiting with a driver alongside a road that used to lead south to An Hoa combat base and now provides tourist access to the ancient ruins of My Son. Something beside the path caught my eye. Laying in the rust-red dirt were some artifacts that proved the war wasn't all just a dream: a piece of olive drab Fiberglas with a rubber switch cover attached to it—probably part of a LAAW—and a piece of sand bag fabric. I stuffed them into my pocket and continued down the overgrown trail.

A LONG DAY IN THE ARIZONA TERRITORY

Bronze Star

On 13 December at Phu Lac (6), the pre-dawn glow of the eastern horizon silhouetted Marines of Second Platoon preparing for a company-sized combat patrol. The only sounds were low whispers; the dull clank of body armor, weapons and helmets; the jangle of machine gun belts thrown over already burdened young shoulders; the *chink* of rounds driven home in the chambers of M-14s as groggy warriors passed through the concertina. A sticky film already forming on the backs of our necks foretold another stifling day. Today, G Company would move out in a "reconnaissance in force" to challenge the R-20 Main Force VC Battalion in its own lair: the mysterious and untested terrain east of grid line 94—

"Arizona Territory."

By mid-morning, we were two kilometers northeast of Phu Lac (6) crouching beside sandy hummocks of dry reeds and grasses along a tributary of the Song Ba Ren. We had moved well along the sandy riverbank. Even so, as we passed an enemy position we had come to call "Ambush Site Two," a couple of rounds buzzed overhead from the far tree line. Kneeling behind me, Dau thought it might be a warning to other VC units, since they had no radios. I sensed the same VC unit that had hit us numerous times was bunkered in at Le Bac (1), so I had the forward observer put about ten 81mm mortar rounds in there, just for drill. The radio net was jammed for a while, so I moved the platoon down the riverbank slowly until it cleared. Meanwhile, we could watch the "fire for effect" thud into the village we had burned twice already.

Corporal Crum held up Third Squad at the banks of the Song Ba Ren. Beyond, I could see 400 meters of open sand marbled with ribbons of slate colored water. On the far side was a tree line that would be perfect for a classic R-20 Battalion ambush—resist the temptation to open fire until the hated "Thuy Quan Luc Chien My" (U.S. Marines) had entered the kill zone and had no cover. I swore I would take every precaution to avoid handing the enemy that kind of advantage. With satisfaction, I noted the platoon had heeded my orders that morning—leafy twigs and grasses sprouted from their helmet covers.

None of us relished the idea of being the first in the company to cross that open expanse of sand and water that was dominated by a tree line. We imagined VC soldiers sweating in the still air as they settled into fighting holes hidden among the vegetation, NCOs adjusting their positions for better fields of fire, sighting in their AK 47s, SKS rifles and RPGs and arranging their ammunition within easy grasp. They were preparing for targets they could hardly miss.

This time it would be different. When Captain Gruner agreed to a brief 105mm artillery barrage into the tree line, I asked that the last few rounds be "Willy Peter" (military jargon for white phosphorous—a substance that creates not only horrible burns

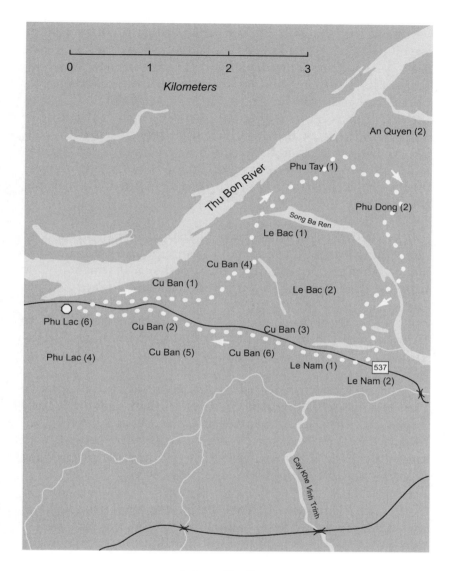

Arizona Territory

on human skin, but creates gigantic billows of white smoke). The battery at An Hoa rumbled like distant thunder, then six artillery rounds shrieked overhead and detonated on target throwing up grey clouds of smoke and debris. I told Crum to get Third Squad ready to move.

Immediately after the Forward Observer announced, "Last rounds out," I yelled, "Move out on the double!" We were 50

79

yards out into the Song Ba Ren when brilliant white cumulus enveloped the far banks. Some of the machine gunners were sinking up to their ankles into the wet sand. The water was cold, but not as deep as it had looked at first. I noticed the white phosphorous smoke was drifting too fast, so I yelled, "Hustle it! Move it out!" Soon we were climbing the far bank and setting in among the dunes, waiting for First and Second Squads to catch up. We were so winded, I just pointed to positions and Marines stumbled wordlessly into them. All of us were drenched in sweat and river water. So far, not a round had been fired. Then all hell broke loose.

A machine gunner was moving into position behind a locked gate when the tree line beyond a pasture ignited like a row of stage lights at opening night on Broadway. Instinctively, he dropped to the ground and unleashed a stream of red 7.62mm tracers, taking a shard of metal in his ring finger from enemy bullets that were ricocheting off the grillwork in front of him. How he survived the initial fusillade, I'll never know. The VC gunners had him dead to rights.

Third Squad was now heavily engaged. As I began to move First Squad behind them towards the left flank, leaving Second Squad in reserve, a tall rifleman took a round in the right leg. I swear I saw it streaking in from a high angle: probably from a sniper in a tree. "Doc" Salisberry crawled over and stopped the bleeding with a tourniquet.

I called, "Snipers up!" Two Marines scuttled over, keeping low in the grass, obviously eager to go to work. I directed them to a gap in the hedgerow, which afforded a view across the opening. They positioned their scoped Remington sniper rifles and watched for targets of opportunity. Three more Marines went down, but I continued to move the squad left to broaden our front facing the enemy. As our volume of fire grew, that of the enemy slacked. I briefed Captain Gruner on the radio and suggested Third Platoon assault on our right flank, as we were blocked by a thick hedgerow and fence.

Soon we had linked up with the assaulting squads from Third Platoon and were examining several enemy prisoners, including one we located in a fighting hole covered with a nylon camouflage cape. He couldn't have been older than sixteen. My machine gunner had pumped a round into his left shoulder. It was swollen and purple and you could tell he was on the edge of shock. His Chinese submachine gun lay next to the hole with several dings in it from the encounter. Later we learned from Third Platoon they had seen several "khaki-clad soldiers" on the far side of the pasture. Thinking they were South Vietnamese or Korean, the Marines held their fire. In fact, they probably were North Vietnamese advisors to the R-20 VC Main Force "Doc Lap" (Independence) Battalion. The captured VC soldier winced as we pulled him from the hole and dragged him towards a group of wounded Marines and prisoners that soon would be flown by medevac helicopter to Danang.

I peered over his shoulder as Dau examined some documents taken from the prisoners; one appeared to be a list of names. Sure enough, he confirmed it was a paymaster's roster with names of his former VC comrades.

After the *whup, whup, whup* of the medevac helicopter faded in the distance, the radio crackled with orders to continue the reconnaissance in force. The company moved southeast through banana groves, open fields, and rice paddies, occasionally finding abandoned and destroyed villages. Always we sensed the presence of small armed bands of VC tracking us on the periphery, anticipating and preparing the best ambush sites.

As the platoon snaked single file along a well-beaten path through thick woods near an abandoned village, a tall corporal in the fire team ahead of me began making frantic exaggerated motions, pointing silently to our right towards something he could see, but we couldn't. He finally settled nervously on the hard-packed trail, sighted his bipod mounted M-14, and cut loose with a startlingly loud burst of automatic fire. When no return fire materialized, we checked the impact area and found a web belt holding several Chinese "potato masher" grenades lying on the trail, neatly cut from its owner's body by the Marine's bullets. There was no blood, no evidence the VC had been hit. The Marine swore he sighted in squarely on at least three guerillas. He was as baffled as the rest of us were skeptical.

81

As the day wore on it became obvious it would be a long one. The company had just turned the bend on a long looping route to the northeast from Phu Lac (6) across the western tip of Go Noi Island. In the span of 10 hours we had fought our way through grid squares 9654, 9753 and 9652. Sensing our homeward vector, the VC stepped up the pressure. Twenty-five yards ahead of me in a bend in the trail, I saw a lance corporal dive into the bushes just as a sniper bullet tore through the air and smacked into the trail beside him. Our fusillade of return fire silenced him. Somewhere along the way we acquired another prisoner: the paymaster whose ledgers we had captured earlier in the day. He was not a happy camper. Corporal Charles "Chip" Mohney, right guide for Third Platoon, found himself on point again, dealing with the complexities of land navigation and exposed traverses across sandbars...

"We were going through this really, really big village. I was point and I came to a trail junction and, quite frankly, I was lost. I wasn't sure where the hell I was. I'm getting told over the radio, 'Move it out. Move it out.' They're pushing, pushing, pushing. I'm thinking to myself, 'Shit. You ought to be up here.' When you're on point and these guys are getting killed day-in and day-out and you're getting told on the radio, 'Move it out. Move it out,' you get to a point where you start taking things in your own hands, going as slow as you can, going as carefully as you can. Lost in this ville at a trail junction, I stopped. I put my men out in a hasty one-eighty defense. I'm kneeling down with the map, trying to figure out where I was, catching hell on the radio. I'm next to a hedgerow and here comes all this crashing through the hedgerow. So I'm thinking it's Captain Glasgow or Captain Gruner, you know, to get me unscrewed on where I'm at and get us moving again. I didn't pay it no mind until I look up and there is a NVA soldier holding a rifle. There he is, bigger than life, holding the rifle. One guy, all by himself. I jump up, stand straight up. This guy looks at me. I'm telling you I can smell his breath, I'm that close. He looks at me and throws his brand-new SKS rifle up in the air. I'm so freakin' flabbergasted I watch the rifle going up in the air as he takes off running down the trail. I slap my M-14 up into my shoulder, ready to let loose with a 20-round burst but he's running right toward my men so I stop squeezing the trigger. They don't see him 'cause they're looking outboard in the hasty one-eighty. I start yelling, 'Turn around!

Turn around! Get him! Get him!' Well by the time my men realize what's going on, he's gone. Disappeared down the trail. Well then, Captain Glasgow does come up, picks up this SKS rifle. I get chewed up one side and down the other. Number one, I guess, for getting lost. Number two, not killing this guy. Well, if my men weren't in front of him, he would have been dead.

Captain Gruner and Captain Glasgow get me squared away on where I'm going and we started moving out again. We go through this big, open stretch of elephant grass. Over your head tall. Comin' out of the grass there at the river, me and my point fire team hit the river. We're waist-deep in water holding our rifles up and they hit us. Rounds are hitting the water everywhere. The fire is coming from a tree line across the tributary. Me and the men make it to a little island in the middle of the river. We're going no further because we can't run, we can't maneuver. I turn around and look back at this tall elephant grass and don't see a soul. Nobody. It seemed like forever, the rounds kicking sand up around me and the fire team. I'm thinking, 'Why isn't somebody giving us some cover fire? Why don't I hear the popping of 60-millimeter mortars?' I thought we were doomed. I kept wondering would it hurt worse when the bullet hits me if I'm tense or if I'm relaxed? So I'd relax and then I'd tense. Then I see the platoon guide, Sergeant Morrill, stick his head out of the elephant grass. He was a character from Boston. Had the heavy accent. He hollers, 'Hey, Mohney!' he says. 'Do you need some help?' I started laughing. 'Yeah,' I says, 'I could use something.' Then the 60 mike-mikes finally starting hitting that treeline. When they did, I told my men, 'All right, let's hit it. Let's get to the bank.' We got to the bank without any casualties and set up there and started laying down fire so everybody could start coming across. Then we moved out again."

Behind Mohney's platoon, Second Platoon moved out onto the undulating dunes of the Song Ba Ren riverbank, through hummocks of tough grass and low bushes. When they hit us again with harassing fire from 150 yards to our left rear, I sprinted across another dry wash with Second Squad, up the far side of the bank, almost colliding with the company command group who were flattened like road-killed salamanders in the sand. "Get down, lieutenant! Snipers!" yelled the captain. Too tired to comply, I chugged on past him and flopped down gasping like a catfish out of water. With darkness approaching, Captain

Gruner decided to move as swiftly as possible back to base. Throughout the day, the company had pushed aggressively through the flat countryside, looking for trouble in Go Noi Island and finding it from small, scattered bands of VC. It had been a rearguard fight since we began looping back home. Now it was time to break contact and move back to the relative security of the trenches and bunkers inside the concertina at Phu Lac (6).

Captain Gruner designated a squad from Second Platoon as point element for the move across half a kilometer of open riverbank that sloped gently south towards a dark tangle of trees and underbrush on the opposite bank. It would be a long exposed traverse, but the road back to Phu Lac (6) lay hidden in the far treeline. I assembled my squad leaders and issued orders: 2nd and 3rd Squads would remain with the main body of the company and join us once we secured the far riverbank. I reminded the Marines of First Squad who would be with me in the traverse to move quickly, to keep an eye on the tree line and avoid bunching up. Since we would be exposed to enemy fire the whole way with not even a pebble for cover, our interval spacing would be extreme. I instructed the squad to concentrate fire on the first enemy position that engaged us, then traverse to the next obvious target.

"Move out," I ordered.

We walked briskly across the sand in wedge formation, senses on full alert despite our exhaustion. After about 400 yards the tree line loomed malevolently before us beyond a steep, narrow gully like a voracious green monster waiting to devour us.

Crack! Crack! Crack! …The unmistakable report of AK-47 rounds snapped around our ears, throwing each of us into an evasive roll on the sand, followed by a bounce onto our feet to fire from the hip in unison, then a desperate sprint forward into what could be our salvation or our ultimate destruction—a thick wall of jungle. Marines crashed though the underbrush and flopped down beside me into firing positions gasping for air and scanning the canopy for snipers. Silence enveloped us. Nothing moved.

84

We regrouped and moved cautiously uphill, still in wedge formation. Beyond the open country we had just traversed, we could hear G Company engaging small bands of VC who were firing from the tree line behind them. Then the thunder from An Hoa rolled, heralding a volley of 105mm howitzer rounds that tore through the air above us, making a sound like ripping fabric, then falling against the darkening horizon to detonate in impressive explosions of smoke, sand and tree limbs. I hustled my radioman Shipley into the entrance of a nearby bunker until the mission ended: no sense both of us falling victim to a short round. Half a dozen volleys gave the company a chance to resume their movement towards us.

Back on the other side of the river, Sgt. Dale Farnham, the Second Platoon Guide, was soon to receive a promotion and a decoration courtesy of the Viet Cong…

"I was near Gruner; we were crossing some little stream there and I says, 'I'm not getting wet.' There was a couple of railroad tracks up farther. So I got up there and I was going to cross them when they started shooting at me, so I had to lay on top of the railroad tracks. There was barbed wire and I got hooked and I lost my helmet and it flew down to the creek and finally I just fell into the water to avoid getting shot.

So then as I was getting out of the water, Lieutenant Jones was in a hole. He reached down and he says, 'Come on, get up in here with me.' I says, 'Lieutenant, every time we get together, we get hit. I'm not getting in there with you. As a matter of fact, get out of there.' They started dropping mortars on us at that time. He says, 'What do you mean?' I says, 'Lieutenant, if you don't get out of that hole, a mortar round is going to come in there.' He says, 'You think so?' I says, 'You betcha.' I says, 'I'm going down the road here.' He says, 'Well, get your helmet.' I says, 'I don't know where it's at.' So I ran down a trail and him and his radioman climbed out of the hole and just as they climbed out of the hole, a mortar round went down into it.

Instead of going the opposite way, he come running down the trail. 'Sergeant Farnham! I gotta thank you! I gotta thank you!' I says, 'Get away from me!' I told him. 'Every time you're around we get hit. Go

85

away!' It was that big whip antenna his radioman was haulin' around. Just like a big flag pole.

We were on the sand bar and we got hit as we were going across. A machine gun was in the sand bar and…they were shooting at us and we made sort of like a frontal assault across an open area. One of the machine guns, and I think it was from Barry's Squad, jammed up. They couldn't get it to fire, so I ran up there and I says, 'What's wrong?' And he says, 'Well, the sand's clogged it all up, you know.' Well, in the citation for the Bronze Star they said I poured my canteen water on it. I didn't. I pissed all over it. I just pissed on it, washed it off, and it started firing again.

About that time, Lieutenant Jones, here he comes right behind me. Him and his radioman with the big whip antenna flailin' everywhere were coming on over. And about then they shot his radioman. I ran over there to take care of him and was yelling for the corpsman to come up and that's when we got, what, two or three corpsman? We got a bunch of corpsman. A corpsman for every squad if I remember right. At least two platoons. Anyway. We had two young ones. They were just fresh out of school. They were scared like anything. I think it was their first patrol out. And they wouldn't move. They would not come up there. After it was over I jumped all over the black-haired one. They wouldn't come up so I didn't have anything to work with. I mean, I didn't have no medical stuff. I tore the kid's tee shirt off and started sticking it right in the hole. He got hit right in the chest. I don't know what shot him because it was behind me when it happened. We were pinned down for a while. Nobody could get to us.

Jones' battalion radio is shot out, so he called the arty people. He got a hold of the arty people and asked them to send the chopper up, which they did. They tried to get to us, but they couldn't get down because there was so much fire. Second Lieutenant Jones, he was a fantastic artillery officer and good at what he did for a second lieutenant. You know, everybody worries about second lieutenants coming straight out of school, but he was really good and he liked to do what he did. He could not quite read the map as good as Lieutenant Buchanan could, but he could read it. He was using the old grid maps and the lieutenant gave him a pictorial map. So he had both of them, there. He told me he knew what gun could shoot where, because he would go back to the 105 battery and talk to the sergeant and tell him which one was having problems and all that other stuff. So he could discriminate one gun out of six on line. 'Cause every time we'd get back into the battalion area, he'd go over and talk to those guys and find out which gun's firing good and everything. He could call up a fire mission without even any spotting rounds a lot of times. He would just fire for effect and it would be right on."

After witnessing his heroics, Lieutenant Jones recommended Sgt. Farnham for a Bronze Star medal. But Sergeant Farnham himself witnessed a heroic act...

"When the mortars came in Bruner, the radioman, jumped on Captain Gruner. And what had happened on that was after Lieutenant Jones pulled me out of the river, Bruner and Captain Gruner was right down the trail. We started getting mortars in and everything. When those mortar rounds came in, Bruner just jumped on Gruner and laid there.

We had a VC prisoner and the Company Gunny killed him. Our platoon had caught him. I think he was the paymaster for the VC company because he had all these Piasters. And after the operation, we went out and took care of our laundry and all that stuff with the VC money. I think the Gunny, the Company Gunny killed him because he took off and headed back towards Go Noi. I think he hit him with a fleshette round from his shotgun."

Second Squad leader Joe Barry, left behind with the G Company command group, remembers a feeling of extreme vulnerability.

"I was on one side of the riverbed. Sergeant Mack was standing on the other side, his radioman down behind him. Standing next to Sergeant Mack down on one knee was a, it might have been a lieutenant, calling in an artillery mission. And you know, he was getting the coordinates, and the whole tree line was lit up. A .30 caliber was firing on us. I'm out on a sand bar with one of my men and the VC, they're getting the range. Now they've crossed back and forth with their traversing mechanism, crossed the sand with machine gun fire, and they just keep creeping up trying to get us. What I didn't see was that the radioman was facing us and he's just getting ready to shut his eyes. He told me this later. He says, 'There were mortars walking in

closer behind you and I could see the machine gun fire getting closer. Any moment,' he said, 'I thought I was going to watch you be killed, either by the mortars or the machine gun fire.'

"Just about the time it would have happened, the fire mission finally was, you know, successful …no spotter rounds. They immediately fired for effect. The whole tree line lit up. You know, really good coordinates. Sergeant Mack wouldn't let me go across over the river to join up with Lieutenant Buchanan. He said, 'Already too many people over there.' He didn't want us bunching up. Where I was, I didn't realize how dangerous it was. The guy with me got a "John Wayne" wound, I called it. The round just creased his shoulder and, you know, you could see the whole ball of the shoulder. And I didn't—I'm no medic or anything—I just pulled out a compress and covered it the best I could. But on your shoulder like that, it's not going to stay. And, I mean, when the action was all over, he was praising me up and down: 'You saved my life. You saved my life.' And I said, 'Hey, look. That's a "John Wayne" wound. That's nothing. It didn't even hit the bone, you know? You're going to be fine.' But it did rip the muscle and well, later on, I don't know if he talked to the medic or what, he said, 'You could have killed me!' I thought I did what I could, you know. I covered it up and…what are you going to do with these Marines?"

On our side of the river, AK 47s firing in the direction of the beleaguered company headquarters broke out from the edge of the trees not 50 yards downhill from us. I formed the squad on line, then moved them through the darkening trees with hand signals towards what sounded like more than one automatic weapon. As soon as I could see light through the undergrowth, I gave the signal for a sustained rate of fire, indicating they should shoot low to compensate for the slope. The smoke and falling vegetation from our fusillade cleared and the enemy fire fell silent.

Lieutenant Marc Glasgow, the company Executive Officer, remembers the extremely exposed position the headquarters group was in as they tried to cross the open sand towards us…

"When they opened up on Buchanan's squad, they were pretty far through it. Before that happened, I did not want to go through there, so I discussed with Gruner about going 'round. But we didn't have *time; it was getting late in the day. He deemed that we had to go through that open space while Second Platoon was going forward. When they hit the CP, Gruner and I and the radio operator, we dove behind big anthills that were there. And an enemy machine gunner was off to the east. He was just takin' out the anthill that my radio operator and I were behind; and I couldn't understand—the thing was just coming apart. Pretty soon we had to move, or the bullets were going to come through. He was just taking it apart, and I couldn't understand how he knew where I was with the radio operator. Gruner was up behind another one. That's the first time I recall seein' what we called a Marine Corps gunship. It was a Huey with machine guns on the side. They called that in. That's what they sent for air support. That's all they could get to help us get out of that mess. By that time, I think Buchanan and the Second Platoon squad was in the treeline. We were stuck in the middle.*

There was a platoon behind us. I turned around and this VC machine gunner that was taking the Goddamned anthills apart, was going to get the whole CP. I told Staff Sergeant Carter, the Platoon Sergeant, 'Go kill that guy.' And he did. They went and they killed the machine gunner. They circled around on his flank and killed him. But I couldn't understand how the guy knew where we were until I realized he was aiming at the big whip antenna. He was just shootin' where the whip was. I turned around to grab the whip and a bullet came through and hit me in the leg, but it was a spent bullet. It didn't penetrate; it just broke the Goddamned...pants. That's it. Just left a bruise—nothin' but a mark. But it shocked me so much I jumped. And I didn't know it at the time, but I popped a disc. I was turned around grabbing the big whip when it happened. And from that time on, my left thigh was numb. Couldn't understand why, but I didn't find out until, I don't know, some years after the Marine Corps. I had a busted disc. By the time we finally got out of that field it was dark...and we were holding on to the guy in front of us trying to go back the east road to Phu Lac, just in a world of hurt. The reason we kept going, trying to make Phu Lac, is we were out of ammunition. And Gruner decided it was better to try to make it by doing that than staying here. Of course, then we made it. I was never so happy as when we hit Phu Lac."

Back in our position across the river, Shipley's radio came alive. "Sir," he said to me, holding the handset to his right ear.

"Sergeant Mack has been hit. Some more Marines are down and they had to shoot that VC prisoner who was trying to escape. Bruner says they're almost out of ammo." By that time, we could barely see across the Song Ba Ren.

The dank night air, alive with insect song, enveloped us like the shroud of death itself just as the rest of the company arrived and we linked up finally with Second and Third Squads. Soon we were in column formation on the road to Phu Lac (6). It was so dark we almost had to perform what Staff Sergeant Bill Curt, my Platoon Leader's Class drill instructor at Quantico, Virginia, delighted in calling "The Elephant Walk"—grabbing the entrenching tool of the Marine in front of you—as punishment for failing to keep a regulation interval. Progress was agonizingly slow, allowing me to take stock of my gear, myself, and my mental condition. We were under strength, exhausted, and almost out of ammunition. My utilities emitted a sulfurous stench like a pile of rotting cabbage. Everyone was braced mentally for an ambush by a VC unit that had maneuvered into an ideal position during the skirmish by the river. That would be the final straw. Much to my dismay, I noticed the luminous dial of my field watch, which I had hung from a buttonhole in my collar for some stupid reason, was glowing like a miniature full moon right over my chest, providing a perfect bull's-eye for an enterprising VC sniper. I ripped it off and plunged it into my pocket. Soon we could see the bulk of Phu Lac (6) rising against the sky before us, could feel the ground tilting upwards towards home. Sergeant Farnham remembers a feeling of overwhelming relief...

"We got hit seven different times that day—truly a long day in the Arizona. Seven different times. I mean, major hits. We got into fights all the way up through there. Just like a, you know, shooting gallery. Goin' back to Phu Lac (6) that night I was so scared. We were so afraid that if we let go of the guy in front of us that we'd lose the guy behind us or something. I said to myself, 'Boy, I tell you what. We got the most fantastic platoon commander of all time.' Because there was no one else that could have brought us out that night. Nobody. We were on point and he had that magical compass that the lieutenant's dad sent and Gruner put the best one up there on point and it was him. Oh, it was dark that night. The darkest night of our lives. Guys

were falling down and runnin' into stuff and everything else. They were so tired that they didn't even care."

Corporal "Chip" Mohney recalled a very dicey situation...

"At the end of that day, just about everybody was out of ammunition, so we redistributed ammo. But there was no sense in me getting any because I could not kick my chamber open. I got the operating rod handle on the M14 on the ground and I'm kicking it but it won't move. It was full of sand. Whoever had them, fixed bayonets and then we made the long walk home in the dark. Thank God nobody hit us. Not one round. Well, they might have ran out of ammo, too. Oh, it was dark."

The real point of the spear that night was Charles Gutierrez, a 22 year old corporal from Albuquerque, New Mexico who found himself leading the column home through the menacing darkness...

"Man, it was so dark the trail was just a little white blur I could barely make out. We tried to move as quiet as we could so we wouldn't get ambushed. Many times the trail would turn, then I would have to kneel in the dark and wait to hear the footsteps of the man behind catchin' up with me. It was nerve wracking. We were all just tired as hell, but we had to pay attention so the Marines at Phu Lac (6) wouldn't shoot us when we got close to the wire."

Despite the casualties, the feeling was G Company had entered the dreaded "Arizona Territory" and had tested the enemy in his Go Noi Island lair. We had shown them they no longer were masters of that sanctuary; that we would hunt them down beyond grid line 94 on our own timetable. As I stood at my traditional spot that night, ushering my Marines through the gap in the concertina, one of them remarked, " God damn, lieutenant. We kicked some butt today!" So much for the myth of the Arizona Territory, or so we thought[5].

[5] Future forays into that same area in January 1967 once again would test the myth of the Arizona Territory and its dreaded beating heart—Go Noi Island. An excellent book on the subject is *Operation Tuscaloosa* by former 2/5 Marine John J. Culbertson.

PFC JOHN RICHARD BATES

Early morning of 17 December, two kilometers east-northeast of Phu Lac (6), Second Platoon was on point again, leading the company from a warren of abandoned hamlets and the cover of trees out onto exposed banks of a tributary of the Song Thu Bon. Hummocks of sawgrass still wet with dew festooned the undulating dunes. Before reaching the apron of the stream bank, we had encountered some resistance from small bands of VC soldiers, but had taken no casualties.

I crawled forward with 2nd Lieutenant Jones, the artillery observer, and peered over a sand dune to assess the possibilities of a 105 mm howitzer barrage. Beyond the sharp bank of the tributary lay open sand for 75 meters, then a ribbon of water, more sand and another sharp bank. Beyond that was a wall of green hiding the supposedly abandoned hamlet of Le Bac (1). My instincts and our past experience warned of an enemy ambush. Jones' radioman was behind us with the enormous whip radio antenna thrusting into the air like a flagpole. About halfway through our discussion about coordinates and fuses, a puff of smoke erupted at the base of the trees across the wash. I thought to myself, "That's curious, why would…" A split second later, a stream of bullets shredded the air a foot above our helmets, sending us plunging face down into the sand. Then we heard the characteristic stutter of a Soviet machine gun. The VC gunner dropped his sights and tore up the sand dune in front of us. Then all hell broke loose.

Although our immediate response was vigorous, the VC unit had planned the encounter well; a 60 mm mortar crew north of us, aided by a 12.7 mm machine gun crew, peppered our position with a deadly crossfire. Well dug in and superbly camouflaged along the banks, the VC soldiers uncharacteristically stood their ground. For John Richard Bates, a lean twenty-year old PFC rifleman with farm boy good looks from Little Rock, Arkansas, that was an unforgettable day …

"At daybreak the rains had stopped, but the sky was still overcast. We wolfed a can or two of C-rations and saddled up to move out. Soon Golf Company was moving northeast of Phu Lac (6), keeping up the momentum of aggressive search and destroy patrols we had maintained since our arrival at An Hoa.

Within Second Platoon, we leapfrogged positions every thirty minutes or so, walking both point and flank security to share the stress and danger equitably. As we slowly passed through what we knew to be the actual village of Phu Lac (6), it was strikingly quiet. Usually, these villages were occupied by children, mothers and the elderly. Sweeping quietly through the narrow paths between the grass huts, we realized that there was no one in sight. Chickens and pigs were still going about their morning routines. Fires were still smoldering as if left recently unattended. A thick blanket of cloud pressed the pungent smell of wood and cane smoke low to the deck. Laundry had been hung to dry on the walls of the hootches. A water buffalo was staked to the ground by a short rope fastened to a nose ring. We searched every hut and the immediate surrounding area carefully. Under one of the large straw rice mats, a Marine found a cache of money. As it was not a significantly large amount, it remained unclear as to whether or not it was personal belongings or perhaps that of the VC. The money and site were reported to the battalion S-2, Intelligence.

94

Our suspicions were that the villagers had been told by the VC that we would be coming that way and if they didn't want to be in a crossfire, they must leave immediately. We had the ominous feeling that our every move was being watched and that any moment we might be walking into the kill zone of an ambush. As the point man, my senses were on high alert. Because of the dense jungle foliage, upon transit through the village, there was a collective sigh of relief that perhaps the VC had decided to choose another day and place for a fight.

Shortly after clearing the village, we spotted three young NVA soldiers wearing green uniforms, black rubber sandals, and carrying AK's on a trail intersection about 20 feet away. Apparently they were unaware of our presence. I put a magazine of 20 rounds into two of them in a four second burst leaving them sprawled dead on the trail and the third running blindly across the sights of Sergeant Alberto Alvarez, my squad leader, who dropped him with a single shot.

The next few minutes were laced with raw emotion. For the first time, I had actually seen the enemy we were fighting. Had they been more alert, it might very well have been our bodies lying in a pool of blood instead of theirs. Upon seeing them up close, it bothered me that they seemed so young, probably about seventeen or eighteen at most. The thought that they, like us, had families also disturbed me. They were at least someone's son, probably someone's brother, or even perhaps had children of their own. My squad seemed jovial about the kill and finally seeing what had up to then been an unseen enemy ....except for me; I just wanted to throw up. Until that moment, the fights had been protracted and at least for me, somewhat distant. Now Viet Nam had a personal aspect about it that would change others and me forever.

It wasn't long before the trees and brush gave way to sand dunes and grass hummocks and we began to receive small arms fire from across the river. It was apparent that the enemy was occupying an egg-shaped, vegetated peninsula, covered on three sides by sand and bordered in the rear by the Song Thu Bon River. To the flanks and front was a large heavily foliated sandbar about forty meters in depth and a couple of hundred meters wide. Our position had occasional scrub brush providing little concealment, and no real cover. Orders were passed for us to pull back a short distance and get down in a covered position while air strikes were called to soften the enemy fire.

The firefight slowed from both sides temporarily. Within a half an hour, an F-8 Crusader arrived on station. After a low level pass to confirm the target which was marked by white phosphorous mortar rounds, the air was shattered with the explosion of MK-82 bombs, 20 mm cannon fire, and on the final pass, what had become my personal favorite, napalm.

There was little hope of anything being able to survive the air strike. Anyone not killed by the bullets or concussion and shrapnel of the larger munitions, would surely have been burned to death or been suffocated by the napalm. Even from our distance in the hasty positions we occupied back in the tree line, the sounds were deafening and the heat was scorching. As the air support was leaving, we were ordered to prepare to sweep the "former" enemy site.

Our platoon commander, Lieutenant Buchanan, had us moving towards the objective in fire team rushes. To our collective great surprise, we received an ever-increasing volume of fire. In the open sand we had little cover and no concealment.

Suddenly something slammed into my chest, propelling me rearward onto my back, leaving me wondering what the hell had happened. There was no doubt in my mind that I had been hit. I just didn't know with what. I could best describe the feeling as standing over home plate and having Mark McGuire try to put me over the fence with a full swing of his heaviest bat. Although there was nothing that I could identify as actual pain, my entire body buzzed as if I was holding a low voltage live wire. I thought it best to call for a corpsman since the firefight was raging with growing intensity and I had no way of knowing if anyone had seen me go down. As I opened my mouth to call for a corpsman, a froth of bloody bubbles swelled from my throat and popped. Then I knew that I had the dreaded "sucking chest wound." My body felt heavy and nearly immobile. My mental tachometer was redlining. In rapid sequence I realized that I was in the open, I might be shot again, and help might not be able to reach me in time.

Two Marines dropping at my side distracted me from my morbid train of thought. At first I thought that they too had just been hit; but it was Lieutenant Buchanan and his radio operator. The radioman was wearing one radio and carrying another while the lieutenant called for an emergency medevac. Enemy rounds continued to crack past our heads and I fully believed that any moment, one or all of us would be killed.

Now back up on one knee, Lieutenant Buchanan directed the rest of the platoon to provide overwhelming fire into the enemy, which from my vantage point were holding their own. One of our corpsmen, "Doc" Salisberry, soon was lying beside me trying to assess the damage. He kept asking me where I was hit but I couldn't tell him. I had this strange idea that if I didn't open my mouth, I would lose less blood. As he stripped off my flak jacket, I could hear him reciting a Catholic prayer while beginning treatment of my wounds by plugging them with plastic compresses. Corporal Barry, my fire team leader, arrived at my side. Corporal Barry, who thought I was as good as dead or soon to die, was telling the corpsman that a Marine whose name I don't remember, 'Was shot just like that at the DMZ before I had arrived in-country, and he didn't live until the medevac arrived.' I wanted badly to tell him that I had no intention of dying, but again, I didn't want to open my mouth and lose more blood. My thirst became intense. Thoughts flashed through my brain of old cowboy movies where the fatally wounded cowpoke would ask for a canteen of water just before he slipped away. Becoming more convinced of the severity of my situation, I kept saying to myself over and over, 'I don't want to die like this.'

Lieutenant Buchanan, who had done all he could for me, returned to directing the platoon against the objective. Doc Salisberry pumped blood expanders into my veins and broke smelling salt ampoules at intervals to try to keep me conscious and alert and to maintain the "cough reflex" so I would not drown in my own blood.

Less than a half-hour later, I heard the distant "whump, whump, whump" of rotor blades. I knew, or at least hoped, that it would be the medevac. Doc had me lying on my side to keep blood from draining into my lung and drowning me. I don't recall any real pain, but I had learned enough about "shock" that I didn't want to go into it. Soon, over the tree line to our rear, I could see an H-34 medevac bird supported by a UH-1 "Huey" gunship."

I knew by then that several other Marines had been hit besides PFC Bates: a 3.5 inch rocket man from weapons platoon with a flesh wound in his buttock and several others. Even though the incoming fire continued at a fierce rate, we had to

97

get the wounded out of there, and fast. Bates looked particularly bad. Bloody froth was bubbling out of his mouth and onto his chest where I could see he had taken a round or two. My radioman gave me the handset and said, "Cassandra Golf Six, Sir. Chopper inbound." I briefed Captain Gruner, then ordered the platoon to intensify their fire in order to protect the medevac helicopter. Then my radioman added with some exasperation, "Sir, the chopper can't see us. He doesn't know where we are!" I looked up to see the Huey veer off and circle out over the southern banks of the Song Thu Bon. PFC Bates was devastated...

"I then witnessed a spectacular and horribly disheartening event: the helicopters turned away. What optimism I might have had that I would ever see home again evaporated. I kept thinking that I really didn't want to die here in Quang Nam Province. I wondered how my family would take the news. I pictured my sisters crying at a funeral being held in the bright hot sun. I wondered if the camera I had bought at Camp Pendleton before coming to Vietnam would be inventoried in the rear and sent back to my folks. I was hoping that they would develop the film in it. Neither the Huey gunship nor the H-34 were in sight and I had to assume that the zone was "too hot", and I would just have to wait longer."

A smoke grenade would only mark our position more precisely for the VC mortar men on the opposite bank; we had no air panels. Frantic to get the wounded evacuated, I told the radioman, "Tell Cassandra Six to bring him back in. He should look for a signal which I will mark." The whump, whump, whump of helicopter rotors grew louder, then the olive drab bird was floating over the trees a hundred meters away from us, keeping low to avoid enemy fire.

"Mark, mark, mark," I yelled at the radioman while flashing the mirror of my Silva compass towards the pilot. "Sir, he sees us," the radioman shouted. "He's coming in!" PFC Bates' hopes soared...

"Probably two minutes later I heard the familiar "whump" of rotor blades—a distinctly "Huey" sound. Now the bird was headed directly for my position. It was flying very fast, and very low. As it got to

where I was lying, the pilot pulled the collective and pushed the cyclic which for a moment made the bird look as if it were trying to stand on its tail. For the next few seconds, everything was chaotic. The rotor wash blew sand, grass, and debris, limiting visibility to only a few feet. The door gunner from the gunship ran out to help Doc haul me aboard, overshot in the low visibility, then did a quick U-turn back to my position. Doc Salisberry already had rolled me onto a poncho and the two of them grabbed the sides and ran about two steps before dropping me hard. Had one of them taken a round, I thought? But they had just stumbled, losing their footing in the sand. Regaining their grip, they took off again and literally heaved me onto the floor of the bird. Doc Salisberry tapped me on the helmet and ran back to attend to other casualties."

Over the roar of the turbine engine and rotor wash, I could hear enemy rounds snapping around us. We would have to hustle it to avoid more casualties. As Sergeant Farnham, my Platoon Sergeant, prepared to load the wounded Marines aboard the Huey, PFC Bates turned to me, his chest and chin stained red with frothy blood, and blurted out, "I'm sorry, lieutenant!"

"We want to hear some nurse stories when you get back, Bates. No lollygaggin' in the hospital, you understand? You'll be okay," I yelled. "Hang in there!" My platoon sergeant, Dale Farnham recalled later…

"When Lieutenant Buchanan and I were putting Bates on the chopper, VC rounds were pingin' the thing all over the place. I didn't think the pilot was going to stay on the ground long enough for us to put him in there. The enemy fire was so hot and heavy and everybody's laying down fire and he and I were about the only ones that weren't shooting. The rest of them, everybody else was just laying down a cover of fire to get the chopper in. We had Bates and we put him in head first and as he was going in he raised his head up and he says, "I'm sorry." The lieutenant commented on it later that night, on the hill. And my response was, ' Boy, I tell you lieutenant, we've got some good Marines.'

A 3.5-inch rocket launcher Marine got hit in the butt because he was lying down on the sand dune. The round went right through the crack of his butt. When we peeled him open, it looked like sombody'd took a razor blade on the inside of his cheek and scraped it. Somebody commented, and I don't know if it was Carl or not, he said, 'We ought to get a rag to put up there.' And they put one of those pressure bandages up there, something like Kotex. It just scraped him. Went through his clothes and everything, but it was like a razor blade."

In a hurricane of blown sand and debris, the bird lifted off, keeping low until it was beyond maximum effective small arms range and could safely gain altitude over the slate colored river. For PFC Bates, it was the ride to salvation...

"As we lifted up and the pilot transitioned into forward flight, I could hear and feel enemy rounds hitting the fuselage. Looking up, I could see holes opening in the overhead and daylight shining down through them. The pilot was twisting and turning the bird radically to reduce his vulnerability to ground fire. The door gunner was firing his M-60 into the jungle below while using his feet to keep me from falling out the open door. Although on the verge of doing so, I never actually lost consciousness. I kept thinking that maybe my risk of being shot again would be reduced if I could just slide over a bit closer to the centerline of the helicopter. Because of the loss of blood, try as I might, I just couldn't move my body. My mind was whirling with emotion and the thought that this surrealistic scene could not be happening to me.

Each meter of altitude gained provided more safety from enemy ground fire. The door gunner, wiping the grit from his face, looked me directly in the eye as if he was trying to recognize me. But we had never met until that morning. He kept slapping me on the boot and telling me 'Hang in there, Marine. You are going to make it just fine.' But his eyes betrayed his words."

With the wounded on their way to the hospital in Danang, I refocused our efforts on the enemy positions. Staff Sergeant Wallace Carter from Centerville, Iowa a handsome Marine built like an NFL fullback, crawled over to me and said, "Lieutenant, the captain wants me to assault through your position as soon as 81s finish the mission across the river." Carter was platoon commander of Third Platoon when I joined the company at Con Thien and was known for his aggressiveness and iron discipline. Sergeant Farnham was equally impressed with Carter's performance, the way he ran his platoon, and how the two platoons worked together…

"Captain Gruner then ordered Third Platoon to assault through our lines. I don't know why, but we always worked better together with Third Platoon than we did with First Platoon. The lieutenant over there, he wasn't as friendly as Marc Glasgow. Of course, Lieutenant Buchanan and Glasgow talked a lot and everything. I don't know. Maybe our Marines were more professional than the First Platoon was, or something. It was just the idea that they couldn't do exactly what Captain Gruner wanted them to do, so he always picked on us first. Gruner knew that we were good and we were so proud to be the first platoon out on point and we didn't mind being on point because we knew we had a good leader and he knew we weren't going to do anything that was stupid and would get somebody hurt unnecessarily."

I passed the word down the line to prepare to support Carter's move with a "mad moment." Just before Carter jumped off, we opened up with two M-60s a 3.5 rocket launcher, M-14s, and M-79 grenade launchers. I clinched my fists and cringed internally as I followed Carter's progress across the dry wash. He was totally exposed. The Viet Cong 12.7 mm machine gun 400 meters to our left front had cranked up again, throwing mini geysers of sand into the air. Carter was doing some impressive broken field running, pausing at a large driftwood log, briefly gauging the situation, then splashing through the shallow stream and charging up the opposite bank into the village. Just before he cleared the sand dunes on the other side, one of his riflemen took a machine gun bullet to the head and went down like a rag doll.

Soon we joined Carter's platoon inside the village and took over the point. Doc Salisberry was tending an unconscious VC soldier who had a bandage around his throat. What should we do with him? Leave him there? Call for another medevac chopper? While we were scratching our heads and discussing it, he solved our problem by passing away peacefully. We folded his arms down by his sides and left him by a fighting hole. I moved Third Squad forward through the village we had come to know as a VC stronghold. This was a "free fire zone" from which the population had been removed and resettled months

101

ago. To our surprise, within 250 meters we came upon the only inhabitants of that area we had seen all day. Despite the raging firefight that had erupted relatively close to them, three Vietnamese women were preparing lunch for an elderly man who had to be helped to his place at a wooden table under a palm-frond veranda. Two small children chased a rooster around the hard packed dirt yard. A young woman had just placed a bowl of "pho" and a pair of chopsticks in front of the old man when the radio crackled.

"Lieutenant," my radioman said. "It's Cassandra Golf Six Actual. He says burn the whole fuckin' village. He sounds pissed, Sir."

Before I could pass the order on, one of the Marines in Second Squad flipped open his lighter beneath the eaves of the thatched roof. A tongue of flame burst from the dry fronds and began to lick its way up the roof. The old man looked confused, but continued to eat his "pho." His shaky hands resembled gnarled roots; his face was a roadmap of misery. Without further thought, I grabbed the Marine as he moved towards the veranda, lighter in hand while Dau beat out the flames on the roof with his hands.

"Belay that, Marine. Not this one, " I said. "Go on down the line: those hootches down there," and I pointed down the trail.

"But lieutenant. I heard the captain…"

"Do it now, Marine."

"Aye, aye, Sir."

AMBUSH AT THON BON (1)

Silver Star

After spending the night back at Phu Lac (6) patrol base, we left early the next morning, 18 December, on an even more ambitious operation with Echo and Foxtrot Companies, most likely prompted by intelligence reports of sizeable VC Main Force units maneuvering along the river east of us. Moving east along the road from Phu Lac (6), toward Cu Ban (3), at first we made light contact and took no casualties. Marc Glasgow, the Executive Officer, also remembers only light contact—at first...

"When we were ordered to do the search and destroy with all three companies, we went out with two platoons; we left one platoon back.

103

We were just to do an overnight patrol to the east and be back the next morning or something. That was the objective, so we were fairly light when we went out. We were less than 100 strong. I want to say 94 total, because as XO, I tallied such things. We didn't take anything heavy for a long period of time. We were kind of foolish. We should have carried more ammo. As we were proceeding east on the road, we took intermittent contact. There were trench lines on either side that had been dug. I started to get a foreboding. We didn't make much contact as I recall until Captain Gruner decided we were going to go into the village."

We spent the night next to the road a couple of clicks from Phu Lac (6) then the next morning, 19 December, proceeded east once again. Company E was about 3 clicks north-northeast of us along the banks of the Song Thu Bon while Company F was bivouacked around 3 clicks south-southeast of us near some railroad tracks. Villagers along our route of march informed us 100 VC had passed through earlier. At about 1730, we were in company column formation with Second Platoon on point, traversing open, sandy terrain. A tree line ran parallel to the road on our right. The Song Ba Ren flowed parallel to our march route, a hundred meters from our left flank. Suddenly a single sniper round shredded the air over our heads, sending us onto the sand to consider a response. It had come from the vicinity of a small hamlet called Thon Bon (1) that was further east along the road, beyond a bridge.

Over the radio, Captain Gruner demanded to know what was holding up the show. " Sniper in the tree line, Sir," I replied. We were so exposed I was reluctant to move toward the road without preparing for covering fire. Soon more pointed urging from Gruner—"Lieutenant, move on down to the road,"—sent us down a sandy slope and into the trees without further incident. The road took us to the far side of a footbridge that spanned a small stream where I crouched shoulder to shoulder with my First Squad leader, 23-year-old Sgt. Wayne Eugene Dawson, a lean, seasoned fighter with hawkish features from Champaign, Illinois. Sgt. Dawson had just started his second tour in Vietnam and we had begun to work well together. We didn't like what we saw.

Beyond the bridge a trail on top of a dike traversed a flooded rice paddy, angling towards a hedgerow 300 meters away that marked the perimeter of the hamlet of Thon Bon (1). We both agreed it looked too quiet; an enemy unit would hold all the cards when we moved from our covered positions out onto the exposed dike. My extrasensory perception screamed mortal danger, but I sensed the company piling up behind us and, more importantly, Captain Gruner's impatience and the lateness of the day. My gut instinct told me the sniper round had been planned to lure us in a specific direction. Nevertheless, Sergeant Dawson and I formulated a hasty plan. I fastened my helmet strap, zipped up my flak jacket and told Sergeant Dawson, "Put Hamm's gun team next to that hummock to cover us. Last rounds after the 105 HE will be Willy Peter. As soon as those rounds are in the air, we move out on the double, and I mean on the double, towards the village. " Dawson concurred with the simple plan.

Thunder from the direction of An Hoa soon delivered six 105 mm high explosive rounds that threw smoke, trees, dirt, and bamboo frame structures into the air. Lieutenant Jones, the artillery forward observer, yelled, "Last rounds out."

"Move out on the double," I ordered.

In the face of modern day Vietnamese government intransigence and secrecy about military matters, we can only speculate what might have been transpiring on the Vietnamese communist side[6]...

Nguyen Lan[7] a 29-year-old "returnee" from North Vietnam and commander of Company Two of the R-20 VC Main Force "Doc Lap" Battalion, tracked three members of a reconnaissance/intelligence squad led by Sergeant Sau as they slithered, crawled, waded, then ran towards

---

[6] As I write this, Don Duong, the Vietnamese actor who played the NVA general in the movie *"We Were Soldiers,"* is under house arrest in Saigon.

[7] A real person who is identified in my platoon commander's notebook dated January 1967.

his position in Thon Bon (1). They were so well camouflaged with grasses and leafy twigs that it was difficult to follow them in the oblique light, even with his East German Zeiss-Jena binoculars. They had done a superb job tracking the American Marine Company G since their bivouac, then luring them down to the road. It had taken only one shot to turn them towards his carefully laid ambush.

Company commander Lan brushed the palm of his hand across the smooth reddish brown leather of the Tokarev TT33 7.62 mm pistol that swung from his belt and surveyed the three-man cells that made up three platoons of his 96-man company. Each was positioned in camouflaged and reinforced fighting holes facing the Marines. A 7.62 mm Soviet Dugtarev RPD light machine gun covered the northwestern quadrant across the rice paddy and another covered the northeastern quadrant toward the low sand ridge this side of the Song Ba Ren. Each gunner had several 100-round drums within easy reach of his fighting hole.

Mai Van Hung, the R-20 Battalion Commander whose headquarters were 1500 meters to the north across the river near the village of Thanh My, had entrusted this important assignment to Commander Lan because of his tenacity and tactical adroitness during previous engagements with the Marines. Lan had proven himself skilled in inflicting casualties on the Marines while minimizing his own by anticipating the use of airplanes and artillery and maneuvering his troops quickly out of the impact area. Battalion Commander Hung would be proud of his deployment this afternoon.

Once reconnaissance reports delivered early that morning made it clear that the Marines were moving east again, Commander Lan conceived and executed what he considered a workable plan to attack the Americans; he brought two platoons of his company from their base in the foothills near Nui Dat to the village of Thon Bon (1) in three-man cells. The third platoon preceded the Marines as they progressed eastward along the road. He positioned his men in such a manner that a tributary of the Song Ba Ren would trap the Marines if they committed themselves to an advance along the paddy dike. He would train an automatic weapon along that avenue of approach and hold his fire until the Marines were well within the kill zone. An 82-mm mortar team across the river in Dien Phu already had fired registration rounds and stood poised to saturate the kill zone with deadly missiles. *A sergeant with the sapper platoon had carefully hidden an American 105 mm artillery shell rigged with an electronic blasting cap next to a gate along the trail on one flank of the kill zone. The detonation of that shell by the sapper sergeant would be the signal to spring the ambush.*

By 0900 they had completed almost all of the preparations, including pre-positioning security cells along the escape route to the south. A rough semi-circle of fighting holes faced the ambush kill zone. Another semi circle of bunkers with bamboo tree reinforcement lay 30 meters behind the first holes. The decoy platoon had done an excellent job that morning luring the Marine company in the right direction by moving quickly east down the road. Surely informers among the villagers in the Cu Ban hamlets and Le Nam hamlets—those settlements that straddled the road—would report the passage of a large body of armed VC. Commander Mai had reminded Lan to, "Grab the Americans by the belt whenever you can. Deny them the use of artillery and airplanes."

It was 1800 and the light was fading when he first spotted the Americans. Three of them were crouched at the near end of the bridge, pointing and talking. When the shortest of the three spoke into a radio handset, he knew what was coming.

"All platoons to the secondary positions now !" he commanded. " Artillery!"

Like camouflaged sand crabs, the cells of each platoon scuttled back to the protection of the inner circle of bunkers in choreographed sequence. Then Lan heard the rumble of artillery at An Hoa. He dove into a nearby bunker just before six shells struck the hamlet, throwing hot metal, vegetation, the hindquarters of an unfortunate pig, and a heavy wooden table into the air. Through the smoke and dust, he could see that eight soldiers had been wounded by the barrage, some slightly, others more seriously. Another muffled ba-ba boom echoed from the southwest followed by an ear-splitting shriek and six more concussive blasts that sent razor sharp fragments ripping through the vegetation and into three more of his men. One of the Dugtarev RPD machine guns was lying on its side smashed by shrapnel. Two of its crew lay dead. Although the blasts had almost broken his eardrums, and he had a nosebleed, Commander Lan peered over the top of his bunker. Along the trail where the Marines had been, he could just make out movement.

"Primary positions now!" he commanded.

His platoon leaders began moving their cells back towards the fighting holes they had vacated just as a final report rumbled from An Hoa. Lan immediately realized he had miscalculated; the moving Marines had convinced him that the artillery mission was over. Not so. The incoming shells burst into thick clouds of white smoke that enveloped his position and sent meteors and comets of burning phosphorous streaking through the air, smacking into one of his machine gunners and a senior sergeant. The NVA political officer did a little dance while swatting ineffectively at a glowing coal that was eating into his thigh. Inexperienced fool, thought Lan. No matter, it was time to trigger the ambush.

"Fire the artillery shell, " ordered Lan. Nothing. "Fire the artillery shell," he repeated. Silence. "What happened?" he demanded of the sapper senior sergeant.

"I do not understand, Commander Lan," the sergeant answered with a great amount of distress in his voice. "I laid the wires carefully."

We took off, following the narrow dike out into the open, body armor and linked machine gun belts clanking. Clouds rising over Nui Hon Chau mimicked the brilliant spiked cumulus of white phosphorous rounds that had begun to blossom in the village. But the squad was moving too slow for my taste. The smoke was drifting. "Double time!" I yelled, gesturing forward. Alarm sirens in my head were shrieking imminent contact.

"Ban! (Fire!)" ordered Commander Lan. "Ban Luc Nay" (Fire now!)" And his soldiers unleashed a storm of automatic and semi-automatic fire towards the exposed enemy, some from AK-47s, some from Soviet SKS rifles, the remaining machine gun, and a Browning automatic rifle. Lan saw two Marines fall hard on the trail. Cell four had done a good job focusing on what appeared to be a Marine commander and his radio operator as they disappeared from sight behind a bush.

Sure enough, we were a hundred and fifty meters from the village when a firestorm of automatic weapons erupted from the hedgerow, cutting down Corporal Horn, PFC Frost and Corporal Gutierrez instantly. My reflexes threw me into a depression beside the trail chased by a swarm of enemy rounds that shredded the air above my helmet and trimmed the vegetation around me; once again, VC gunners were double-teaming an American commander and his radioman. I rolled into firing position and unleashed a 20 round magazine from my M-14 towards the enemy positions in the hedgerow. When I jammed a five round stripper clip into the receiver and fired it off, the metallic "ching" of the ejected clip prompted me to feed in another, then another from my bandoleer. I rolled from cover to see Corporal Robert Hamm hunched over a bucking M-60 that was pouring a veritable cascade of tracer-laced steel into the village. Hamm's fierce concentration and his tight grip on the weapon made it appear man and machine were one lethal device spewing certain death toward the enemy force. I watched in awe as he traversed back and forth across the hedgerow, chewing up the VC fortifications. Dirt and vegetation flew up from the impact area, punctuated by an occasional crimson ricochet that caromed off at a high angle. His barrel was so hot it had begun to smoke, yet he continued to fire. Prone on the trail at Hamm's shoulder, the assistant gunner fed a helaciously long belt into the M-60. Had they linked several 100-round belts together? Then for a heartbeat there was complete silence.

"Pour it on!" I yelled. "Don't let them get away this time!"

A few Marines echoed my words with, "Yeah. Pour it on! Get some!" as the volume of fire resumed. *'Don't let them get away this time'?* What the hell was I thinking? They had us cold. My verbal bravado did not match the deep concern I felt for our predicament and for the three Marines whom I could see and perhaps more who had fallen 30 meters down the trail. My premonitions about this being the prototypical VC killing field had come true. What had I gotten my platoon into? 82mm mortars started falling behind us and walking in our direction, killing one man in Third Platoon and wounding Lieutenant Jones, the artillery forward observer, in the neck.

109

As the First Squad 'point of the spear', Corporal Vernon Horn had an unobstructed view of the ambush. He thought he was a goner...

"I was the point man and got wounded in the left leg. My fire team leader behind me, a lance corporal, got his leg almost shot off. He screamed he was hurt so bad. A new man in the squad named Frost got the firing mechanism of his LAAW blown up under the skin of his upper arm."

Corporal Charles Gutierrez had placed himself near the front of the platoon, so he could closely supervise the bunch of new Marines who had just joined the outfit. A BAR bullet through the right leg dropped him on the hard dirt of the paddy dike...

"I went down with the first volley. I knew I was hit, but tried to put out some rounds anyway. Then my rifle jammed and I couldn't get the damned thing firing again. Greg Valness flopped down beside me and started puttin' out some heavy fire towards the ville. Then I looked back at my leg and there was blood all over everywhere: a femoral artery wound. The corpsman crawled over and put a tourniquet on it and stopped the bleeding, but we were in a world of hurt."

Even though Sergeant Joe Barry of Second Squad didn't observe the initial contact directly, he remembers...

"Now, Hamm was the machine gunner. They said it's a wonder he didn't melt the barrel. They might have even changed barrels. But they had 200 rounds. You know, two belts hooked together. He just wouldn't let up. I mean, other people were pinned and couldn't fire and he just kept going. The VC had a 12.7 mm gun, like a heavy machine gun. It was going right through the paddy dike. A paddy dike's what, 18 inches? 2 feet? Right through it, splashing the water on the other side. I remember charging down a hill and I was in a depression-like. I had an M79 but the bushes were just too close in front of me. It only takes four right turns or 14 feet to arm that projectile. I fired one round in the direction of enemy flashes, but it didn't make it. It hit 15 feet away, far enough to arm the shell and shrapnel came back on our own guys. Somebody yelled out, 'Hey, you're wounding us.' So I took myself out for a short period there."

110

"Second Squad up!" I screamed. No response. "Second Squad up now!" I repeated. Nothing. Finally the Third Squad leader, a Marine with a compact build carrying an M-79 grenade launcher and a pouch of ammunition for it, appeared pumping his arm up and down in the "double time" signal. " Let's go, Third Squad," I heard him say. As he approached my position, he pulled a compass from his pocket and took an azimuth on the VC 82 mm mortar crew across the river, calling it and the distance out to my radioman for relay to Cassandra Golf Six. With some satisfaction, I heard 60 mm mortar rounds leaving their tubes at the company command group behind us. Weeks earlier, I had prevailed upon Captain Gruner to include two tubes and the Marines to operate them on significant operations. My confidence was bolstered by each successive detonation in the village. Third Platoon also had not been idle all this time; they were pouring their own high volume of fire into the village.

Commander Lan could see the kill zone now; the smoke had thinned. Not only had the booby-trapped artillery shell failed to detonate, the ambush had taken down only a handful of Marines. He could see their commander, the one who should be dead, marshalling his troops, conferring with a black soldier, and preparing to assault. An unexpectedly fierce barrage of semi-automatic and automatic weapons fire, as well as mortar fire from the rest of the American company had taken out one of his machine guns and damaged the other. The cursed Marine gun team could not be stopped. He had never seen such tenacity and fire discipline in Marine units they had opposed previously — the hated Thuy Quan Luc Chien My (American soldiers who fight from the sea). A sheet of hot steel swept his position.

Another miscalculation had caused severe casualties; after the initial burst of fire into the kill zone, he had ordered a fallback to secondary positions. Somehow, the maneuver had not been done incrementally, but all at once. A silence was followed by a yell from the Marine commander and a storm of fire that cut down his executive officer, a platoon commander, and three other men. From that point on, withdrawal was chaotic. They had to leave the bodies of two fine soldiers behind, so fast were the Americans moving. Battalion Commander Mai would not be pleased.

Bill Gavin, a PFC rifleman in Sergeant Carter's Third Platoon,

111

was at the rear of the column when we ran into the buzz saw...

"When the shit hit the fan, Second Platoon was on point and we were behind the company CP. We were ordered to move up and came to a creek that had a small one-man bridge. A hand-bridge. It was quite a swift creek, only about 30 feet wide, but deep. They were sending men over the bridge and some were walking though the water underneath it to get to the other side. I got about halfway across and the current got me and swept me off my feet. I held on to my rifle and my helmet while I tumbled underwater. When I came up, another Marine ran over to the bank and helped me out. I got to the other side and the whole company was along this rice paddy dike firing across into a tree line. I hit the deck right next to a machine gunner and we were all fucked up as far as squads and platoons. Everybody was all mixed in together, scattered along that dike. I hit the deck next to this machine gunner and his assistant, fired one round with my M14 and it jammed from the creek water in it. So I ran down the dike until I saw somebody in my squad and hit the deck next to him. The firefight was continuing and here I am with a jammed rifle. This was just before dark. They were dropping M1 rifle grenades in on us. One of them hit right next to where this machine gun position was, where I was laying, and killed a Marine who had a shaved head."

I prepared Third Squad and what was left of First Squad for an assault on line into the village. We had no choice; it was either move forward or get chopped up piecemeal. But where the hell was 2nd Squad? Then I heard whooping, yelling, and hollering from the direction of Captain Gruner's command group. It was Staff Sergeant Wallace Carter leading his Marines towards us like Pickett's charge in the Civil War. Carter flopped down on the trail beside me and we agreed on a quick plan to move into the darkening village. Only a few bursts of fire from the enemy, meant to delay us, met our advance. My Third Squad leader found a wounded VC who had been left behind. We found one more body and three Browning automatic rifle magazines, as well as dozens of well-constructed and concealed fighting positions. The next day Foxtrot Company would locate and blow in place an unexploded 105 mm howitzer round the VC had rigged with wires not far from the bridge where Sergeant Dawson and I had been plotting our moves into the village. So intense had been our concentration, we hadn't even noticed it.

2nd Plt. Right Guide Dale Farnham at Nong Son

Dan Day at Nong Son

Strong Back Tents at An Hoa

Lieutenant Glasgow with Viets at Nong Son

John Peterson at An Hoa with Automatic Weapon

Lieutenant Bill Harvey with Mortar

**2nd Plt. Radio Man
Shipley at An Hoa**

**Ron Carbone with
M-14 Rifle**

Rick Wilhite in Japan

**1st Sqd Leader Wayne
Dawson**

Recon Mountain Near Nong Son

Dan Day on Patrol

Lt. Glasgow and Capt. Gruner

G Company Combat Patrol

Bill Gavin and Local Vietnamese Family

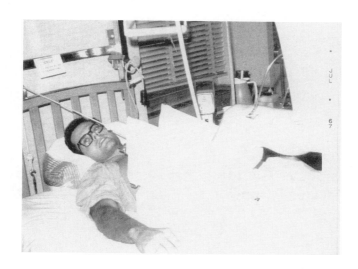

Bill Gavin Recovering from Leg Wound

Bates, Barry, Briggs,
Garza, & Greeves

John Peterson Recovering
in Japan, March, 1967

John Bates Guarding
An Hoa Perimeter

John Bates after
Nong Son Patrol

No sooner had we secured the village than company Gunnery Sergeant Mayberry walked up in the twilight and asked me, "How in the hell did you get that far along the trail, so quickly, lieutenant?"

"We had no choice, Gunny. We had to close as fast as we could," I answered. "And where the hell was my 2nd Squad all that time? I had no maneuver element."

"Well, lieutenant, we held 'em back for CP defense. We were catching a lot of stuff back there."

Mystery solved.

Sgt. Joe Barry was relieved we had broken the back of the ambush, but disturbed by another event...

"Once we decided to get up, we assaulted one side, broke through and set up a perimeter. In fact, when we did break through one of the other squad leaders, you know how we carried a .45, an M79, and a K-bar, right? Well, I remember looking over and...you know you think you know these people a little bit. But this guy was on this NVA's chest, and he was stabbing him in the chest over and over and over again. But it was such a frenzy that somebody else could have just walked over and killed him. It was like he was in another world."

The village was dark by the time I deployed Second Platoon in defensive positions. The captain was not happy with my arrangement.

"Hell's bells, lieutenant. You can't cover the whole goddamned village. Pull those people back in a ways," he said with some exasperation.

I had seriously overextended myself. While I was readjusting the lines, pointing out sectors for the squads, a senior NCO stopped and asked what the hell I was doing, Marine? No rank insignia and my M-14 had confused him. After a nearby fire team leader set him straight about my identity, I thought to myself I wished the VC commander had been so easily fooled.

121

Suddenly a single M-14 shot ripped the muggy night air and made everyone duck for cover. I ran towards the sound and within fifteen meters found Sergeant Dawson lying on the ground bleeding from a wound in his chest. As I approached him, he groaned, "You've killed me, Private Hagerty.[8] Why the hell did you do that?" A private, newly assigned to the platoon, cringed nearby, clutching his smoking rifle and looking absolutely devastated.

"What in God's universe possessed you, Private Hagerty?" I yelled at the man. "Have you lost your mind? Look what you've done!" Then I said some stronger things at an even higher octave that caused him to sink deeper into misery and despair. But my immediate concern was for Dawson. The call for a corpsman brought Doc Salisberry on the double. He crouched over Dawson, who appeared to be drifting into unconsciousness, and placed a compress on his chest. He gave me a very unreassuring look as we placed him in a poncho and carried him to a hastily chosen landing zone; the pallor of death already had begun to tint Dawson's features.

"Hang in there, Sergeant Dawson," I whispered. "You're going to be okay." The command group already was on the horn for an emergency medevac.

"We set in for the night and Dawson had his squad set up in a sort of like a semi-circle." Sgt. Farnham recalled years later. *"In order to stay on line with everybody, he had to move Hagerty back a little bit, but he forgot that he had moved him back. So Dawson and Doc was walking the line. Because he'd moved Hagerty back, he forgot and he walked right in front of him. Hagerty heard noise and just greased both of them."*

Joe Barry, of Second Squad, remembers the incident clearly...

"After Lieutenant Buchanan dug that round out of Sergeant Dawson's flak jacket some weeks before, it stuck in my mind, like, wow,

---

[8] Not his real name.

God was telling him, 'You're going to die today. Prepare yourself.' I don't know why, I just always thought of that. I thought, wow, you're very fortunate. But then that night his own man shot him. We set up a quick perimeter, expecting a counter-assault from the enemy and that's when Dawson didn't give the password or didn't give it quick enough. The new man had only been there two days and shot him right in the chest."

Twenty minutes later, an H-34 from Danang was settling into the landing zone, more or less in formation with eight 82 mm rounds from the persistent VC mortar crew across the river. Before he was able to lift off with Dawson and some of the other seriously wounded, the pilot caught a shard that ripped right through the canopy. Corporal Horn, the wounded point man, remembers a feeling of extreme loss...

"Sgt. Dawson's death was a great tragedy. It is now something of a mystery also. I lay wounded at the LZ waiting to be medevaced out when I heard the single gunshot that signaled his death. Because I was not critically wounded, I had to wait till morning to be medevaced, as the choppers were taking intense incoming fire. At the time I was in no condition to deal with anything like his death, even if I had known that he would not make it. On a C-141 bound for Subic Bay, Private Frost told me that after the ambush was over, Sgt. Dawson was busy setting up a defensive line, trying to get every one linked up. He came through some brush and Private Hagerty shot him through the chest. Frost's story was that Private Hagerty had been so shaken up by the ambush (all of us getting shot) that he had fired his weapon before seeing who it was that was coming through the brush. Frost and Private Hagerty had only been in the squad a few weeks and hadn't seen any major action."

Corporal Gutierrez remembers viewing the scene through a morphine-induced fog...

"I was lying on someone after being thrown in the medevac chopper and the crew chief was yelling, "'Get 'em in here! Hustle it!' as enemy mortars started dropping into the LZ. Then the pilot got hit by shrapnel and he started screaming to get out of there now."

Mark Glasgow, who by then had assumed the billet of G

123

Company Executive Officer, recalls the skirmish…

"After that fight Second Platoon was in, I went to pick up a man, and I realized you can't pick up a dead Marine with a flak jacket and all of his gear on. I was just too weak. So I got a couple of guys to help get him on my shoulder, and I carried him back to where we had the CP near some little house. I laid him on what I thought was a little hill, and I didn't realize it was an anthill 'till the morning. The next morning ants were all over him, and it just made me sick that I laid him there. Then we got that man out on a helicopter the next morning and got re-supplied with ammo and so forth."

In his typically conscientious way, Sgt. Farnham was trying to hold things together…

"We put our CP into a pigpen. That was the only place that was covered and that's the only place I could find. As far as the pigs, we booted them out. It was sort of a thatched roof type thing and low to the ground. We put the radios in and Shipley says, 'I'm not getting in there!' And I told him, 'Get your butt in there!"

The H-34 chopper was setting there idling next to a big hedgerow and we started putting the medevacs on and the pilot got hit with mortar shrapnel. One of our Marines, I think he was a hillbilly, another slow-moving individual; he was one of Shaw's assistant gunners. Big huge guy. Always carried an M-60 and about three or four belts of ammo. He jumped up there into the chopper and started putting bodies in and next thing we know, away the chopper goes with him still in it. They hauled him to Danang, then they took him back to An Hoa. When he joined back up with us, it was a week later. Sort of a 'friendly flier casualty.' Sure could have used him the next few days."

After the medevac chopper augered itself into the thick night air, we adjusted defensive fires and hunkered down. I settled in with the rest of the group in Sgt. Farnham's fragrant CP, hoping a scorpion, millipede, bamboo viper, roof rat, or king cobra would not snuggle up as a bunkmate. I already had enough company—thousands of sanguinary mosquitoes hovering six inches over my head. Wrapped in my poncho, with my pack for a pillow, I fought desperately for sleep that yielded reluctantly.

Every time I drifted off into the penumbra of dreams, Sergeant Dawson's words, "You've killed me!" jolted me awake to the sound of crickets, frog song, the whine of mosquitoes and the hissing of the AN/PRC-25 radio.

I was having a hard time dealing with the loss of one of my most experienced and resourceful squad leaders. Over the months, we had developed a good working relationship that had led me to appreciate his enthusiasm and professionalism. I could always depend upon him in a firefight. Was there something I had done or failed to do as a platoon commander that might have prevented his accidental death? More indoctrination? More training? Closer supervision? A different way of setting in the lines that night? I had this nagging feeling that if Dawson didn't make it, he would be distressed about dying at the hand of a fellow Marine rather than from enemy fire. Then I convinced myself if the cold aluminum of the vibrating helicopter deck, the pressure of the web restraints, and the mottled sky rushing past the door telescoped into a smaller and smaller circle and he began to drift down that long transcendent tunnel of pure light, that his last images would be of cornfields waving in the heavy July wind outside Champaign, Illinois and chilled lemonade on the porch swing with Mary while lightning bugs floating over newly mown grass created pulsing constellations of their own.

I couldn't help wondering what had happened to the other fine Marines who had fallen along the way: Bates, Horn, Frost, Mihalcik, Gutierrez. Had they made it, and would Dawson? My gut told me it would be a long time before I saw some of them again, if ever. In two days of action, the company had sustained light casualties. How would those numbers change up the road?

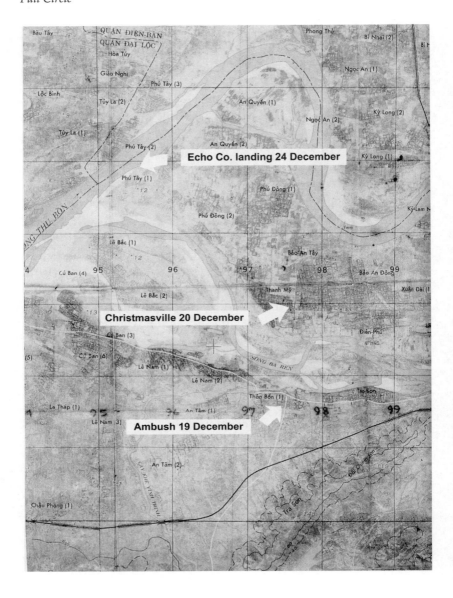

CHRISTMASVILLE

Navy Cross

D awn illuminated ribbons of mist floating over the Song Ba Ren and pieces of pale blue sky showing through overhead. I felt like a maggot-riddled pile of buffalo crap. The lack of sleep compounded a profound sense of loss and an unexplained foreboding about what lay ahead of us. For some reason alarm bells were sounding again, much as they had just before the ambush. I lit off a chunk of C-4 to heat a can of "Ham and Eggs Chopped," finished it off with fruit cocktail and a John Wayne cracker and stirred up a mixture of coffee and cocoa in an effort to fire up the neurons and dissipate the funk I was in. Then I walked over to join Staff Sergeant Carter, the Third Platoon commander, at Captain Gruner's briefing.

"Echo Company is four clicks north of us along the river," Gruner told us, pointing to grid square 9655 on the 1/50,000 topographic map. Company F is just south of us. "We'll move north across the river to link up with Echo. Third Platoon takes the point."

While we were fighting our way out of the ambush the previous day, Echo Company was doing some fancy footwork of their own up along the sandy banks of the Song Thu Bon. They were crossing an open space near the hamlet of An Quyen when the R-20 Battalion sprang a highly disciplined ambush on them. Echo Company commander 1st Lt. Terry Ebbert from Belvedere, Illinois, was 24 years old at the time and remembers that day vividly...

"When we crossed that open area I spread the company out and we must have been 200 meters on line with 20 meters between people. They let us get all the way through the water and up on the other side so close that I thought there was nobody over there. When we were about 25 meters away they opened up. But the problem was they were in a space of about 40 meters, and we were spread over 200. They couldn't take us all under fire. The CP hit the deck and the two platoons on the end just charged. They never went to ground. Eventually we overran the whole VC position. But for a moment they had the CP pinned down. The radio antennas and everything were drawing all the fire. Their mistake was they let us get too close. We were fortunate to have sustained only a couple wounded. We killed some enemy troops that day and found some weapons and equipment."

After an H-34 helicopter from Danang resupplied us with food and ammunition and hauled out the dead and wounded from the fight the day before, Captain Gruner told Company G to saddle up. We were on the move again.

Marc Glasgow had some reservations about the plan...

"I had a conversation with Gruner about going across that open area to the northeast. My map showed we were headed more or less for this village called Dien Phu. I said, 'Captain, we don't want to do that. We don't want to go across the open.' And he said, 'We're going to go

across in the open.' It was bright sunlight and—it must have been Third Platoon—I watched them going across because we set up the base of fire if need be, and I watched the first guy almost make the bank going up into the ville, and there was a 'pop' and I just knew that shit was going to happen."

After we crossed the river and linked up with Echo Company, we began moving through thick woods criss-crossed by well-beaten trails and pathways. Echo was on point, with Golf following in column formation. Abandoned villages appeared and disappeared through the clearings, menacing in their silence and formidable for their potential to hide sizeable units of VC or NVA. A relentless sun streamed down through the canopy overhead, casting weird shadows on the ground. The heavy smell of rotting vegetation and acrid sweat filled our nostrils. Silence was so palpable the only thing you could hear was the rhythm of your heart. We definitely were in the belly of the beast now: the dreaded Go Noi Island. Every step forward heightened the anxiety of our Vietnamese "Chieu Hoi," a colleague of Dau's. He gestured at a mulch of leaves and twigs that littered the trail ahead of us.

"Captain," he said to Captain Gruner. "Beaucoup VC ahead. Many, many VC. You see, captain? Leaves from them." We had been pushing some unit so hard, the camouflage was falling off of them onto the trail. He was reluctant to move forward. Captain Gruner seemed interested, but not convinced. After all, Echo Company hadn't sounded any alarm, and they were on point. It was 1530.

"Move it out," ordered the captain. "Stay alert up there."

Sergeant Joe Barry also had seen ominous signs…

"It might have been lined with hedgerows or something like that, but I remember a trail so wide it was like a sidewalk. A well-beaten path. But that path, which would have been all dirt because it was so well used, was covered with—and this is what was pointed out by the Kit Carson Scout—these branches; the sap's still wet, they're all green. These VC were using this in their clothing so that they wouldn't be spotted from the air. They'd just go down on one knee and look like

129

hedgerows. But we were pushing 'em. We were runnin'. We were moving faster than we normally would, trying to run these guys down, and he's saying, 'The captain won't listen to me. There must be 100 of them. This isn't good. This isn't good.' This stuff was falling off the VC troops they were movin' so fast. The scout, he's just looking for anybody who will listen to him. I listened to him, but there's nothing I could do. I'm only a squad leader. When we got caught up in that big ambush, it became evident that it wasn't just a few...it was a lot."

We hadn't gone two hundred yards farther before the world ahead of us exploded in a cataclysmic exchange of fire. What sounded like Little Round Top at Gettysburg erupted with a roar of automatic weapons, both enemy and friendly, punctuated by incoming mortar fire, swelling to a deafening crescendo.

My radioman blurted out, "Lieutenant, Captain Gruner wants you to attack forward and link up with the right flank of Echo Company. They're in a world of hurt!" Vague forebodings that had whispered to me that morning had materialized into screaming reality.

"Third Squad!" I yelled over the racket. "Get up and follow me in this direction. First Squad on my right, Second Squad in trace." I took off running east just as two mortar rounds detonated ten meters from my Third Squad leader. I thought he was goner. Instead, he shrugged off the near misses as if someone had cut him off on the Santa Monica Freeway. Pumping his arm in the "double time" signal, he rallied his squad and we all ran together towards what sounded like certain doom—the beaten zone of enemy fire.

After a hundred yards, we broke out into a sunlit clearing. To our right was a small stucco structure. Ahead of us was a shallow trench line leading straight towards a gap in a low hedgerow. Before I could react otherwise, I was scuttling along the trench behind a Third Squad fire team. Then we stopped. The fire team leader, a Hispanic corporal, calmly began to assign targets and monitor the rate of fire. At regular intervals he pointed at different Marines and ordered them to reload. His composure in the face of what appeared and sounded to be a very large enemy unit was impressive. I began to take stock of our situation.

On our left flank a slightly built Echo Company platoon commander with a fair complexion yelled over, "Lieutenant! Watch your ass. There're a couple of machine guns in the tree line. They took out my whole fire team. Just blew 'em back on top of me!" Promoted from staff sergeant to second lieutenant, he had been with Echo Company only a few weeks. I could see eight wounded Marines and two dead lying in a depression behind the lieutenant's front line. His troops were pouring fire into a thick tree line not 50 meters away across a meadow that looked like the 8th fairway at Pebble Beach: flat, with a tight carpet of short grass. A single banana tree stood halfway across the clearing. The tree line pulsed with muzzle flashes. White smoke enveloped a concrete way marker four meters in front of my fire team. Puzzled, I looked at it more closely. Then it dawned on me; a hail of fire from an enemy machine gunner across the clearing was chewing it up; the smoke was pulverized concrete. It was obvious our battlefront was way too narrow. All we had facing the enemy was the volume of fire from a single fire team.

Although grazing fire swept our position, and my stomach knotted up at the thought, I ordered my platoon sergeant Dale Farnham to pass the word to First Squad to move on line 25 meters out across the clearing and occupy firing positions on our right flank. It would be a risky move, but we had no choice; only by increasing the breadth of our line would we be able to take the pressure off Echo Company and begin to chew up the VC positions across the field.

"Guns up!" I yelled at the Marines who were huddled behind me. Soon we had two M-60s chattering away, providing some cover for First Squad's desperate move. I yelled, "Mad moment!" as Sergeant Farnham and the First Squad leader maneuvered towards a hedgerow that bordered a shallow ditch off to our right flank. The enemy gunners responded with a furious fusillade. Miraculously, all the men made it to their positions without taking any rounds and the volume of fire towards the enemy began to swell. A junior corpsman who had made the rush with First Squad yelled over jubilantly from behind a fence

131

post, "Lieutenant! We made it okay! A bullet bounced off my flak jacket, but we're okay." Thank God, I thought to myself.

With typical alacrity, Sgt. Farnham galvanized his Marines...

"Lieutenant Buchanan said to get a squad over into a little stucco house that was sittin' in the middle of a big tapioca field. They were just shooting like crazy all over the place. So I told everybody, I said, 'We're just going to do one squad rush and I don't want to goof around. I don't want to give them a chance to figure out there's other people coming after the first group goes through. No fire team rushes. A whole squad rush,' I said. 'Everybody will get up when I tell you to go. The first person that stops I'll shoot you.' I says, 'Everybody run straight toward the house. The tapioca field—there's no tapioca that's going to protect you. Run like crazy.' I says, 'Lieutenant wants us to go over and get the machine gun set up in that house.'

So we all got up and we got ready to go and I said, 'OK, Go!' And everybody was goin' and I looked behind and here's Biberg the radioman on his hands and knees. I says, 'What are you doing, Biberg?' And rounds were zipping all over the place. He says, 'I lost my wedding band and my wife will kill me if I come home without it!' He was on the ground looking for his wedding band! I reached down and grabbed him about the same time he grabbed his wedding band and I pulled him up and said, 'Get your ass forward!'

So we got over to the house and we got the M-60 all set up. The VC/NVA were using Chinese rounds because every tracer round that would come through the windows and the side of the house was green. We were sittin' there for a while, providing cover fire and everything. The lieutenant was still up at the hedgerow behind a cement village signpost and he yelled, 'OK, bring them back over here and link up with me.' I says, 'Where you at?' And the lieutenant said, 'Up by the village sign.' I said, 'OK.' So we moved from the house towards the hedgerow, leaving the M-60 team in the house.

As I moved the squad along the hedgerow, there was just a small break in it. Every time I sent somebody across, they drew fire. But I didn't dare send more than one person at a time through that little break. So I set everybody up and I said, 'OK, Biberg, it's our turn now.' He says, 'OK, you go first.' And I says, 'No, I'd rather you go

*first.' He says, 'No, you go first.' I says, 'No, I'd rather you go first.'
So finally he went, and as he went across, they fired, and a round went
right through his radio. I thought it killed him, but away he scooted,
then he fell down. I said, 'Oh, Christ he's dead.' I ran over to him and
I says, 'You OK?' He says, 'Yeah, I'm all right, but they got my radio!'
I said, 'Get up! Keep goin'!' At that time they started throwing in
concussion grenades. I don't know how many times I picked myself up
from those damned things. One of those rinky-dink corpsman that we
got after Kerry Bice left got smacked in the shoulder with a round
when we made that move across the field. Bice took care of the whole
platoon for a long time; but when he left, they gave us two or three
corpsmen. One was a sort of a skinny guy with a needle nose, but the
one that got hit, he was scared. He never even carried a magazine in
his pistol. He had toilet paper shoved up in there."*

Second Squad would have to remain in trace; there just was
no reasonable cover on First Squad's right flank: only sun beaten
grass. Someone tapped me on the shoulder. I turned to see the
senior sniper of the team that had been assigned to my platoon,
cradling his Remington sniper rifle with a Redfield scope. He
had an eager expression on his face. As I was giving him
instructions to maneuver around the stucco structure on our
right so he and his buddy could begin to work the tree line for
suitable targets, a series of enemy rounds struck the ground in
quick succession a meter away from us, spraying dirt and grass
in little puffs. The roar of battle masked the reports, but it was a
tight group no bigger than your hand shot by a VC sniper up in
the trees across the way. Only his windage error had saved us:
just the target for my eager snipers. I gestured at the impact
area, patted him on the helmet and he scuttled back down the
trench line intent on his mission. I have no doubt the VC sniper
met a quick and honorable end.

But for the time being, the enemy machine guns were giving
me a headache. With a "heads up" to the nearest fire team leader,
I hurled an M-26 grenade past the banana tree and towards the
tree line. It detonated with a satisfying "crump!" and a nice cloud
of smoke and debris. I pulled another grenade from my belt
and tossed it in the same direction. Nothing. I took another
grenade from a nearby rifleman and threw it. "Crump!" Grass
and areca leaves flew into the air. He passed over another one. I

threw it. Nothing. "What the hell's going on with these grenades, " I grumbled. "Who's making these damn things? Is this sabotage, or what?"

Sgt. Farnham recalled an interesting field expedient to snipers who had begun plinking away at us again from high trees across the way...

"Then the lieutenant got ahold of Barry's M79 and we finally found an idiot up in a tree someplace. We was behind this village sign. He took the M79, put his foot down on the stock and pulled it back and used it as a mortar. Just about the time the lieutenant would get the trajectory on it, Barry would pull the trigger. First round didn't even hit the tree. Second round blew that sucker right out of the tree."

My radioman patted me on the shoulder and handed me the handset. Over the cacophony, I could barely hear Captain Gruner say, "Lieutenant, I want you to prepare to assault the enemy position." I thought I had heard him wrong. Surely he had said he wanted me to assess the enemy position, or mark the enemy position. I had him repeat the order. He did, and there was no mistake; the critical word was "assault." I looked over at the Marines of First Squad who were firing measured bursts monitored by their fire team leaders, as were the Marines in Third Squad around me. The sun, swinging over us, had passed zenith, throwing us into silhouette and illuminating the meadow between us and the VC bunkers like a Broadway stage. This could be our first and last performance. I passed the word down the lines: "First and Third Squads prepare to assault. Second Squad reserve." I thought about HE followed by Willy Peter rounds from the 3.5 inch rocket teams and a barrage of grenades from each Marine before our desperate wind sprint. Should we fix bayonets? Had Echo Company been alerted to our move so they could support? Where was Third Platoon? My stomach churned and my heart raced as I contemplated the sheet of grazing fire before us. Like broken field running at rush hour on the San Diego Freeway, it would be a costly, if not fatal maneuver. From the position he had flopped into after the flanking maneuver, Sergeant Farnham shot me a glance as if I had lost my frigging mind. I played my last card. If this didn't work, we would go. I grabbed the handset.

"Cassandra Golf Six Actual," I yelled over the racket. "We are preparing to assault, but I thought the captain might want to come up here and take a look before we go."

Three minutes later, Captain Gruner and his radioman scuttled up the trench line, heads held low. I described how we had maneuvered into position after the initial contact and where the enemy fire was pouring from bunkers across the meadow. He gazed out at the twinkling underbrush across the way and said, " Jesus Christ, lieutenant. Hold what you've got. You're not going anywhere!" Then he disappeared to the rear.

It wasn't long before the ghostly wail of an F-4 Phantom maneuvering into position high overhead grew into the ear-shattering roar of twin Pratt and Whitney engines driving the airframe across our front lines as load after load of 250 pound bombs, 20 mm cannon fire, and napalm fell into the VC positions. It was hard to comprehend how any living being could survive the ghastly eruptions of orange flame and boiling black smoke which we could feel as a warm glow on our faces and hands even at that distance. Even this relentless pounding did not quench automatic weapons fire pouring from the camouflaged bunkers enough so medical evacuations could proceed. It was no surprise to us that after-battle assessments by S-2 (battalion intelligence) gauged the enemy unit at 350 to 400 men—a VC battalion at least.

Marc Glasgow, the Executive Officer, recalled assessing the situation from the vantage point of the company command post…

"So we had two companies minus on line: Echo minus and Golf minus. But it was a curved line and that's when we just couldn't move. We were more or less stopped dead after shooting our way into that place. We were in their trench lines. And that's what saved our ass. They let us get too close. Either we surprised them, or their lookout shot too late. They weren't ready for us when we came across the open. I remember having a discussion with Gruner about, you know, it's not a question of assaultin', it's a question of us survivin'. That's when he was working with battalion."

135

"Battalion decided they were going to envelop from south to north with Fox Company. I remember looking down to the east when Fox assaulted, when they came jumping over the trench line—it ran east-west—I thought, 'Wow, that's just like a John Wayne movie or something.' They were assaulting right into that Goddamned village and they were taking horrendous fire. But they actually got partway into the village. Keegan, our gunny, he and I were working to try and get all the casualties out."

It had been a long afternoon, but the sun finally set and dusk was beginning to blur the features around us. By 1930 the enemy positions across the meadow were quiet, sinking ever deeper into shadow. Word came down the line from our right flank friendlies were approaching. Sure enough, a lean, medium-sized officer from Foxtrot Company hobbled over to my position, using a stick for a cane. A dirty handkerchief encircled his right thigh where he'd taken a round. He reminded me of an officer from the Lost Battalion of the French Foreign Legion—maybe a survivor of Dien Bien Phu.

"Hit the deck, lieutenant!" I whispered urgently. "There's a machine gun crew across the meadow. Get your ass down!"

The lieutenant shrugged off my concern and asked where the company CP was located. I pointed to the rear, then watched as he and his command group strolled off into the twilight, casual as hell. Marc Glasgow soon was enjoying a light show...

"After it got dark, somebody called in one of those Spooky gunships. Puff the Magic Dragon. It was shootin' in front of us, just peppering that village. We couldn't gain much forward momentum at all. Every time we tried to get out of the trenches, that horrendous fire would come. Plus we had six or seven wounded and dead laying behind us up on the birm. We couldn't get them out. Someplace in there, the chopper that tried to evacuate them got shot down."

An enemy soldier in a spider hole became quite adept at tracking movement across our position. Each time a Marine moved laterally along the trail marking our front lines, BOOM! —a VC "potato masher" grenade hurled him into the air. He

136

would land hard on the ground, jump up, brush himself off, and scuttle on down the trail. Sergeant Farnham was airborne three times before he reached my position. Although unscathed, he was furious.

We dug in deeper for the night. Sometime before midnight, the word came down that a chopper would try to take out some casualties. Soon an H-34 helicopter was hovering over a hasty landing zone near the company CP, creating a debris-laden windstorm. At my signal, the platoon opened up on the enemy positions in order to cover the pilot and crew. While the chopper was hovering behind us about thirty feet off the deck, a beam of bright green tracers streaked out from a concealed bunker in the tree line and slammed into the side of the craft with a metallic "th-th-th-thunk." The engine sputtered, backfired, fell silent, then dropped the airframe hard on the ground. Although neither the pilot nor anyone in the crew was seriously injured in the crash, it soon became obvious we had a whole new set of problems unless someone could make that bird fly again.

The next day dawned gray and drizzly. No sound came from the enemy positions in the dripping trees and bushes across the meadow. When orders came down the line to prepare to check out the area, we deployed gun and rocket teams with a covering squad, clenched our teeth, buckled our chinstraps and zipped our flak jackets, then struck out at a lively pace across center field at Comisky Park. Much to our delight, there was no resistance. Our search into the trees bordering the meadow revealed well-designed and constructed zigzag trenches that would warm the heart of an engineer like Marc Glasgow. Bunkers constructed at intervals along the trenches had roofs reinforced with banana tree trunks. We found no equipment, weapons, or bodies. The battlefield was clean. The ghostly Doc Lap Battalion had faded into the mist.

Although it wasn't funny at the time, years later Sgt. Farnham recalled with a chuckle, doomed efforts to make the wounded bird fly...

"That was interesting why we was there in the village, because the chopper was down and then they brought in some guys on 21 December

to fix the dumb thing. It was so funny because the chopper dropped them outside of our lines and they were off-loading the repair stuff and everybody had on brand new flak jackets, just shinin' like anything. The minute we told them they were outside our lines, they left all their gear and came running with their little grease guns.

After that incident, Gunny come up and he says, 'OK, send some people out and get their gear.' So we just went out and picked up all their gear and brought it back. They got up on the dumb chopper to try and fix it and the snipers started bangin' on them. Then they decided, 'Well, we'll fix it at night.' So they went to work on it during the nighttime and it was raining and raining, you know, more rain than we really needed. They were supposed to fix the chopper. Did they ever fix that thing? No."

We returned to our original positions and passed three more soggy days without any C-rations. Monsoon rains kept helicopters lashed to the runway at Danang, unable to resupply us. Gaunt-looking Marines wearing disintegrating utilities began probing through trash piles with sticks looking for a can of peanut butter or a piece of cracker—perhaps a salt packet. One Marine with a dark growth of beard resembled a Barbary Coast buccaneer with his trouser leg ripped lengthwise and tucked back up into his web belt in sort of pantaloon fashion. On the second day without food, one of my fire team leaders found a small cache of rice stored in metal tins. Using the skills we developed on Operation Mississippi, we processed the rice, then boiled it over open fires until it was palatable. It was enough for a couple of cups of rice per man per day, but far short of our caloric requirements. Sergeant Barry had the foresight to bring along bouillon cubes, which he used to create what seemed at the time no less than a culinary masterpiece.

Dan Day was helping another Marine pluck a skinny chicken they had caught when Bill Gavin, a Marine from Sergeant Carter's Third Platoon, sauntered over and said, "Why don't you skin it like the Hoosiers do?" Day said, "Hoosiers" Where are you from?" And he answered St. Louis. Since Day also was from St. Louis, the two Marines compared notes and discovered both had attended high schools in the area, taught by Brothers of Mary. Gavin was an alumnus of McBride and Day went to St.

Mary. Small world. Private First Class Gavin also remembered the short rations, the feeling of abandonment, and small bands of enemy soldiers lurking in the dripping underbrush...

"I got sent to another position on the lines and that's where I met Dan Day from Second Platoon, Lieutenant Buchanan's platoon. And we got to talkin,' since we're both from St. Louis, Missouri. When Echo humped back across the river on 23 December, every man walked over my hole going out of the perimeter. It was raining like hell. After they left I was watching down this trail and noticed a tree 30 yards down with a big thick bush about 10 feet high growing out of it. I had just taken my M-14 apart and lubriplated it to make sure everything would work. I snapped the trigger guard back in and as I was watching down this trail I swear to God I was thinking, 'I wonder what I'd do if a gook stuck his head out from behind that tree?' This thought no sooner left my mind than this gook leans out. He had a blue shirt on and black pajama pants, parted his hair on the left side, had an M-1 carbine over his shoulder and was wearin' Marine deuce gear; I could see this shit hangin' off him. We spotted each other at the same time and I came up with my M-14 on semi-automatic. As soon as I brought my rifle up, he disappeared into this bush and I fired off 17 rounds or however many I had—we never loaded the magazines full. Anyway. I emptied this magazine into this bush. I was a good shot. I knew I'd killed this guy. So the guys in the holes to the left and the right of me said, 'What are you shooting at?' From where they were, they couldn't see."

With the other Marines providing cover, Gavin searched the area behind the bush, but found nothing: no blood, no gear, no body: a veritable mystery, given Gavin's high marksmanship standards. Bill Gavin recalled that despite the wretched conditions, the VC provided some entertainment that night...

"That night, the 23ʳᵈ, we got quite a few sniper rounds coming in and the gooks were hollering at us. They were beating on 55-gallon drums or metal drums and hollering, 'Marines, you die. You're going to die, Marines.' That kept us awake all night long. We were in two-man holes, 50% watch, and bailing our holes out with our helmets 24-hours a day."

By that time, Captain Gruner had grown tired of the constant sniping from small bands of VC. Evidently, remnants of the main

139

VC force had stolen away to the east, leaving fire team-sized groups of infantrymen behind to harass us. The captain decided to send his best marksmen out to hunt down the VC and neutralize the annoying incoming fire. It was no surprise when the chore fell to PFC Bill Gavin, an avid and capable wild game hunter who had honed his skills at the St. Louis dump, where no rat, squirrel, or pigeon was safe from his pellet gun after school let out. Later forays into the backwoods of Missouri taught him the patience and skill necessary to bag more illusive quarry such as deer. Bill's grandfather, John Francis Gavin, joined the Marine Corps in 1917 at the age of 30. As an infantryman in the 75th Company of the Fifth Marine Regiment, he carried an Enfield rifle against the Germans at Belleau Wood, Argonne, and St. Mihiel thus earning the right to wear the cherished fourragère. Over Bill's parents' concerns about his deployment to a combat area, he enlisted in the Corps, tore through MCRD like it was summer camp, then volunteered for Vietnam. He had a reputation for being the best point man and the best shot in the outfit. His squad leader, Corporal William "OB" O'Brien, called him "Dinger." When Lieutenant Bill Harvey, the Third Platoon commander who took over from SSgt. Carter in January 1967, asked Gavin why he always volunteered to walk point, Gavin answered since he was the best, he could keep other Marines alive. Even the hunger and continuous combat at Christmasville never dulled that spirit of professionalism and sacrifice. As Gavin remembered it…

"24 December came along and even though the Christmas truce was supposed to be in effect, the morning started out with sniper fire from the tree line that I was watching. About 10:00 in the morning Captain Gruner said that he was going to send out a four-man killer team to get these goddamned snipers. Well, I got the assignment. With me was Royer, another Marine by the name of Moore, and a radioman."

Captain Gruner told the Marines he wanted them to proceed cautiously 300 yards down the trail, move off to the side, and camouflage themselves. "There's nothing but gooks out there," he said, "Nothing but Indians—no civilians." He told them to watch and listen. After an hour, they should call on the radio. Gavin steeled himself and shifted into his deer-hunting mode…

"I said to myself, 'Oh my God. I am dead.' But as soon as we moved out it was just like I was hunting deer in the hardwood forests of Missouri again. It was a small patrol and I wanted to see those gooks before they saw me. So it took us probably a half-hour to get out 300 yards; I counted the steps."

After an hour, Gavin's patrol reported no activity. The CP ordered them to move out another 300 yards. "We want you to go out another 300 yards and do the same thing," they told him over the radio. Gavin led out again at his deer stalking pace, scanning the dripping understory for any hostile movement. The Marines settled in, camouflaged themselves, and waited. Soon Gavin spotted his quarry ...

"I was looking down to my left and there was this gook wearing dirty white pajamas squatting against a tree 25-yards away, probably half asleep. He had an M-1 rifle across his knees. I had my rifle on full auto so I put the peeper right down at his feet and give him a burst. He went over. As soon as the shot rang out, all hell broke loose. A hundred gooks huddled around a cooking fire just out of sight charged across the trail straight into the jungle."

Gavin's lethal bead just missed one VC soldier. Another paused in the trail and fired off a round towards Gavin, whose short burst sent him flying backwards, "Like he was superman." The trail became a target rich environment: sprinting VC chased by swarms of Gavin's 7.62mm rounds. Headquarters came on the radio and told the fire team to sweep the impact area, collect weapons and search for documents. By purposely making a lot of noise and reconning by fire as they advanced, the Marines strove to give the impression they were larger than just a fire team. One of the wounded VC soldiers made a move and Gavin finished him off. Then he approached another one farther down the trail. This man was wearing a blue shirt, black trousers, and Marine 782 gear as well as M-26 grenades on a web belt and an angle-head flashlight. His hair was parted down the left side. It was the same VC who dove behind the bush the day before, the one Gavin thought he hit. He made a move for his M-1 carbine and Gavin pumped a round into his midsection, sending a geyser of steam shooting into the air. Startled, Gavin dropped to the ground...

"I thought I hit a grenade so I hit the deck. I waited for this grenade to go off and after five seconds, nothing happened so I got up. What had happened is, a Marine gave me a magazine full of tracers and one of them hit the VC's bladder. When the tracer hit his bladder, this big column of steam shot up from his belly. Scared the hell out of me."

The patrol collected the weapons, ammunition, and a souvenir—a knife that appeared to have been made in the jungle. Bill Gavin saw it as a heck of a keepsake…

"It had some type of a wood handle and aluminum and copper rivets holding it on. And it was Parkerized. It hadn't ever been sharpened and the point was bent over like it had been used to open a can of C-Rations. Through the handle was a bullet hole from one of my rounds."

When the patrol arrived back at the CP, Gavin asked Captain Gruner if he could keep the knife. Gruner acceded, then handed Gavin two Camel cigarettes: a bonus for outstanding combat performance. Gavin was overjoyed…

"We had been out of cigarettes for four days and man, that was like heaven. Then I opened this gook's pack and found a handkerchief with a rice ball about the size of a softball wrapped inside and it was soaked with blood."

In their emaciated condition, Gavin and the other Marines didn't hesitate; they carried the rice ball to their fighting holes and wolfed it down. Then Gavin smoked both Camel cigarettes, letting the tension from the last few hours drain away like pus from a boil.

Sgt. Dale Farnham had a similar nicotine transaction with the captain, though at less personal risk at the time. By then, even a smoke provided an illusion of caloric satisfaction…

"We were pretty much out of food the whole time. We did find some rice in tins or something like that. Garza from Barry's Squad went out and found a couple cans of brown rice or something. We were

thin. Not only body wise worn-out, but morale wise and everything. We were, you know...sort of at the end of our rope. We were losing the clothes right off us. I was down to my shorts. I gave somebody my trousers to wear because he didn't have any trousers. But I still had a couple of cigars; SSgt. Mihalcik got me smoking on the cigars. Captain Gruner called me up on the radio and said, 'You ready to smoke that cigar of yours yet? Bring it over. We can pass it around. We just want to smoke it all up. We didn't want to wait to get another one.' "

Echo Company remained with us until 23 December, then began the long trek back to An Hoa, crossing the swollen river and losing a man in the process. John Peterson, an 18-year-old rifleman from Salt Lake City, Utah was in Echo Company at the time. He remembers the incident clearly to this day...

"When we left that position 23 December and went to My Loc patrol base, we got into some fire fights and we lost some people. On the way out there was a big black machine gunner next to me. They always wanted you to carry the gun ammo in the boxes rather than Pancho Villa style and it got all fouled with mud and everything. Well, most of us said, 'Fuck you. We're going to do it Pancho Villa style.' 'Cause otherwise you had to walk with those boxes bangin' against your legs. This guy was very conscientious, and he tied these things on him: probably four or five of these 100-round belts of machine gun ammo. He tied them on him to the point where he couldn't just throw them off real easy. So we're crossing this river, and they're shooting at us, and he is probably four or five feet in front of me, just to my left. He stepped in a hole, and he was gone. I mean, he was just swept out of there, and he couldn't swim, because of all the weight on him. We tried to grab him and stuff, but they found his body down in 2/1's area a couple of days later. It was traumatic as hell."

1st Lt. Terry Ebbert, the Echo Company commander, was scratching his head about this maneuver...

"We had to fight our way all the way back. That was one long trek across there because we got delayed crossing the water. Then all the way back to My Loc small VC units shot at us. The frustrating thing was leaving Golf out there for the damned helicopter, which was a worthless piece of junk! We had been operating out in that area for several weeks. I knew what was going to happen. You had two reduced-

143

*strength companies that made up about one company between them.
Take half of us and walk out of there and leave the other half out there
all alone? Why anybody would have thought that nothing was going
to happen, I'll never know. Because I'd been out there long enough to
know this was a bad place to be."*

One soggy, foodless day followed the next without any sign
of a break in the weather. The rain poured down with Biblical
intensity. Rivers and streams encircled Go Noi Island like a nest
of pythons, bloated and writhing, throwing watery coils across
the land, choking us off from sustenance and reinforcement.
After an aborted attempt to reach us by fording the swollen
waterways, Hotel Company retreated back to base. Meanwhile,
the H-34 helicopter sat grounded and forlorn, unfixed and
perhaps unfixable, like a rotting albatross around our collective
necks. On Christmas Eve at the Golf Company CP, Lieutenant
Marc Glasgow, the executive officer, was tracking events over
the radio. He heard what he thought was shaping up to be a
mini Iwo Jima...

*"So the enemy was starting to withdraw by that time. Air support
spotted fleeing units to the east of us and blew the crap out of them.
Echo pulled out on 23 December, Foxtrot had already gone. That left
us. From where I was in the CP listening to messages, I couldn't
understand why they were going to leave 90 people out there. We were
getting illumination from the 155s from An Hoa, but that was max
range. Then on 24 December, battalion ordered Echo Company to get
into Mike Boats at Phu Lac, and come up the river and try to link up
with us by moving south from the river landing. What I remember
distinctly on the radio—now I'm in the CP, listening over the battalion
tactical net—they're coming up the river and they come into the bank
in one or two Mike Boats. The ramps went down, and the gooks had
machine guns. They shot right into the Goddamned boats. They got
creamed coming right off the boats, which meant to me that the VC,
they were listening to the radio. They knew exactly where Echo was
going to put ashore. That's where Ebbert, the company commander
got hit. So, when that battle broke out, I just thought we were in a
world of shit."*

That afternoon of Christmas Eve, Echo Company was
following battalion orders to march south from My Loc combat

144

outpost down Liberty Road towards An Hoa when Battalion Commander Airheart ordered them to reverse course. Without hesitation, 1ˢᵗ Lt. Ebbert responded...

"By the time we got saddled up and moving from My Loc, it was already later in the afternoon. We could hear the gunfire out in the G Company area as we were marching back towards An Hoa. We were probably about halfway to An Hoa when battalion radioed, 'You got to move down the river and go back to Golf Company. They're running out of ammunition and need ammo, reinforcement and food.' They didn't want to risk a helicopter going in. So we crashed north all the way up to the river and they said they'd be sending Mike boats down to pick us up and bring in a resupply of ammunition for ourselves as well as for G Company. It was already getting dark when we loaded on those boats. We loaded up with all the ammo and food we could carry and they pushed us back down the river. The problem was, it was dark by then, and it was raining. The last definite landmark that I could recognize was Phu Loc (6) when it slid by on our starboard side. We only had about 94 people on board so I knew we were going to be in for a bad time. First of all, it was dark. Second of all, we were already in this truce that the VC weren't abiding by. I'd been out there long enough to know that the VC were deployed in great numbers and that if we did not get any help they would just find the remains of two Marine rifle companies. The volume of fire that they'd leveled at us those previous three or four days proved we were operating against numerically superior forces. We were physically beat. We knew what was coming, but we pressed on."

Darkness and sheets of cold rain conspired to obscure Ebbert's progress down the river. Soon, through the murky twilight, he spotted the open area near where the company had assaulted VC trenches on 19 December. He ordered the Mike boats towards shore. The VC were waiting for them...

"We got off the boats and we hadn't gone a hundred meters when the whole world opened up. My radioman, a Marine by the name of Franklin, knew I had a habit of having him relay most of the messages in the field. But this time he gave the handset to me without hesitation. Someone at battalion had countermanded my order for a 155mm artillery barrage. I was trying to send the fire mission in and they were telling me it was a Christmas truce and they couldn't shoot it.

145

That's when I got rather colorful in my language. I said, 'We're getting the shit kicked out of us here. If there's a truce, these guys don't know it. If we don't link up, don't bother sending anybody out here unless you just want somebody to pick up the pieces.' Then Colonel Airheart got on the horn. He was screaming for a sitrep—one of the last things we should have been talking about. So I said to him, 'If I could get my fucking head up high enough to tell you what's going on, I'd let you know what was going on. But if you want to know, just listen to my calls for fire. I haven't got time to talk to you. We're trying to stay alive out here. We're trying to keep moving and I don't have time to talk to you.' He told me, 'You can't say that to me.' With that, the heat rose a bit and I said, 'Well, you know, if you want to get somebody else out here, I'll turn it over to them. Get off the air because I need this artillery.'

"*Finally somebody from First Marine Division headquarters chimed in and gave the okay for the 155 battery at Hill 55 to deliver fire support. General Nickerson told me later that he had given the word to go ahead and release the artillery. I guess the way they heard about it was they were sitting back there on Christmas Eve listening to these two company commanders basically fighting for their lives in the middle of this truce, so they jumped right in on the tac net. Once we got hooked up with Hill 55, the rounds started dropping in on VC positions. We would fire a mission for effect, get up and charge for 50 yards, add 50 or add 75 and fire the next mission, then go again.*"

Ebbert's company broke through the first VC unit and proceeded towards the beleaguered Marines of Golf Company. They were halfway there, but the VC were not ready to take their marbles and go home. They had one more play in the game...

"*They hit us pretty hard a second time and we were pinned down. So I led a squad down a low trench line to get around what would have been their left flank. Then I got hit in the chest. Two rounds knocked me over like a bowling pin. I rolled over and said to myself, 'I've been hauling this flak jacket all these months and finally it's worthwhile.' I didn't have a shirt on. I was cold. I rolled over and got up on my knees and could feel all this blood running down my stomach and I said, 'You know Ebbert, this is not very good.' At first I thought the flak jacket had saved me and the rounds had just knocked me end over end but I was hit in the chest and the stomach. One AK-47 round went right through the jacket, through the left side of my chest, and out through the back of the flak jacket. The other one, it just sort of tore up my diaphragm and lodged in there. After that I couldn't stay conscious. I tried to continue to adjust fire, but I couldn't even move myself anymore."*

We got the company moving again and Sergeant Cerralo, a West Virginian, would grab my flak jacket and pull me along the ground. Every time they'd get up to move, I'd say to myself, 'Oh no, here we go again.' I knew if I took itsy-bitsy little breaths, I could survive the ordeal. From that point on, it all blurs out until we get into G Company lines. Once we made the link up, Captain Gruner came over and said, 'Well, we're going to get you out of here.' I said, 'Hell, I've been trying to run medivacs all night and we're not going to get any helicopters in here. I brought you your chow, now get me out of here.'

The last thing I remember is Sam Williams (Echo Company platoon commander) standing up like the Statue of Liberty with a strobe light trying to guide this helicopter in and rounds zinging all around him. Then they threw me on the helo. I'd been all right until then, but I thought I was going to die because they threw people on top of me. Once we got airborne I managed to kick the gunner, because I couldn't talk. Then he finally started prying everybody apart once we were out of the LZ. The only way I could breathe was to get up on my bad side so I could breathe out of my right lung."

1st Lt. Ebbert's heroic efforts to break through to his fellow Marines in Golf Company on Christmas Eve would earn him a well-deserved Navy Cross. John Peterson, a rifleman in his company, watched the whole drama unfold with sickening certitude…

"I remember every truce we had over there whether it was Tet or Christmas or whatever the hell it was, the VC broke it. But you can't do a fire mission 'til you get hit, I suppose. But it was just like, 'OK. We gotta go, you guys. Let's go.' And we didn't go more than a hundred yards from the Mike boats before the shit hit the fan. Not long after that, Ebbert got hit, probably by a round and shrapnel from a mortar round. The enemy unit got in between Company G and my company and that sort of neutralized them helping us out, although I remember

147

they did come to our support there. The guy next to me got killed. His name was Surber. He was a rifleman. I remember looking up and actually seeing enemy 57mm recoilless rounds flying through the air. They were black against the sky. To this day I have an image of that. There were tracers and bullets flying all over the place. It was probably a VC unit of about equal strength. I don't think we were overwhelmed by any stretch. I think, to the best of my recollection, that we finally did get some 155 support. I guess that Ebbert arguing with the battalion commander probably did some good in the big picture.

"We finally did hook up with Company G. I have a recollection of these guys coming towards me and everything. Ebbert was in terrible shape. He may have lost a lung. We thought he was going to die. Once we got inside G Company lines, I spent the coldest night I've ever experienced; I was next to Sergeant Batteo who was the platoon sergeant at the time. We were just exhausted, so we went to sleep in this mud puddle. I mean, the whole area was flooded. We were hugging each other for body warmth all night...very unashamedly, I would say."

Ron Carbone, a nineteen-year-old rifleman in Third Platoon, G Company, found himself at the point of the spear trying to link up with Echo Company...

"Bill Gavin and I were right up front, trying to link up with Echo. That was our famous thing, and of course it stood out in everybody's mind because it was Christmas Eve. We got the order to move out and find Echo Company. Course it was pitch black; it was raining. There was enemy all around the woods. We were just boldly going through it. I mean, there could have been booby traps; there could have been an ambush. We would have walked right into it if it was set up right. Anyway, when we finally got close and we were in contact by radio, Gavin was out there literally just going, 'E-e-e-c-c-c-h-o...E-e-e-c-c-c-h-o.' Just kind of singing out 'Echo' to make voice contact."

According to PFC Bill Gavin, Sergeant Carter, the platoon commander, passed a curt, truncated order for a very dangerous mission...

"Carter didn't tell us anything. That is what really pissed me off. He just said, 'We got to find Echo Company'. That's all he said. 'And they're in this direction and what they're going to do is they're going *to pop up flares.' We knew that they were coming in with food because it was still raining and they couldn't get any choppers in. So there I was on point again. All I had to do was move through the villages and aim toward those popup flares. So then I knew we were all going to get killed because the gooks were between us and Echo Company. They had just gotten ambushed and I knew I was fucking dead. Me and Carbone had the point. I started weaseling my way in the general direction through villages going a little bit north or south just to keep from traveling in a straight line. It was really spooky. I could see candles lit in the little Vietnamese hootches and we were moving very, very slowly because I was moving very slowly. It took me probably an hour and a half to get to where Echo Company was. Then I saw some popup flares from Echo Company a click, two clicks away. It was pitch black, eight or nine o'clock at night. Echo had wounded, they had killed. Finally we got to where it looked like we were within 200 yards of where the last popup flare came from. I said to myself, 'I don't know how accurately these dudes can shoot at night. I've made it this far, but I'm sure as shit not going to walk up on a Marine company that's just been ambushed in the middle of the night. Somebody's not going to get the word if we radio.' So I started hollerin', 'This is Golf Company. Don't shoot. This is Golf Company. We're coming into your lines."*

The battered and exhausted Marines of Echo Company materialized out of the dripping darkness like ghosts of Christmas past, each carrying a pack board with extra C-rations lashed to it. Along with several other wounded and dead, the Marines carried Terry Ebbert, the company commander, on a makeshift poncho litter. Soon the gunnery sergeants and right guides had distributed the food to ravenous Marines standing watch on the lines.

Back home, the San Francisco Examiner Sunday, December 24th 1966 edition reported the following:

The Truce Remains Troubled

Saigon (Sunday — AP). Rifle fire and exploding shells shook the uneasy two-day truce in a dozen areas of this war-torn land on Christmas Eve. Saigon spokesmen blamed the Communists. Allied forces responded to some attacks sharply, in the case of a strike with mortars and small arms at a U.S. Marine company 12 miles south of

149

Da Nang. They ignored others...A U.S. military spokesman said the attack on the Marine company was of considerable importance. He declined however, to call it a major violation of the cease-fire. Viet Cong riflemen fired about 1000 rounds and mortar crews lobbed 20 shells at the company.

Once everything quieted down, I bunked in on a hard wooden shelf or piece of furniture in a thatched hut we had commandeered as the platoon headquarters. Sergeant Farnham had settled in below me and Shipley, the radioman, was on first watch rolled up in a poncho against the wall, listening to the AN/PRC-25. Starvation began to take its toll, inducing bizarre dreams that flickered across the penumbra of consciousness. I drifted into a half sleep that coalesced into holiday scenes— cylindrical lights suspended from the arched ceiling of the United Methodist Church of Los Altos, California cast amber light across rows of poinsettias and garlands of cedar boughs. The fragrance of candles permeated the air. Reverend Cox, tall and serious, looking a bit like the Hollywood actor Gene Hackman, reminded us that hope kindled by the birth of The Savior burned brightly on this special day. The celebrated choir, accompanied by concussive bass from a two-story high pipe organ, softly sang, *"Silent night, holy night, all is calm, all is bright."* Then the congregation joined the choir in belting out the jubilant strains of *Alleluia* from Handel's *Messiah* until the stained glass windows rattled in their frames and the sound reverberated across arched trusses, pulsing and swelling in intensity. Someone in the pew behind me brushed his program against the back of my neck, startling me awake to the needle-like claws of a rat that had just scurried across my head and down the wall of our miserable hootch. Outside the rain moved in misty curtains across the defensive perimeter. I threw off my poncho and swung down to check the lines.

All the Marines answered my challenges. The lines seemed secure, so I returned to the hootch and rolled up once again in the greasy poncho. Just before dawn an angry explosion thirty yards away shook us awake. When we discovered what had happened, Sgt. Farnham was highly agitated. It had been a serious breach...

150

"Then early one morning we had a bad incident. Second Platoon had a hootch for a CP. There was some big furniture in it. Lieutenant Buchanan was sleeping on top of a three or four dresser thing. We had Biberg and Shipley and somebody else in there on radio watch and lieutenant got up to go check the lines. I was sleeping right below him and he just about stepped on me. Shortly after he checked the lines and came back, the VC came in. They came through and hit a position down the line. I think it was a grenade that got one Marine—new people that hadn't been with us very long. They were sleeping. The VC came through the lines and they found them asleep. They took a rifle. That was a mess because they actually got inside our lines. It was a miracle we didn't start shooting people. I just about shot one of those Kit Carson Scouts. We had to call in a chopper to get the wounded Marine out. Gruner caught a little static from his medevac request; they told him that all we wanted was just food, that really there was nobody up there that was hit. He said, 'I'll blow this goddamned chopper up if you don't get the medevac in here.' He was getting to the point where he was going to blow that wrecked chopper up."

Over at the company command post, Marc Glasgow finally heard something that sounded more like a Christmas carol...

"Christmas Eve, Major General Nickerson, Commanding General, First Marine Division, came up on our company tactical net with the call sign Cassandra and he said to tell Gruner that he'd put every plane he had in the sky the next day and to be prepared to go out by chopper. The next day the choppers showed up just like he said. We both went out together, Echo and Golf. We had them loaded in the sticks, Gunny Keegan and I. I think it was the first CH 46 that landed and the appropriate unit got on it. Troops by that time looked pretty ragged. There's no way we could have walked out of there. The troops were in such bad shape, the feet, the boots. Their feet were swollen outside of their boots. Some didn't have pants on anymore. There was actually a guy walking around with VC pants on because his trousers got all torn. There was barbed wire all over that village. I had sores for quite some time from running into barbed wire at night. Now, I don't know who wired the village, the old French or the VC, or whatever, but we ran into it.

As the first chopper started lifting off, some young trooper in the second stick going out just couldn't take it. And he ran and he jumped

151

on the back of the 46. He went out. They didn't kick him off. Gruner and I expected the crew chief to kick him off, but he just broke ranks with his unit and dove in that chopper. He wanted out of there so bad. Gruner and I discussed what to do when we got back. And you know what we decided to do? Nothing. He'd just had enough. Choppers got in and the planes could fly—probably by radar—dropping bombs around us. I don't know if they could see much. Why the enemy didn't close with us, I'll never know. But they didn't want a piece of us and we managed to get out."

Sgt. Farnham had had all the fun he could stand for a holiday season. To him, those birds looked like angels from heaven...

"Then the 25th, Christmas day, the clouds opened up just enough for everything to come in. The first set of choppers that flew in, they dropped off 50 caliber rounds; but there wasn't nothing that we could do with them. Gunny got mad. He said, 'What the hell are we going to do with this stuff? Throw it at them?' They left us the ammo, but we had no fifties to shoot it with. They brought in CH-46s and there was 12 of them—four across, three deep. They landed in that big field near the village over there to the south of us. That was some impressive sight. We were the last platoon to go out. As we started out, they started shooting at us again, so they brought in some air support. I think they were A-7s that morning and they just dumped everything that they had off to the north of us."

The last bird wobbled into the LZ, jousting with the wind for mastery of the air. Captain Gruner had designated I be with the last unit to board, so I sent first one fire team, then another across the field. When our turn came, distant alarm bells tolled in my head once again. I had the creepy feeling VC were waiting for the last unit to begin boarding before they opened up across that soggy billiard table-like field. While running pell-mell for the ramp of the CH-46, I surveyed the dark tree line beyond the LZ, watching for winking lights that would signal an assault, an assault I sensed might come—but never did. Then we were in the helicopter, tossed this way and that, enduring the wild ride by holding on to the sides of the seats.

Marc Glasgow was impressed with the reception party at An Hoa...

"When I landed with Gruner, there was General Nickerson, shaking every one of these young troopers' hands as they stumbled out of the helicopters. I bet quite a few didn't have boots on. Their feet were swollen up. Their clothes were torn to hell — they were filthy. He made such an impression. I heard him talking to the troops, thanking them for their effort."

Like most of the Marines in Golf Company, PFC Bill Gavin's clothes had just disintegrated during the weeklong operation, leaving his appearance a bit short of parade field resplendent. But elation over finally escaping the rain-swept gloom of Go Noi Island trumped any embarrassment he might have felt when he stepped off the ramp of the CH-46 chopper and spotted a high-ranking reception party…

"I was one of the first guys to get off the chopper because I was among the last to load on at Go Noi. I saw this general standing on the runway to greet us. Then I realized I didn't have any trousers on. All through the operation I was wearing the same pair of cotton utility trousers and they just rotted right off, more and more each day. So there I am standing on the ramp before God, the general, and everybody wearing my flak jacket, helmet, and two, maybe four white pockets, a few buttons and a belt. That's it. My dick was hanging out. So what the hell. I walked over, shook his hand and he said, 'Merry Christmas, son. It looks like you lost something.' I said, 'Yes sir, I sure did.' And that was the best day of my life."

I was just one more mud-smeared, bearded apparition walking off the ramp of the helicopter that Christmas Day. I was carrying an M-14 rifle, half a bandoleer of ammunition, and the North Vietnamese field pack I had found near the DMZ. The crotch in my trousers was missing. After seven straight days of combat, my normal body weight of 158 pounds had dropped to around 142. A Pancho Villa-like mustache dribbled down both sides of my mouth. When I walked up to General Nickerson, the only thing that saved him from malodorous anaphylactic shock was by then we'd been rinsed off somewhat by the rain. Regardless, we were a rank bunch of warriors. His aide, an officer in my Basic School class, introduced me to the general, who shook my hand and asked, "You're not Buck Buchanan's son are you, lieutenant?" I assured him I was. When the Fourth Marine Division assaulted Iwo Jima in 1945, Dad went ashore as an artillery and Naval gunfire officer. The refurbished Model 1911A1 45-caliber pistol that hung from my web belt had borne silent witness to those historic battles. "Your Dad's a fine Marine from the Class of '35," said General Nickerson. "He would be proud. Great job out there, lieutenant. Carry on."

Marc Glasgow wasted no time getting the logistics squared away...

"I was carrying a shotgun that was rusted shut. It wouldn't fire anymore. And they had a pile of weapons...I threw my .45 and shotgun both in the pile of the ruined weapons. When Gruner got off, General Nickerson said to him, 'You people are going to get two weeks off, looking at your troops. You're not to be used. You're to stay here at the CP—at the battalion back at An Hoa.' And the next thing we were arranging with the cooks to serve a peanut butter diet for the next week and a half at all meals. They were feeding a lot of peanut butter, every meal. Wanted everybody to eat peanut butter. I never knew peanut butter could put on that much weight, but it was about 10 days. We didn't leave the compound. We had perimeter guard."

Sgt. Farnham was delighted to learn that, thanks to a thoughtful and generous company commander, an appropriate alcoholic libation would compliment our substitute Christmas dinner...

"When we got back to An Hoa, we had missed Christmas dinner, so General Nickerson, the First Division Commanding General, said that he was getting some steaks down or something for us to eat because we didn't have a chance to enjoy Christmas dinner with the rest of the battalion. We got back in the company area and Gruner went and got his private footlocker and opened it up and passed the bottles around. Took a bottle to each platoon. I don't know how many bottles was in there, but he said, 'Here's a bottle for each platoon.' That was our Christmas of 1966. "

LINCOLN

Golf Company spent the next two weeks at An Hoa with another company, guarding the airfield, improving perimeter bunkers, doing limited patrolling, and consuming prodigious amounts of peanut butter. New blood began to trickle in slowly, filling the gaps that constant patrolling and combat operations had opened in the ranks of Second Platoon. New layers of skin began to grow over the bottoms of our ravaged feet. The jungle boots worked well, but pulverized silty clay had a way of seeping into the drain holes, working its way into our socks, and before we knew it, wearing holes in our feet just like emery paper. We were at a loss to prevent it.

When Bill Gavin's leg swelled up inexplicably a week after Christmasville, he found himself headed towards a paradise that he never imagined in his wildest dreams...

"From Christmas Day for about the next ten days, my right leg started to swell up. I didn't know what the hell it was, especially my knee. I had boils all over my legs because I had no trousers on at Go

155

Noi. But my right leg and my right knee kept swelling up and swelling up. Then I remembered that when a Marine fired an M-79 round on Christmas Eve when we were going out to get Echo Company I thought I felt a thorn in my knee when I hit the ground. So I reached back there and sure enough found a little sliver of M-79 round. The leg kept swelling up. Then just as Golf Company was going to leave (our 3rd Platoon was going to support Operation Tuscaloosa) during the first week of January, my knee was swollen up like a basketball. So they medevac'd me to Charlie Med in Danang. The doc said, 'We're going to have to draw the fluid out of it.' So they put me in a bed and I spent two weeks at Charlie Med waiting for the swelling to go down in this knee. The swelling didn't go down to their satisfaction, so they flew me from Charlie Med in Danang to an Air Force hospital at Cam Ranh Bay. Oh my God, it was like heaven! Air-conditioned wards, round-eyed women. All around was white sand! When I got ambulatory to where I could walk, there was an ice cream smoothie truck that would come around and sell ice cream to the guys in the wards. It was just wonderful. They had an enlisted men's club that was unbelievable. They imported Australian strippers. They'd dance. And when I got ambulatory, there were about five Marines in this hospital and we'd get on our blue hospital robes and we'd walk over to the enlisted men's club. We were sitting right on the aisles that the performers would use to come in and this Australian stripper came in and one of our guys reached out and grabbed her ass. Then two Air Force MPs threw all of us Marines out. So we were walking back to our hospital and some fucking Air Force puke, he throws out a whole string of firecrackers and every Marine hit the deck and rolled in a ditch. Incoming we thought. Damned right! You know, just a reaction. The Air Force guys, they just laughed at us. 'What the fuck are you guys doing?' Then my knee healed up and it was back to An Hoa."

While it lasted, we savored creature comforts: having a cot to sleep on, hot meals served in a mess hall. The secure environment also meant not getting shot at when we went about our daily routine. Easy patrols took us looping out to the north and east. Then the Life of Riley ended when the word came down another search and destroy operation was in the wind. This one, it turned out, had a bit of a twist to it.

Once again the Shangri-La of Antenna Valley was calling to us. G-2 (1st Marine Division intelligence) had learned a local force

Viet Cong battalion was in the valley, supported by an unknown number of guerillas. Villagers had seen a local force Viet Cong platoon operating regularly along the main road a couple of kilometers west of the river. A task force comprising battalion headquarters (Lt. Col. W. Airheart commanding), along with Company F (Captain Burgett) and Company G (Captain Gruner) was assembled, along with the necessary supporting arms. The plan called for Company G to move south into Antenna Valley, establish a base of operations, and wait for Company F to march in the next day from Nong Son Coal Mine, eventually linking up with us.

For added operational security, and to avoid signaling our punch as we did on Operation Mississippi, Company G would shove off from An Hoa while it still was dark, without informing the South Vietnamese soldiers who manned a portion of the southern perimeter near a reservoir. It would be risky; a threatening sound or the sight of unidentified troops moving through the darkness in front of their positions might signal enemy attack to the Vietnamese and they would open fire on us.

At 0530 on 5 January we strapped on our gear, checked our weapons one last time, and began to file out to the south, threading our way between buildings and through the concertina, the minefield and finally the shoreline of the reservoir called Dap Thich Nuoc Khe Cong. It was a cool, foggy morning. With a sigh of relief, the last platoon cleared the South Vietnamese positions and we began to climb into the foothills. My map showed our route following a trail over a constricted pass at an elevation of about 100 meters. With a little advance warning, a sizeable unit of VC or NVA could unleash a devastating ambush on either side of the pass, or at any number of places on the other side where accuracy of artillery fire would be impeded by slope angle. Mines also would be an effective impediment.

To our immense relief, we traversed the pass without incident, moved down the south side, and settled in on a brushy slope about three clicks north of the valley itself to await developments. Sunrise illuminated the ridges and began working its way down into the rice paddies, evaporating light mist that had crept in from the river. NCOs admonished sleepy Marines were who beginning to stir to observe noise discipline. As battalion headquarters group flew from An Hoa by helicopter to establish itself at Nong Son, we began to move towards our next objective, the west end of a small airstrip next to the road that bisected the valley. By 1700 we had dug in our defensive perimeter and were setting up listening posts and ambushes.

Late morning the next day the Second Platoon radio crackled…"Sir, its Cassandra Golf Six Actual. He's seen some VC setting up a heavy weapon and they're calling in a 105 mission." Perhaps our stealth approach had worked and the real show was about to begin.

Captain Gruner sounded excited. "Lieutenant Buchanan, we can see a trench line about 300 meters southeast near the road. It's full of VC. Move down there and assault as soon as the fire mission ends."

I briefed my squad leaders, then began moving down the hill. We had just reached the valley floor when a phalanx of artillery rounds came screaming in over the ridge to the north of us. I hadn't heard the gun reports, even though An Hoa was only 8 kilometers away, well within the 11 kilometer range of a 105mm howitzer. Geysers of water, trees, bamboo structures, and dirt flew up into the air near a paddy dike that angled out from the hamlet of Ap Ba (1) a hundred and fifty meters away. After all rounds had fallen into the near edge of the hamlet and the smoke began to clear, I ordered the platoon to move out.

Second and Third Squads were on line, with First Squad behind us bringing up the rear. "Move it out now!" I yelled, and Second Squad began slogging through a flooded paddy. On our right flank the Third Squad leader moved his men down the road in column formation towards the objective. They looked like a green picket fence—five meters apart. I couldn't believe my eyes: like frigging British redcoats. Enfilade fire from the trench line would take them down like bowling pins, but correcting their formation at that point would have triggered confusion so I kept my fingers crossed. But the Marines around

158

me still were moving too slowly.

"Let's see some hustle," I admonished. "Move, move, move!"

The pace remained the same: a desultory, uninspired slog through the watery mud. Then we were on dry ground, moving toward the village, which we could see nestled in among banana trees and hedgerows. The trench line turned out to be more of a ditch. Although we found pools of blood, it was abandoned. By 1600 that day we had linked up with Company F and formed a defensive perimeter.

By 0800 the next day, we were sweeping east along the north side of the valley, with Company F and the battalion command group following in trace. We moved carefully and deliberately through the rice paddies towards Ap Ba (1) challenged only once—by a cranky water buffalo one of the Marines threatened to shoot until I admonished him to talk to it in low tones and fire only in self-defense. "Niiiice water boo." City boy. No use signaling our presence to otherwise clueless enemy forces after all this hard won subterfuge.

Ten minutes later an explosion twenty-five meters to my right front followed by outgoing M-14 rifle fire shattered the morning quiet. Moving forward past a grove of banana trees, I saw a VC soldier lying face down on a rice paddy dike where one of my fire teams had dropped him as he tried to escape after tossing a grenade at the point man. His buddy, wounded in the exchange, took off to the northeast. Then my acting platoon sergeant walked over holding his face. "I'm hit, lieutenant," he said as he pulled his hand away, revealing a dark gray grenade fragment embedded solidly in his cheekbone just below the right eye.

"Damn, sergeant, you're going to miss the hike out," I told him. "That's an evac wound. Can't have you walkin' around here with a piece of a grenade stickin' out of your face."

Soon a medevac helicopter was hauling him back to Charlie Med in Danang. One of the riflemen showed me a World War Two carbine the guerilla had dropped when the bullets cut him down. A piece of bailing wire held the stock to the receiver. What

159

could he and his comrade have been thinking to take on a heavily armed platoon of United States Marines?

The middle of that afternoon, the VC managed to shoot down a resupply helicopter three kilometers southeast of us in grid square 9136 and rake with automatic fire a second chopper sent to retrieve the crew and supplies. I prayed this was not a prelude to another "Christmasville" exercise in short rations. As things worked out, patrols scoured the area where the bird was reported to have crashed, but never did find it: chopper-sitting assignment cancelled, thank God. We spent the night without incident in a battalion perimeter just south of the road and a click east of the supposed chopper crash site. The next morning we mounted out and moved west toward the river, keeping the road on our right flank and a wary eye out for main force or NVA units that reportedly infested this valley from time to time. Two kilometers from the river, in the area where intelligence sources had predicted VC activity, snipers started pinging us from low hills to the south of us, wounding three Marines. We responded with small arms fire and a 105mm howitzer barrage that threw an impressive Old Faithful-type geyser of water into the air from a short round that fell into the Khe Le, a sizeable stream that flanked the road. A quick adjustment into the far trees calmed our nerves somewhat and quelled the sniping. Corporal Charles "Chip" Mohney of Third Platoon drew the short straw of providing flank security as the company made its move along the exposed road...

"Coming out I was behind the point squad. I was still a squad leader and I had two machine guns with me. At the end of Antenna Valley before you cross that little bridge is a big knoll to your right. I took the guns out and set them up to give overhead fire for the companies that was goin' by. The VC opened up from across this wide rice paddy and we spent a long time there covering two companies as they moved down the road. At first, we took some friendly fire because they thought we were the bad guys. We got that squared away pretty quick. After the two companies had passed by, we had to maneuver off that little hill and rejoin the main body. But enemy fire was still poppin' all around us. Now I got a lot of rice paddy to cover and to get those Marines on the road and then get out of the valley. So I tell everybody. I said, 'Listen, we're not all going to get out in the rice paddy and make a big

long line getting out of here and back over to the road.' I says, 'So we're going down the back side of the hill.' I was thinking the gooks in the ville wouldn't see us. It didn't work out that way. We're movin', but rounds are hitting everywhere. I mean at one point I'm watching the steam come off the rounds hitting between my legs."

Corporal Mohney had his hands full with the functional Marines in his squad. Then Lady Luck dealt him a bad card with one who wasn't so functional...

"Well, we all got to the road and then of course we had that burm there so you can get down behind the berm. I turned around and there's a Marine that shouldn't have been in the Marine Corps—PFC Philip J. Kimpel. He is sitting out there, exposed to enemy fire. It looked like he wanted to die. He wasn't a coward. He just sat down. What the hell was I going to do? I had to get him out of there, so I stripped everything off: belt, flak jacket, helmet. I laid my weapon down. I ran back out there, grabbed him, and pulled him to his feet. I would shove him and he would go two or three feet and stop. I ran back up and pushed him again. He'd go two or three more feet and stop. The whole time rounds are throwing up little sprays of water around us. I hauled him like that all the way back to the road bank, crossed the bridge and rejoined the squad. As soon as we got back to An Hoa, I went to see First Sergeant Moore about Kimpel, who I had to drag out of the rice paddy. I said, 'First Sergeant Moore, I'd like this guy to have a psychiatric, evaluation.' First Sergeant Moore said, 'He's a Marine, like anybody else.' Since he was one of my Marines, I keep him as close to me as I can. Everything I do, I have him with me. Later we took over the coal mine at Nong Son and for some reason or another, they let him go out on patrol one day. I didn't go. That was the day he killed himself."

Without Corporal Mohney's rearguard action, we would have taken a larger number of casualties than we did. Regardless, we helped several blood-spattered walking wounded hobble into the village of Khuong Trung. Then they rode medevac choppers into Danang, leaving the battalion to dig in a perimeter along the resort-like shores of the Song Thinh Yen. White sand beaches flanking turquoise waters of the river, a backdrop of rich green jungle mountains, and some puffy cumulus turning lavender in the waning sunset comprised an almost surreal scene.

161

Ron Carbone recalled great expectations at the beginning of the operation...

"We were supposed to be looking for fifty weapons and 80,000 pounds of rice, but found only a couple tons of rice: no weapons. The operation was supposed to last three days, but it was five days before we got back. There was a downed chopper near us and we had to go look for it. After a day of searching, they decided to let it go. The next day we walked back to An Hoa. It rained the whole time and my feet were really sore. After the doc checked my feet, he gave me two days no duty."

By the middle of the afternoon of 9 January, Company G and the battalion command group had finished the hump back over the pass to An Hoa and Company F had climbed back up to Nong Son. No one ever mentioned whether the South Vietnamese soldiers on perimeter duty at An Hoa were surprised to see us return when they never saw us leave.

Marc Glasgow, the Executive Officer, recalled some years later...

"Although the company had converted to M-16s shortly before this operation, we kept a few M-14s as a reliability factor. While we were moving down the main road towards the river, VC snipers shot at us from beyond the 1000 meter range, so the M-14s came in handy. M-16s just didn't have the effective range. Back at An Hoa, Captain Gruner, Gunny Keegan, and myself made it policy to carry two M-14s per squad, the drawback being that each man could carry only 300 rounds versus 600 rounds of M-16 ammo. After the horrendous shoot-out at Christmasville (Go Noi Island), the standard ammo allowance was 600 M-16 rounds per man and 2000 rounds for each M-60 machine gun. That was a heavy load, especially considering our depleted manpower. However, the fear of running out of ammo was forever on our minds after Christmasville."

As on Operation Mississippi, the battalion had reacted to intelligence about sizeable enemy units in Antenna Valley with an excellent plan, but had come up empty. In five days we had scoured the valley floor, moving first west to east along the north side of the valley, then east to west along the south side without engaging any units larger than a squad. Second Platoon took credit for the one VC killed—the pathetic *Du Kich* (local guerilla) with a World War Two carbine held together with bailing wire: not exactly a worthy adversary.

REWIND

On 11 January 1967 we packed our gear and mounted out for Phu Lac (6) company patrol base once again. It was our turn in the rotation cycle. The wound Sergeant Mack sustained on 13 December during our long day in the Arizona Territory had healed. His return from the hospital coincided perfectly with the medical evacuation from Antenna Valley of my acting platoon sergeant. Having his ornery persona around made the outfit seem normal.

Rumors about the new combat rifle were swirling through the battalion. After one of the armorers showed me the spiffy new M-16, I convinced Captain Gruner platoon commanders should try them out on the next operation. Compared to the M-14, the thing was ridiculously light and had hardly any recoil. I loaded some ammo pouches with about 200 rounds, some of them tracers, and packed them along to Phu Lac (6).

It didn't take us long to recognize a definite shift in VC tactics, since we last had patrolled the area. Late in the day during our first platoon-size patrol off the hill, we were looping back in when we saw a couple of kids take off on a water buffalo a few hundred meters away. They weren't moving very fast, because you don't really "take off" on a "water boo" as the Marines called them. They're definitely built for strength, not speed. Nevertheless, the movement caught my eye for some reason. I had a squad in front of me, and a fire team from the Second Squad providing security for our left flank.

An explosion shattered the bucolic scene and sent metal singing past our heads. A Marine went down clutching his leg.

"Sorry lieutenant," he said when I looked over to see if he was seriously hurt. "I just couldn't see the trip wire. It's monofilament."

"Just be careful, corporal. We need you here with us, not in the hospital giving the nurses a hard time," I joked, trying to keep his mind off his wound.

A dark stain was beginning to spread along his calf. Doc Salisberry patched him up and, since we could see Phu Lac (6) 500 meters away, another Marine helped him hobble along the trail. We resumed our measured pace, knowing that proximity to Phu Lac (6) was no guarantee of safety. We hadn't gone two hundred meters before another sharp explosion ripped through the heavy air. The point man was down.

"Corpsman!" someone screamed. "Corpsman up!" It sounded bad.

I took off along the paddy dike, yelling, "Security out both flanks. Heads up for booby traps."

Within seconds I had sprinted to where a large Marine was sitting beside the trail clenching his teeth and holding his right arm. His helmet and rifle were lying on the ground beside him. Ten feet from the trail, the booby-trapped M-26 grenade had scorched grass and torn up the ground. I lifted the man's right arm and blood spurted out with each heartbeat from a half-inch slit inside it, between the bicep and the tricep—a classic arterial wound.

"No sweat, corporal. I'll just turn this valve and it'll be okay," I told him. When I gripped his arm just above the wound, in effect applying an arterial pressure point, the blood stopped spurting. The Marine turned gray and keeled over onto the dirt path. Two seconds later, Doc Salisberry was beside me. "I've got it, lieutenant," he said, as he applied a tourniquet. Stretcher-bearers from the hill helped us haul him back so he could meet the incoming medevac chopper.

"Victor Charlie," as some of the Marines referred to the Viet Cong, obviously had opted to escalate the use of mines and booby-traps instead of engaging us in full-scale firefights for the time being. Perhaps it was a tactic designed to buy time for training and replacement of soldiers lost during recent battles. These tactics, anonymous yet deadly, were as frustrating to us as our use of supporting arms probably was for the enemy troops. On the next patrol, we lost six Marines to mines and booby traps before we'd traveled 2000 meters. They were just impossible to detect.[9]

On a rare morning with no patrols, my Third Squad leader strolled over to my command bunker and asked me to show him how to reassemble his 45-caliber pistol. I showed him, we talked for a while, then he drifted back to his squad area, leaving me to sit on the edge of a sandbagged fighting hole and enjoy the view: a mosaic of soft green rice paddies, villages girdled by thick hedgerows, Liberty Road snaking towards An Hoa, cumulus clouds forming and dissolving over the Que Son Mountains. The January sun streamed down from the southeast, evaporating the light dew that had condensed overnight, and warming the muscles of my shoulder and back. One of the Marines was playing tug of war with Maggie, using a haversack strap to drag her growling through the red dirt. This short break

---

[9] For an interesting description of VC mine tactics, read *Not Going Home Alone* by James J. Kirschke.

from constant patrolling and search and destroy operations was almost euphoric. I used the time to write letters home, clean my combat gear and get ready for the next foray into Arizona Territory.

Other times of quietude occurred when it was my turn at radio watch and I sat in the bunker at 0200, listening to the interminable hiss of the AN/PRC-25 radio and a symphony of soughing: the radioman, Sgt. Farham, Dau, accompanied by the wheezing and whimpering of Magnolia Buttplate as she drifted through her own canine version of dreamland. At those times the lonely darkness often would glow with bittersweet reminiscences about the ladies who had graced my life over the years since high school—of autumn days in the mountains near Julian, California with Jenny, beautiful Jenny of the chestnut hair and azure eyes, both of us giddy with the tangy scent of Macintosh, Pippin, Fuji, and Astrakhan apples, the orchards bathed in oblique, honey sunlight and the sharp definitions of the season, and the intoxication we felt most of all with each other; or the adventurous tomboy, Elliott, her dark Ojibwa features smoldering with passion as we undressed in our tent 40 miles into the Ontario canoe wilderness. As I sat there, alert for listening posts to check in, I pondered the series of events that had linked me up with Company G and this band of worthy warriors called Second Platoon.

Mid summer of 1965 already seemed like the distant past. Having graduated in June of that year from a six-month officer-training course at The Basic School in Quantico, Virginia, I soon found myself at the First Anti-Tank Battalion at Camp Pendleton, California. Having little affinity or affection for things mechanical (I never owned a hot rod in high school), the assignment surprised me. A further surprise was my billet: battalion adjutant. Surely there was some mistake. A quick look at my own personnel jacket would have revealed infantry-type talents acquired on my own and during Oregon State College forestry field exercises in the dripping Douglas Fir forests of the Coast Range: wilderness travel; mountain climbing in the Cascade Mountains, the Bernese and Valois Alps of Switzerland and the Canadian Rockies; land navigation with topographic maps and magnetic compass; fire fighting; cross country skiing;

168

target shooting; track and field events; backpacking, and canoeing. Thanks to a short language course, I had learned the fundamentals of Vietnamese. I had shot competitively on the Basic School Rifle Team. Would I not have made a first rate reconnaissance platoon commander? All those talents notwithstanding, there I was shuffling duty assignments, personnel jackets, company rosters, pay records, and unit diaries in an anti-tank battalion of all things.

My immediate superior was Major Robert Ernest Harris, the battalion executive officer, a powerfully built mustang with a dark complexion, square features and a rigid, no nonsense manner. He had a habit of crossing his arms when he wore the short sleeve summer uniform, displaying his sinewy forearms. Within four months, Major Harris moved me from the adjutant billet to Third Platoon Bravo Company, perhaps because he sensed my discontent. The company commander was Captain Felker, a tall, affable sort with a freckly face, light hair and eyes and a professional air about him. It wasn't long before Captain Felker was plucking my chestnuts out of the fire on a regular basis. Early one particular morning we found ourselves standing tall in Major Harris' office. The major ordered us "at ease" and we both sat down on a sofa across the room from the major's desk.

"Lieutenant Buchanan, you're here because you let your Marines down yesterday in the company classroom," said the major with a rising inflection in his voice. I could tell this was the warm-up phase of a dressing down. "Your mission was to instruct those Marines in the proper assembling of the field marching pack. They need that instruction so they can be combat-ready at a moment's notice, and so maximum efficiency can be achieved in this battalion through proper loading and assembly of the individual gear of each Marine. They look to you for good instruction, for leadership, for proper procedures. Yesterday you failed to deliver those to them. You let them down." Major Harris' face was beginning to glow. "For the short time I was in that classroom yesterday, I could have sworn I had walked into some kind of GODDAMNED rummage sale. Your NCO fumbled around with that pack until even I was confused. He didn't know what the HELL he was doin'. And when he turned to you, he got a muddled response. Now lieutenant, I don't know what you think this is—some sort of college fraternity where you can slough things off hoping that somebody will take up the slack, but we're headed for a war zone. I want these Marines ready. I'll tolerate no less than excellence all the way down the line and that includes classroom instruction. Have I made myself clear? Dismissed."

Captain Felker gnawed on my butt some more as we walked across the parking lot and back to the company area. After all, his reputation also was on the line. Difficult as it was to endure the major's blast of heated invective, the notion that he was right squirmed in my gut like a bad burrito. I had reviewed assembly of the field marching pack only cursorily the night before the class, leaving detailed instruction to my NCOs. Had I been able to take up the slack when the instructor faltered, my leadership quotient would have risen in front of Major Harris as well as the enlisted Marines, not to mention the practical effect of us all learning something. He was right. I had failed him and them. It would not happen again.

The incident prompted me to do some homework on the Ontos, affectionally called "pig" by the crewmen, many of whom had been assigned from infantry units. I learned it had been designed and manufactured in the early fifties to destroy main battle tanks. A relatively light tracked armored vehicle that carried six 106mm recoilless rifles with a fifty caliber spotting rifle on each one, it was only 12 feet long and 8 feet wide. It was a snug fit for three crewmembers: a driver, a gunner and an assistant gunner. 20" wide tracks supported the 9-ton Ontos on soft soils and sandy shoreline littoral. By participating in preparations for mounting out, I learned a lot about the mechanics of these weapons, their strengths and vulnerabilities.

The platoon, consisting of a light section of two Ontos and a heavy section of three Ontos, seemed stacked with senior sergeants—salty types who pushed the envelope with the butter bar platoon commander. They also were experts at keeping the machines running, and more importantly, training the crews to shoot. My first few training days with the M50A1 Ontos at the firing range were a revelation. Watching the 106mm HEAT (high

170

explosive anti tank) and HEPT (high explosive plastic tracer) rounds roar out of the barrels ahead of a cataclysmic backblast made me glad to be on the delivery end of this formidable weapons system. Like the sky fire of Zeus, tracer rounds streaked as far as 7500 meters towards the target then detonated, creating great clouds of dust, smoke and debris within a 35-meter killing radius.

As the months rolled on, I began to appreciate Staff Sergeant Pridemore, my platoon sergeant, for what he was—the lynchpin of Third Platoon. Tall and thin and in his late twenties at the time, he looked like a piece of beef jerky wrapped in a crisp 100 dollar bill; his utilities were so heavily starched they resembled green fiberglass. His leather boots shined like plastic. His brass belt buckle and insignia were blinding in the sun. He knew the machines and he knew the men. One of his most valuable talents was his nose for bullshit; he could smell it five miles away. More than once, he caught a Marine hauling a load of it to his lieutenant and he stopped him in his tracks.

Summer faded to fall and the leonine hills around Camp Pendleton—125,000 acres of the old Santa Margarita land grant—turned even drier. Then the hills caught fire and Santa Ana winds dropped gray ash like a Pompeii eruption all around the base. By the time our embarkation date for Vietnam rolled around, Third Platoon was as good as they come. Soon we were aboard the U.S.S. Tortuga, a landing ship dock (LSD) with a well deck that could be flooded to facilitate the launching of LVTP-5s, a tracked landing craft, as well as LCM-8s, larger boats that would carry the Ontos to amphibious landings. We churned across the Pacific as part of a squadron made up of troop ships, destroyers, a landing platform helicopter (LPH), and our landing ship dock (LSD). The whole shebang was called Battalion Landing Team (BLT) 3/5.

Late March of 1966 we landed on the island of Okinawa in an epic monsoon downpour so thick it was hard to differentiate the sea from the air. Soon we were creeping through the jungles of the Northern Training Area sharpening our jungle fighting skills. Later we shipped out for the Philippines, dropping anchor in Subic Bay. In late May we fine-tuned our amphibious landing

171

technique and conducted battalion maneuvers further south at Mindoro Island.

Back at Subic Bay, liberty hounds led us across the Santa Maria River bridge into Olongapo, a collection of ramshackle homes, seedy bars, and swarms of brightly decorated jitneys. I was sitting at one of the older bars with a chilled San Miguel beer in front of me when the old hands among us welcomed me in a most extraordinary way.

"First time in Olongapo, lieutenant?" asked a chief petty officer sitting across the table next to a young officer from the U.S.S. Tortuga.

"First time in beautiful downtown Olongapo, chief. The fumes from the river almost ate off my uniform, but my Marine training prevailed. And here I am."

The chief gestured to one of the waitresses, a busty, raven-haired Philippina wearing a low-cut light-colored cotton dress. "Esmeralda," he said, holding her tightly around the waist with his hairy, tattooed arm. "Give the lieutenant here our special welcome to Olongapo." He patted her on the butt and she walked around behind me. To the accompanying uproar around the table, my head suddenly was sandwiched between two bare breasts—plump pillows of satiny caramel skin. She had pulled down the top of her dress to give the new lieutenant the "Olongapo special welcome." The next night I was disappointed to learn you were eligible for only one special welcome per tour.

While the rest of the BLT used the time to consolidate equipment and take care of personnel matters, my platoon linked up with a couple of local Negrito guides, Rosalino Manuel and Jesus Carpio, for a two-day jungle training exercise in the foothills behind Subic Bay. The Northern Training Area on Okinawa had only whetted our appetite for the steamy, insect-infested, dimly lit operating environment we were likely to encounter "in country."

Our Tagalog-speaking guides knew just enough English to be understood. The minute the jungle swallowed us up they began showing us things: how to find fresh, sweet, water in bamboo sections, vines, and trees; how to find and eat quinine, rattan, and other medicinal plants, soap vine for cleansing, first-aid cream from shrub stems, snakebite cure from green bushes; food—guava like fruits, coffee beans from 150 foot smooth trunked coffee trees, tea for dysentery and stomach ache from the leaves and bark of tea trees, frogs from tiny streams, black spiral snails and fresh water shrimp boiled in green bamboo sections and served with steaming rice; shelters—bamboo structures raised off the ground with palmetto thatched roofs or taut ponchos, rattan and butterfly vine cord for lashing and making snares.

Near the edge of a jungle clearing, Jesus, the shorter of the two and seemingly the brighter, more experienced and talkative, stopped and cut a foot long section of stem from a short bush. "This is my medicine for cure snake cut, Sir," he said pointing to white liquid oozing from the severed end. "When snake bite you, you put on cut like so, and by'm by, blood come down, not go up." Then he smiled a gold-toothed smile and reached into his shirt pocket, bringing out a cigarette pack. Wrapped in dirty paper was an inch-long chip of fibrous serpentine-like stone worn smooth with handling. "This is my medicine for me," he said with what I thought was an amused glint in his eye. "Maybe not work for you. Place on cut and be better." He re-wrapped the stone carefully and placed it in his pocket. As we continued deeper into the jungle, I could only wonder at what far-flung ancient mysticism handed down from father to son back in the cloud-shrouded mountains this represented. Was there any scientific validity to it? What part of it was just ignorant witchcraft? What was actually effective, but spurned by the scientific community? Nevertheless, as we chopped our way through bamboo groves and thickets, we listened and noted all these guides had to show us. We faithfully ate the quinine and fruits they gathered for us.

Rosalino, quieter and shyer than Jesus, had long black hair and sharp features. He wore a blue baseball cap backwards and a tan pair of cotton trousers. He shucked off his black sneakers and shinnied up a tall, smooth-boled tree with large fan-like leaves. Shortly, we were covering our heads and dodging tennis

173

ball sized fruits that came whistling down from about 50 feet up. They were yellow skinned with a white, meaty interior surrounding three large nuts that was so tart it made your eyes fall in. I asked Jesus what it was. He didn't know the English word for it, but was eating one, so we followed his example. These were two superb woodsmen. They had that innate sense of direction you find only in experienced professional foresters or hunters.

That night the opening in the canopy far overhead flashed blue-white as a storm moved in from the north. Everyone was secure in sturdy bamboo framed shelters lashed up off the ground with rattan and roofed with a poncho stretched taut over bent saplings. The rain later washed the mosquitoes away and it was a passable night.

Soon the training and liberty ended and we found ourselves embarked aboard the ships, cruising due west. On 10 June we saw the coast of South Viet Nam for the first time: a low broken range of hills filtered by blue haze. Large sand dunes flowed down to the sea in places through gaps in barren, parched looking slopes. A squadron of huge yellow dragonflies, our first glimpse of Vietnamese wildlife, flew aboard the ship.

A week later we made our first actual combat landing on the coast of Quang Ngai Province—Operation Deckhouse One. Everyone from battalion commander down to rifleman was so keyed up that sleep the night before was ragged at best. Reveille sounded at 0430 on D-Day. We loaded up on the traditional steak and eggs breakfast, then listened as the Chaplain intoned over the speaker system...

"Lord on this day give us the strength and courage to carry through the tasks that have been set before us. Help us to realize that it is a good life and that the manner in which we live it determines our value to Thee. Be with the Marines as they land and with our families who wait at home for our safe return. We ask this in the name of our Lord Jesus Christ, Amen."

North of us the attack ship U.S.S. Renville floated solidly in the half-light as the eastern sky steadily brightened. Amphibian

174

tractors growled and wallowed like angry hippos in the light chop. Flat nosed LDM eights and sixes circled slowly on station, waiting for the command that would send them churning at full throttle toward the now obscured shoreline. A fog had covered the amphibious squadron and only two ships were visible through the gray air.

The Navy commander had a round, reddish face, carrot colored hair, and blue eyes. He gave the impression of quiet, relaxed competence. He ran the bridge efficiently; signal pennants were accurate and punctual, and electronic communications with the circling assault craft and other squadron ships were precise. He stood on the port side watching the maneuvering craft, looking very authoritative in his blue baseball cap with "scrambled eggs" on the bill and the word "Captain" embroidered across the back.

Suddenly an amphibian tractor commander stood upright in his cockpit, arms horizontal, signaling his platoon to line abreast formation. The assault wave formed slowly, each vehicle jockeying for position, then riding the swells in a shifting line. At standby one minute the port signalman locked the signal lamp aboard the command/control vessel. Then two pennants darted to the top of the mast, sending the amtracks forward, churning parallel emerald wakes. The formation crossed the line of departure and began the long run to the beach, stuffed full of sweating Marine infantrymen loaded down with body armor, helmets, packs, weapons and ammunition. On the bridge the TACLOG party marked times of departure on an acetate chart as each wave formed on line, then accelerated towards shore. The sun filtered gray-green through the mist, fusing sky and water, ships and boats into one slate colored plane. The sun broke through the milky sky now and again. The ship rode quietly at anchor. The landing was going well.

The pucker factor in our landing craft was at a tolerable level until someone said, "They're taking fire from the beach!" Christ. All I could think of was how the ramp on our Mike boat was designed to drop forward onto the sand, allowing enfilade enemy fire to nail us like rats in a barrel. Someone else said, "Bullshit. That's amtrack exhaust." Pulses dropped a notch. The

175

beach drew still closer, bristling with bushes and pine trees. There were sand dunes and an occasional cactus plant. I remembered the movie *Sands of Iwo Jima* and how the Japanese waited until the Marines were clustered at the high tide line before they opened up. Had the VC ever seen the movie, I wondered? But there was no resistance on the beach.

Operation Deckhouse One supported the U.S. Army's First Cavalry Division "Operation Nathan Hale." Third Platoon left the Ontos on board ship and deployed as a machine gun platoon along the defensive perimeter next to Foxtrot Battery. Infantry units encountered only scattered resistance. On 16 July, we steamed north along the coastline to a point near the DMZ in Quang Tri Province where Operation Deckhouse Two rolled into Operation Hastings that later rolled into Operation Prairie. Again, we left the Ontos aboard and functioned as an infantry platoon armed with 30 caliber machine guns.

At the end of July we offloaded at the First Marine Division base at Chu Lai. They disbanded BLT 3/5 and assigned 1st Anti Tank Battalion to perimeter security at the Chu Lai airfield. Thus began a long, tedious, but not uncomfortable phase of the Vietnam War. We lived in strong-back tents, which seemed like palaces after weeks of living in foxholes. On 31 July they moved us from the airfield further inland to Hill 35 where we provided security for India Company. On the day of our move it rained so hard our fingers shriveled up. We spent the entire morning splashing around in the mud nailing two by fours to plywood sheets, then hauling the completed decking by truck to the new position with the Ontos clattering behind. We ended up bivouacked between two hills in a narrow cleft that was choked with aggressive undergrowth and not a few bamboo vipers, cobras, crocodiles, leeches, and centipedes. Earlier in the day, one of the Marines had killed a bright green bamboo viper on a nearby trail. Plague had broken out in a village three kilometers away.

We cleared brush from the sides of a natural clearing with just enough slope to give it drainage, then sank bomb racks into the soft ground, leveling the decking on top. After a couple of hours with the tent repair kit, the old rotting canvas was up and stretched taut. The monsoon cycle had begun, bringing a drumming roar that thundered over the canvas and hissed across the rice fields, sending rust red rivulets flowing down the road in widening gullies.

The Mayor of Long Phu, the village adjacent to our positions, spoke only French and Vietnamese. He was 32 years old, slender, with a long face and an easy smile. You never saw him wearing the traditional black Vietnamese silk, because he bought his clothes in Saigon. One day I met him on the trail and asked him how much he might charge to build me a bamboo thatch hut like the kind I had seen near the Chu Lai airfield. He did some calculations on a pad and came up with 9000 piasters—about $90. I did some figuring of my own and came up with 2000 piasters—around $20. We never did close the gap, but he invited me to his French-style plaster and concrete house for a drink.

When the mayor opened the double wooden front doors of his house, bright sunlight poured into the room, illuminating a large glass topped table. Underneath the glass was a collage of fleshy torsos and big-breasted Playboy Bunnies interspersed with photos of JFK and the mayor's children. We drank orange soda while black flies used the bizarre table for a runway. Inside, it was cool and musty. The villagers had stacked shucks of newly cut rice in the courtyard and a couple of white ducks were pecking at the loose grain. In the next room a small boy swung in a long curving hammock. Like most of the children in Quang Tin Province, he was exuberantly happy and sort of oblivious to or at least philosophical about the war. In the morning he went to school in the nearest town. Afternoons he spent with the rice harvesters in the fields or selling soda pop to the Marines.

Outside I could hear the rhythmic swishing sound of heavily laden carry poles bending and straightening with the pulse of a shuffling gait as rice carriers hurried along a nearby trail. While enjoying our sodas, we found enough French and Vietnamese words to converse about the South Vietnamese National Assembly, the VC, and women. He seemed reluctant to help me improve my Vietnamese, spending most of the conversation in French and giving me the impression he was a cunning businessman who expended no effort unless it produced a profit

177

for him. Like most Vietnamese of his station, he was polite, but quite reserved.

While we strolled back towards the company defensive perimeter, he confided to me his plan to import hookers from Danang. Of course the India company commander couldn't know anything about it. To avoid encouraging him, I did not tell this entrepreneurial village elder the high command might not have opposed a brothel in the nearby village as long as health concerns could be handled by daily visits from a Navy corpsman.

Mid-morning the next day while I was packing some gear, a giggling gaggle of six-year old girls from the hamlet of Long Phu (2) scurried into the hootch with some batteries for my little tape recorder so I could record their squeaky rendition of a popular Vietnamese song. We had tried it the day before, but the machine ran out of juice, ending the session. I felt like a rock impresario auditioning a budding young group (*The Long Phu Ducklings?*) as they wailed through the same song over and over, just to get it right, accompanied by the bass drum of monsoon rain pummeling the galvanized roof. After the little perfectionists were satisfied, they made me play their performance over and over. They spoke such basic Vietnamese it was relatively easy to understand them when they talked about their families, their studies at school, and what they wanted to be when they grew up. Of course they had to know whether the *Thieu Uy* (2nd Lieutenant) has a wife (answer: yes, I have many wives). Does the *Thieu Uy* have a Vietnamese wife? (answer: perhaps). Does the *Thieu Uy* have any children and if so, how many children and what are their names and what do they look like and does the *Thieu Uy* have a water buffalo like they do? Their shiny raven hair, chestnut eyes, and unaffected innocence were almost excruciating counterpoints to the razor edge of war.

That night my Ontos rolled into firing positions above rice paddies that monsoon rains had flooded to the tops of the dikes. Once in a while, 81 mortars would pop an illumination round in front of our position, just to keep Victor Charlie honest. Thus the green-tinged nights faded into soggy or brutally hot days, then, like the movie *Groundhog Day*, replicated themselves again and again. My letters home tell the rest of the story…

178

August 7, 1966; Tam Ky, Republic of Vietnam

Dear Mom and Dad,

On 5 August, my platoon of Ontos was ordered to leave Hill 35 and join Operation Colorado. This was the first time my platoon would have been on the road since May in Okinawa. I put three vehicles (the heavy section) in the front of a column of 60 vehicles that carried the bulk of BLT 3/5. The light section provided rear guard. The march took about seven hours and we encountered no enemy fire whatsoever. Once we moved into position at the battalion command post, VC snipers fired on one of the Ontos and it fired three major rounds in response. The sniper fire stopped. The VC don't understand these machines. They hear a funny whine and then this hideous monster with tubes sticking out all over comes grinding through the rice paddies. When it fires, they don't know which way to run because fire comes out the back in a devastating cone and projectiles come out the front.

Operation Colorado turned out to be one hell of a big operation — regimental size. We were looking for a PAVN division that was in the infantry training stage. To that point we had encountered nothing but snipers and spent most days locating primary and alternate positions for the Ontos and camouflaging the vehicles.

August 13, 1966: Tam Ky, Republic Of Vietnam

Dear Mom and Dad,

On August 11 we pulled out of the rice paddies and into the outskirts of Tam Ky about 15 miles north of Chu Lai. 5th Marines regimental headquarters and 6th ARVN regimental headquarters were co-located at Tam Ky. Our bivouac was on a huge grassy playing field along with elements of the 5th Marines and ARVN units. Helicopters fluttered in and out while a constant stream of people carrying rice, vegetables, building materials, and the like moved to market along the road in front of us.

The road march from Hill 45 had been done in record time. The day before, I'd taken the heavy section out west of a village in a combined infantry-Ontos sweep. We moved into a blocking position while the infantry drove towards us from the east. I guess we chose the wrong time, because the suspected VC platoon never appeared: only a few

179

sniper rounds on the way back. These snipers work overtime because they're the worst shots in the world! For example, we were all sitting around the CP the morning before we moved out. My radioman, Lance Corporal Wallace, a red-haired kid from Texas, had the radio on and was monitoring some trivia between the line companies up on the hill when a VC sniper fired a few shots at us from a tree line 150 meters away. Wallace stood up and called him all sorts of ugly names, including the ultimate epithet—"non-shooter"—until I pulled him down. The sniper was getting the range and rounds were smacking into the deck around us. But it was impossible to get a clear shot at him. About then a patrol from M Company moved across our front and flushed him. An Ontos would have made short work of him.

Kids buzzing around us like flies do wonders for my Vietnamese because they speak simple sentences and have no slang phrases or weird dialects yet. One little group of boys about ten-years-old whom I'd sort of befriended asked me where we were going after this. I told him we were going all the way to Hanoi. Their eyes grew as big as doorknobs and they all screamed at once, "No, don't go. VC will shoot you!" I told them that Bac Ho (uncle Ho) really was a friend of mine and we'd be all right. This really upset them. Some of them actually got mad until I explained that it was all a joke. Then I delivered a big speech about how the United States and the Republic of Vietnam were joining hands to defeat the VC. They were all smiles after that. The kids really are a kick.

On the way to Tam Ky the Antitank Company stopped at Hill 30, an ARVN outpost. That afternoon my platoon displaced to Tam Ky along Highway 1. Flying along at 30 miles an hour loaded for bear with all Ontos running like Swiss watches put everyone in high spirits. We really tore up the road. That night I put all five vehicles on line facing east across the road. At 0215 on 12 August, 1966 the VC hit us with 82 mm mortars, 57mm recoilless rifles, and small arms fire, inflicting 47 casualties in all: three Marines in Hotel Company died, including a platoon commander, and a company gunnery sergeant. An Army Special Forces Captain also died. The battalion on our left flank lost a whole platoon. They weren't dug in because the ARVN had requested they not damage the playing field. Regardless, within hours of the attack we all had dug deep holes in the carefully manicured turf. My personnel carrier (PC) was sandbagged along the floorboards for road mines so we dug a fighting hole big enough for all four

180

headquarters personnel then drove the PC over it. It created a fine little bunker with firing slits beneath the running boards and a comfortable layer of steel and sand overhead. If that wasn't enough incoming, at 1715 on 12 August, a lightning bolt struck the Co E bivouac position approximately 50 meters from the 2/5 command post, killing two and injuring seven.

2/5 moved out this morning for landing zones northwest of here. My platoon was scheduled to move out also and link up for supporting fires, but yesterday it rained and flooded all the paddies, drowning our hopes for a cross-country run in the Ontos. Last night 1/5 was hit hard with 82mm mortars and 57mm recoilless rifles. Those are the only two weapons besides mines that I worry about. They could really do us some damage with the rifles unless we saw them first. We run with all tubes loaded, so all the gunner had to do is close the breeches, spot with the spotting rifle and fire. The plan now is to wait and see how the ground looks tomorrow, then move to an alternate position for the same mission. I understand Hill 54 at Chu Lai was hit also and overrun. I don't wonder. We're all up here, leaving no one to hold the lines back in the rear. C'est la guerre!

Now we're sitting around drying wet gear in the already pleasant morning sun. The rain yesterday flooded everything. But now the sky is blue and marbled with only a few cirrus clouds. Tomorrow morning will come soon enough. We're ready to go, mechanically and ordnance-wise. The weather is the key.

August 20, 1966: Chu Lai, Republic Of Vietnam

Dear Mom and Dad,

We cruised into the company area this morning in a great rolling cloud of rust-colored dust. Operation Colorado is a thing of the past. My last letter was written on Hill 29 after we had moved south from our last position. We stayed there on that Godforsaken sun-baked, rock-strewn hillside until 18 August. About all we accomplished was running a few recon patrols with the infantry. This of course gave drivers, Ontos commanders, and section leaders excellent training. We showed the "grunts" what the Ontos can do and instilled that much more confidence in our ability. Most days we sweltered under the heavy sun, then moved the camouflaged vehicles to alternate firing positions on the perimeter at night. I have seen the results of Charles

181

*the Cong's marksmanship with the 57 recoilless all around me—thinned
ranks of infantry with staff sergeants as platoon commanders and first
lieutenants as company commanders—and didn't want the same thing
to happen to us.*

*On the 18^{th,} we moved back to Tam Ky, a staging area for the
forthcoming Operation Jefferson. The day before we left Hill 29 (or 35
depending on which peak you choose), an ARVN second lieutenant
invited me to his "house", a thatched affair walled with 105mm ammo
boxes, for a beer. He spoke little English, but we got along well enough
in Vietnamese. It turned out he was the supply officer for 4th Battalion
5th Regiment and had taught philosophy at Danang. His fiancée also
taught school at Danang. We sat in the hootch while his housemaid
served us a noodle-beef lettuce dish that really was delicious. I had
some problems with the chopsticks, but lunch-mouth that I am, I found
a way. You pick your pair of sticks out of the common stack (that
everyone uses) in a small vase in the center of the table. Hot tea finished
off the meal, and I strolled back up the hill to face the afternoon onslaught
of heat. It was a fine respite. Often a lonely ARVN soldier would wander
near our CP, and I would grab him and trade the B-1 and B-2 units
from the C-rations and old beefsteak and potato rations nobody wanted
for a big sack of rice. Since then we've had terrific chicken and rice
casseroles, fried rice, boiled rice, rice mixed with ham and limas and
rice pudding. Any fool can be uncomfortable in the field. It takes
ingenuity to survive comfortably.*

*We set up in Tam Ky on the 18th, but Operation Jefferson never
came together. So today we came home. My platoon was set in on the
playing field again, on the opposite side from the last mortar attack.
ARVN officers and government officials housing was across a dusty
road and one roll of concertina. One evening I began chatting with
some of the officers and their wives about the Ontos. They had never
seen one before and were curious. The conversation rolled on, finally
ending late that night after many cups of tea. They offered me a bed,
but I declined. We were expecting a mortar attack that night, and they
had seen a main force battalion west of us earlier that day. I didn't care
to have a heavy tile roof come smacking down on my gourd, so I politely
retired to my very deep foxhole—the 14th day in the field. My utilities
smelled like an ancient pile of rotting cabbage and my right knee was
hanging out. C-rations long ago had lost their appeal and we were all
tired of flinching at every little noise. Home, humble as it may be,*

certainly is home.

Someone in the infantry company killed a VC the other night. He was in the wire and a corporal opened up on him with an M-14, then finished him off with an M-60 machine gun, just to make sure he was really dead.

September 14, 1966. Chu Lai, Republic Of Vietnam

Dear Mom and Dad,
We're still at the Chu Lai airstrip. The same old sun comes up at six; the same five A-4 fighter jets blast overhead; the same 14" long purple and red lizards come around at noon looking for lunch scraps. The same old thunderstorms growl over the mountains to the west; and the same old mosquitoes chew on us at night. Each evening I hear the men say they hope the VC hit us tonight, just to break the monotony. If they caught one, I swear they would tear him to pieces barehanded out of sheer frustration.

They're transferring four infantry lieutenants from 1st Anti Tank Battalion. I'm one of them. I hear we'll be going to 1st Marines at Danang or Phu Bai. I also hear a rumor that because of my Top Secret clearance and Vietnamese language, I may be transferred to Division G-2 here. We'll see.

September 19, 1966: Chu Lai, Republic Of Vietnam

Dear Mom and Dad,
We're still south of the airfield among the sand dunes. Fall is a barely noticeable phenomenon. The wind blows a little harder from the ocean, drifting long fingers of sand across the roads. The surf is higher now. Nights are cool and dew stains the sand dark around the tent. The Vietnamese are stacking bundles of twigs against their shacks as insurance for the long monsoon season. After the farmers burn through the dry sticks they've been gathering they switch to more expensive charcoal. Birds are gathering ripe fruit from the trees in preparation for a migration somewhere. Of course days are shorter, mornings darker, and evenings descend with a noticeable swiftness. It's not uncommon to wake up two or three times during the night to adjust the blanket. Days are breezy with a sea wind and not as sweltering as a month ago. Winds have kept the afternoon thunderstorms at bay high in the

183

mountains. Last night the VC mortared the airfield not far from here and damaged some aircraft.

Actually, security duty at the Chu Lai Airfield had its rewards. First Reconnaissance Battalion had built a pleasant little enclave near the beach with showers, hot chow and movies. One night we saw *The Pink Panther* with Peter Sellers. A week later I cranked up the field telephone and called the theatre. "What's the flick tonight, Corporal?" I asked. *"You Must Be Joking, sir,"* he answered. I pressed him again. "No, I'd really like to know. I was thinking of coming over if it's any good. What's on?" He repeated himself. *"You Must Be Joking, sir."* Just before I said something like, "Do I have to come over there, Corporal?" I realized that was the title of the movie.

September 24, 1966: Chu Lai, Republic Of Vietnam

Dear Mom and Dad,
We're still on duty as perimeter security at the airfield, with four Ontos on the line. The fifth vehicle is in the maintenance shed, having blown up in the field. Lately all I have been doing is getting into trouble. About two weeks ago, the battalion commander told me that four of us were being transferred to 1st Marines at Danang or Phu Bai. The deal was that G-1 (Division Personnel) trade him four 1801 lieutenants (tankers). Well, about three weeks ago, I ran into First Lieutenant Ellermann, an old buddy of mine at G-2 (Division Intelligence). He introduced me to the major in his shop. All I really was after was a pictomap of my patrol area (which I got). They offered me a job up there just like it was a corporation. The colonel wanted someone with an interest in intelligence, a Top Secret clearance and Vietnamese language to augment a new program of going to battalion level and to ARVN outposts to initiate a flow of information towards Division. At the time, I said, "Fat chance at the AT Battalion."

A week later the quota for four 0302 Lieutenants arrived at 1st Anti-Tank Battalion HQ. It just so happened that a lieutenant in G-2 wanted to go to a line company so bad he could taste it: former recon man—a real animal. He wanted to substitute for me and fill the quota to 1st Marines. Despite Major Harris getting all excited and going to see the G-1, orders arrived at Company B assigning me to G-2.

That afternoon, Staff Sergeant Pridemore informed me Captain Felker wanted to see me. I walked over to Major Harris' headquarters hootch and rapped on the door. Captain Felker peeked out and said, "Lieutenant, you've stepped in it again. I'm getting tired of bailing you out. Orders assigning you to G-2 just hit the major's desk and he is fit to be tied. Wait out there until he calls you." Inside I could hear Major Harris ranting in apoplectic rage. This was not going to be pretty. But what the hell could he do, as the saying went, shave my head and send me to Vietnam? I waited. Fifteen minutes flowed by like molasses. I watched monstrous 14-inch long purple and red iguana-like lizards with blue stripes down their spines lurking in the shade. These reptiles were so bold about scrounging for food scraps the Marines in my platoon gave them names: "Stumpy," "One eye," "Godzilla." When they got in a real hurry, they would sprint across the road on their hind legs. After another fifteen minutes, I rapped on the door again. Captain Felker peeked out and growled, "The major said wait until he calls you. He hasn't called you yet, lieutenant." Aye aye, sir. More waiting. A while later, the door opened and Captain Felker led me over to Major Harris like a sacrificial lamb. I snapped to attention and managed to squeak out, "Lieutenant Buchanan reporting as ordered, sir."

Major Harris dropped a soggy cigar into a C-ration can on his desk, wiped his forehead with a green handkerchief and leaned forward deliberately like a Mississippi snapping turtle eyeing its prey. "Lieutenant, you have been a pain in the ass for a long time, but this takes the cake. Who told you to go over my head to Division and request a transfer to G-2?" The major hadn't ordered me at ease yet and I could feel my left knee begin to quiver. I hoped he wouldn't notice. A gigantic blue bottle fly landed on the top of my right ear.

"Sir, I didn't really request a transfer. I was at G-2 a while back to get a pictomap and the colonel told me they needed someone with my background and skills. Someone who speaks Vietnamese and has a Top Secret."

"Your background and skills are needed in this battalion, lieutenant" We're short of people, in case you didn't notice. And

185

in a war, people don't just waltz on over to another unit without telling their commanding officer what the HELL they're doing, especially lieutenants in my command, is that understood?" His face was glowing again.

"Yes sir. It's just that I thought I could be of better use to the Marine Corps with my language skills and clearance. I did not inform the major because G-2 told me they would clear it with you, sir, *if* they took any action."

Major Harris crossed his sinewy arms and glared at me. "Well, they didn't, lieutenant. They just lobbed this paper mortar shell dead center on my position. No warning shot or anything. Arrogant as hell. Trying to steal my people right out from under me. It's not going to happen. These orders are cancelled, lieutenant. CANCELLED! I'll tell you when you're available for reassignment. Now get back to that platoon of yours. That's where you're needed. Dismissed."

Somewhat crestfallen, I shuffled back to the platoon and filled in Staff Sergeant Pridemore on the denouement. He chuckled and kidded me about being sideways with the major once again, reminding me the last time was for running the Ontos along a road in Okinawa, leaving track marks on the asphalt. But this takes the cake, he continued–disloyalty bordering on outright defection. That night, as I lay on my cot listening to H & I fires mimic the booming of the surf, the deterioration of my relationship with battalion command weighed heavily on me. Major Harris and Captain Felker now probably saw me as a malcontent and a schemer. The truth of the matter was I felt my skills were being underutilized. Although I had an admitted aversion to the mechanical approach to war—engines, grease, gas, endless parts shortages, the lumbering, cumbersome, road-restricted, rear area defensive deployment of the anti-tank company—my sense of loyalty to the First Anti-Tank Battalion inhibited an outright request for transfer. I also had a high regard for Major Harris' professional standards. Without knowing the fighting reputation of any particular infantry unit, I was reluctant to initiate the transfer process. Well, I decided, I would just have to ride this flap out to its logical conclusion.

186

Several weeks later, we escorted a convoy from Chu Lai down Highway One south towards Quang Ngai, a coastal town flanked by brown stubble fields standing side by side with the emerald green of new rice. One Ontos from the light section was at the head of the column, the other at the rear. My command vehicle was second in the line of 6x6 trucks. Heavy dun-colored shucks balanced stolidly along the road on the shoulders of lean, brown Vietnamese men, women, and children made a sound like, shusha, shusha, shusha. Kids playing alongside the roads waved and shouted, "Hey-lo! Hey-lo!" to the Marines riding in the trucks. We passed a massive hardwood tree that threw cool green shadow across the road, the upper reaches distant and winding and mottled against the sky. Harvested rice lay drying on round woven pallets and a fresh beef hide laced with twine was stretched on a wood frame in the sun. Like a bloated dragonfly, a Huey gunship circled the rice fields warily, flanking the convoy, then wheeling and banking for another pass to scrutinize rice harvesters, its shadow spooking a herd of gangly cows. Great white cement spans lay unfinished by the riverbank, replacements for the ones destroyed before election day by night-raiding Viet Cong. They had cut the bridge expertly by placing explosive charges precisely at the weak points.

It occurred to me this bucolic scene would be a perfect theater for a massive ambush on the order of the ones the Viet Minh sprang on French Forces thirteen years before. In his book *Street without Joy*, Bernard Fall described the destruction of Groupement Mobile (GM) 100, one of the best and heaviest units of its type deployed against the Viet Minh. Elite battle-hardened veterans of the French U.N. Forces battalion in Korea formed its core. The unit included its own reserves: two Vietnamese companies, Commando "Bergerol", a regiment of jungle-wise French and Cambodian troops, as well as an artillery regiment–all told, a unit of 3,498 men. On 10 December 1953, GM 100 began to move towards the southern part of the Mountain Plateau in Central South Vietnam not far from the towns of Pleiku, Dak Doa and Ankhe. Its mission was to interdict and engage Viet Minh units that had been converging on the area. After catching the French in a series of devastating ambushes along the roads of the region, the 803rd Viet Minh Regiment delivered the *coup de grace* to GM 100 on 24 June, 1954, catching the unit moving

187

along the road near Pleiku and cutting it to pieces with heavy weapons and determined infantry assaults. Survivors escaped through the jungle in platoon-sized units. On 1 September 1954, the French High Command in Indochina dissolved GM 100.

Soon we rolled into Quang Ngai, finding it to be washed by a benevolent sun and full of rushing bicycles, cyclos, jeeps, and hulking six-by-six trucks carrying ammunition, food, gasoline and building materials. Gaudy, cluttered shops displaying cloth, sandals, watches, and books lined the sidewalks. Young high school girls and collegians peddled to class on bicycles dressed in elegantly cut, immaculate white "Ao Dai," their long straight raven tresses flowing from beneath the all-too concealing conical straw hats. Very neat and polite Chinese merchants sold silk and cotton in very neat and clean shops. The convoy turned out to be a milk run.

October 17, 1966: Chu Lai, Republic Of Vietnam

Dear Mom and Dad,
Things have been moving pretty fast the last couple of days. On October 15th , I was transferred from the First Anti-Tank Battalion to 2nd Battalion 5th Marines which is now engaged up at the DMZ. They're working over the same area we covered during Operation Hastings. Today I'm flying up there to take over a platoon or the company executive officer billet, one of the two. I understand that 2/5 is a real fine outfit. It will be interesting to work with them in that area.

At the time of my transfer from 1st Anti Tank Battalion to 2nd Battalion 5th Marines, I had no way of knowing my farewell to Major Harris would be the last time I would see him. On 9 November 1966, at the age of 37, he died in a VC ambush while riding in the passenger seat of a Jeep near the Hai Van Pass north of Danang. His bullet-riddled forearms bore silent witness to his characteristic pugnacious nature. Even though our relationship had been rocky, I was saddened by the death of an exemplary Marine who did his best to hone a young lieutenant's professionalism.

Thus my letters home traced an arc in a circle that closed with my assignment from an anti-tank unit to an infantry unit:

from the alien world of gears and grease and oil and exhaust to the world of mud, blood, sheer terror, exhaustion, elation, depression, hunger, thirst, dust, heat, cold and wet—in short, the world where I truly belonged.

My reminiscence then carried me back to the present on Phu Lac (6) where the day had flowed uneventfully, giving us time to clean weapons and improve our defensive positions. Feisty Maggie was scampering around challenging the Marines to play and getting an occasional taker. The cumulus towering over the Annam Mountains were turning to soft pastels in the waning sunlight.

NONG SON

On 5 February 1967, after returning from a week-long rest and recuperation sojourn to Okinawa and recovering from the effects of the flu and an intestinal disorder, I flew by helicopter from An Hoa to join G Company where it had taken its turn occupying positions at the Nong Son Coal Mine, a company-sized combat outpost 14 kilometers southwest as the crow flies. The rumor mill had it that Nong Son was relatively easy duty in a location with stunning views. When the dust storm from the rotor blades had subsided, I looked up at Nong Son Mountain, the dominant geographic feature rising 200 meters above the Song Tinh Yen, a ribbon of blue water flanked by wide sand beaches that wound north past the base of the mountain. An emerald green pyramid-shaped feature 452 meters high called Cua Tan by the Vietnamese, but "Recon Mountain" by the Marines after the type of unit stationed on its summit, dominated the skyline two kilometers east of Nong Son. Our mission was to defend the mine complex and to

conduct combat patrols in an area where large NVA units roamed at will. Somehow it didn't seem like easy duty to me.

I discovered the defenses at Nong Son started at the bottom of the hill where a reinforced platoon was deployed. Another reinforced platoon occupied the middle section. On the summit was the remaining infantry platoon, along with one or two 106mm recoilless rifles, a 4.2 inch mortar crew, an Army searchlight crew, and a flamethrower section. Like an ant farm, the hill was riddled with linear excavations—trenches and bunkers hacked out of the flinty soil and surrounded by concertina. The northeast slope was almost vertical at the summit and the lower parts reportedly held a minefield. I thought to myself, as I inspected the defenses on top of the hill, an enemy unit would have to be doped up or crazy to try to scale such tilted terrain and mount an attack on reinforced bunkers and trench lines manned by heavily armed U.S. Marines. The future would prove me woefully wrong. Since I was the newly anointed executive officer of the company, my first priority was to check in with Marc Glasgow, the newly anointed company commander. As we chatted in the early afternoon sun, I got the impression that the place got his engineering juices flowing…

"Since I had an engineering MOS, I was designated liaison to the Vietnamese Chief Engineer at Nong Son to see about opening up the coal mine there. They were still face mining there because the river had flooded out the shafts in '64 or '65. The plan was to link up the coal mine with Dai Loc and An Hoa. The generator at An Hoa ran on Nong Son coal. Since we didn't have pumps big enough to flush water out of the flooded shafts, not a lot could be done and I reported that to battalion. They said there was an ARVN minefield on the south side of the hill, so we never went through there on our patrols. I had my doubts about whether there ever were any mines there, especially after Foxtrot Company got overrun some time after we left. I didn't like the trenches at the top of the hill because they were straight-line trenches; one round from an AK-47 would fly the whole length. I would have designed zigzags to minimized shrapnel and small arms. But it was already done so we lived with it."

Intelligence reports of large NVA units moving through the narrow valleys and bivouacking behind the mountains kept our patrols short and relatively close by. Shortly after Second Platoon came in through the wire from such a foray, I wandered over to see how it had gone. Half a dozen Marines were clustered around one of the bunkers smoking and joking and cleaning their weapons. I looked a little closer at one of them and realized it was PFC John Bates, the rifleman in my old platoon who had been so severely wounded in the chest on 17 December. What, I asked myself, was he doing out here? Was he saying good-bye before a much-deserved trip home to the States? I invited him over to my command bunker to talk about it. When he sat down on an ammo box in the half-light, I could see he had lost some weight. Lean to begin with, he was probably down to 140 pounds. "So, Lance Corporal Bates, you're just here to tell us all good bye and torture us with nurse stories then you'll catch the next chopper to Danang for a stateside flight, right?" Bates lit up a Camel cigarette from the C-ration accessory packet he was carrying, then in his low-key, humor-laced manner told me an amazing story. Years later he fleshed out details in the following account...

"After I got hit during the firefight on 17 December, the medevac chopper flew me to Charlie Med ("C" Medical Battalion, Danang). As we touched down at the helo pad at Charlie Med, two corpsmen and a doctor waited with a gurney. They pulled me from the bird and wheeled me rapidly into the emergency room. As we were leaving the landing zone, I heard the doctor yell to the door gunner to tell the pilot to get out of the zone quickly because there were several other medevacs enroute. G 2/5 was not the only unit to take heavy casualties that morning and throughout the day.

Typically, the emergency room was full of activity. But it seemed to me that there were entirely too many people in such a confined space. The first thing they did was to cut off all of my clothes to include my boots. I wondered why they couldn't just untie them? I lay naked on the table as they carefully evaluated my wounds. They kept asking me questions and the answers were clear in my head, but hearing my own response, everything seemed to come out garbled. I kept waiting for them to tell me the worst was over and I wasn't going to die. They told me nothing of the sort. Instead, they wheeled me to the next room and under a harsh glaring light, begin to operate. Because I had received the proverbial "sucking chest wound" they couldn't administer general

193

anesthetic. Instead, they were giving me a local in my chest in the area surrounding the wound. It was surprising to me that the injections were not painful. For that matter, neither was my gunshot wound. I still had a buzzing sensation throughout my body—shock probably setting in—but it was not localized in the vicinity of the wound.

I was able to observe the entire surgery. Quite honestly, I kept thinking that as long as I could stay awake, I knew that I would live. The AK round had penetrated my flak jacket (body armor) passed between my fourth and fifth ribs, punctured my right lung, exited between my fourth and fifth ribs and tore a hole the size of a quarter out of the back of my flak jacket. I was indeed fortunate to be alive.

Following the operation, I was given a sedative. Fighting hard to stay awake, I eventually succumbed to the medication and awoke several hours later scared and confused as to what had happened to me. I tried to convince myself that it was all a bad dream and that it couldn't be real. When I tried to move, I experienced real pain for the first time since being shot. Quickly, the events of the day before began to come back to me. By that time it must have been dark outside, but I had no window to provide clues. I sensed that the medical staff was talking in whispers about someone I guessed to be my new neighbor. There was a privacy drape pulled around my bed so I could not see where I was or who else might be sharing that area of Intensive Care with me. I recall being incredibly thirsty. When a corpsman passed, I tried to ask him to bring me some water. In doing so, I found my throat was raw and even breath passing over it hurt. It began to come back to me that I remembered them shoving a plastic tube down my throat when they started the surgery. Finally the corpsman brought me water. It was ice water, the first I had drank in months. The experience was bittersweet in that it hurt to drink it.

Every hour or so, a doctor or corpsman would come to check on me. They would review the charts and produce an endless supply of medicine that I was required to take, primarily to fight infection.

On 20 December Dr. Virgilio told me that I was improving much faster than expected. Their plan was that once I was ambulatory, probably after the first of the year, they would fly me to the hospital at Clark Air Force Base in the Philippines for follow-on surgery and then eventually back to the Naval Hospital at Memphis, Tennessee so that my family could visit me. A day or so later, they reevaluated my case and decided that I would eventually fully recover and possibly be able to remain in Vietnam. All I asked of them was to promise that I could go back to G 2/5 when well enough to do so.

The morning of 21 December I awoke to another surprise. PFC John T. King, a buddy of mine, now occupied the bed across from me. We had gone through ITR and Staging Battalion together but when we got to Vietnam he was assigned to Echo Company. He had been shot the night before as they were trying to assist Golf Company,. His squad had triggered an ambush and he was trying to pull a wounded fellow Marine to safety when the enemy shot him in the back. John was a big guy who had played football for a state university for a year before enlisting in the Marine Corps. The doctors had already told him he might never walk again.

The morning of the 23rd, the mayor of Danang and his wife visited the hospital. They seemed genuinely concerned for our health and well being. They gave us some Christmas cards to send home and a Vietnamese doll that I sent to my sister Carolyn.

On Christmas Eve we were told to expect visitors on Christmas day—The Bob Hope Christmas Show. Although still on intravenous fluids, I was determined to position myself so I could see the entertainers as they came into the hospital. Much to my delight, I saw Bob Hope, got a kiss from Joey Heatherton, a big hug from Chris Noel (an Armed Forces Network disc jockey with a very sexy voice), and an assortment of beautiful women from the States. Later that day Congresswoman Margaret Chase Smith stopped by. I had met more high profile people that day than I had in my entire life to that point. Following Congresswoman Smith's departure, three other Marines and myself were honored with a ceremony and presentation of Purple Heart medals by Lieutenant General Lew Walt, who was in charge of all Marine operations in Vietnam at that time.

Even though I was ambulatory, I remained in intensive care. The reason, I was told, was because it was the cleanest environment available and the risk of infection was lower. By the first week in January I could get around without too much trouble, so I really felt I should be doing something other than writing letters and taking naps. I was getting restless. By mid-January, I was considered healthy enough to be

195

admitted to the rehabilitation ward. The idea sounded okay, but in fact I soon found out it was not a place I wanted to be. At the sound of reveille, a junior ward corpsman would get us up and have us sweep and swab the deck before breakfast. I was frustrated because of the way I was being treated and I was thinking more and more about my platoon back at Golf Company. Three days of "rehab" and I had had enough. I asked both Dr. Benson and Dr Virgilio if I could rejoin my platoon. They first were adamantly against it, but then appeared non-committal. Since they had earlier talked of the possibility of someday returning to my unit, I didn't think that they had any reason to quibble about the actual date. I was still spitting up blood when I pushed myself too hard, but otherwise felt fine.

In a corner in the ward I found a pair of boots that still had the laces in them. They were close in size to what I wore, so I decided they would do. I found a pair of utility trousers folded on top of a medical locker that had evidently belonged to someone much bigger than me, but they were certainly better than leaving in just a hospital gown. There was not a utility shirt to be found, so I tucked in my gown and left the hospital looking for transportation back to An Hoa. Only one of the hospital workers questioned me as I walked out—asking if I needed any help. I said 'no' and kept moving. It was rather exciting to be 'breaking out of jail.'

I knew where Hill 327 was and that there was a big post exchange near it. That would mean transportation. Emboldened somewhat by then, I walked into the PX and got my lighter engraved, 'John Richard Bates An Hoa 66-67,' then talked a South Vietnamese soldier who spoke passable English into driving me to the airstrip in a military stake bed truck. From there I went into the passenger terminal and told them I needed transportation to An Hoa. I was holding my breath, afraid they would ask to see my orders or an ID card. I had neither. The Corporal at the desk only asked me for my service number to put on the manifest. Soon I was on a chopper back to An Hoa."

I congratulated Bates on his escape from Charlie Med and his promotion to Lance Corporal and welcomed him back to the company. He then excused himself to clean his weapon and prepare for the evening meal. 'Such Marines,' I thought to myself, as I watched him hike back up the dusty hill wearing utility trousers that seemed a bit too large. Such Marines indeed.

As we were prone to do whenever we occupied a new position, G Company turned to and began to improve the defenses and the living infrastructure at Nong Son. Local kids even helped fill the sandbags. In order to maintain a high level of training for replacements, the company held regular classes on weapons and tactics. One bright morning, Third Platoon commander Bill Harvey, a 23-year-old 2nd Lieutenant from Rochester, Vermont, witnessed a tragic incident during a class on the 20mm light anti-tank assault weapon (LAAW)...

"On 6 February Sergeant Tyson, the rocket squad leader, was wrapping up a class on the LAAW. He'd gone through all the procedures on how to extend it and open it up and sight it in and check the back blast area and all those things. Well, when he was trying to collapse it he had one end of it on his thigh and the other end, he had his hand over it. He had one hand somewhere forward of the sight and the other hand was right over the back of the tube. He just went to jam it back together. It wasn't anything that was really ever taught because LAAWs were disposable; you threw them away after you fired them.

All of a sudden there was this huge explosion. The LAAW fired and a round drilled right through his leg, taking out a piece of the femur. From the look on his face when he saw what was left of his hand, I knew he would go into shock immediately. He was my first wounded Marine, so I didn't know much about that type of thing. I remember his hand was what was concerning him the most. It was shredded. Gone as I recall. He might have had the thumb or something still, but it seemed like everything else was gone. We got a medevac in there quickly. Of course, being in a kind of a behind-the-wire environment, the corpsmen were able to work on him right away."

Although a setback and a tragic wound for a dedicated Marine sergeant, this incident paled in comparison with the fireworks that exploded early morning on 3 July, 1967 when Foxtrot Company was deployed on the hill with the usual supporting elements. Having been assigned from Third Platoon G Company to the Combined Action Platoon (CAP) in a hamlet across the river from Nong Son, Art Morrill, a 30-year-old sergeant from Natick, Massachusetts had a front row seat. It was not unusual to place a squad of Marines with a like number of

197

South Vietnamese Army or local militia soldiers to defend a small geographic area and complement larger allied forces. The Marines lived and fought in the village to which they were assigned. In early July, the village chief confided to Morrill, "Many VC and many NVA" had been seen in the area recently. Sergeant Morrill paid a dollar to the ferryman for a ride across the river to Nong Son, where he reported the intelligence to the Foxtrot Company commander. Then he paid another dollar for the return trip back to the village.

The official battalion record paints an ominous picture. At 1000 the morning of 3 July, 1967, First Lieutenant J.B. Souras, the commanding officer of Company F, reported terrified villagers from the nearby hamlets of Tu Xuan (2) and Ninh Hoa (3) were leaving their homes after spotting 200 NVA soldiers moving toward Nong Son with the mission of attacking the Marines there. Souras ordered a fire mission from An Hoa and fifteen minutes later, 300 rounds of artillery fell into one likely target area and another 300 rounds into an adjacent zone. A request to Division for an aerial observer (AO) and a fixed wing aircraft never was fulfilled.

No further enemy activity was seen or reported for the rest of the day. The burning sun dropped into the western hills near Laos. Darkness rose from the valleys like an ebony tide, swallowing up the serpentine windings of the Song Tinh Yen on its way to engulf the summit of Nong Son Mountain. The company settled into its night defensive positions. At 2327 that evening, a Company F listening post reported, "I have movement to my front." Within seconds, two transmissions followed: "They're all around me," and "We've been overrun." At that instant enemy mortar rounds slammed into the topmost defenses of Nong Son, sending fans of hot, razor-sharp steel singing across the trenches. Before the dust had settled from the barrage, Vietnamese sappers, riflemen and surprisingly, a flamethrower section, had scrambled up the impossibly steep face of the mountain, and into the bunkers and defensive positions of the surprised Marines.

The assault was as well coordinated as it was audacious. Satchel charges detonating in defensive bunkers punctuated

198

measured bursts from AK-47s, and responding fire from the Marines. Private First Class Melvin E. Newlin, a machine gunner attached to the First Platoon, Company F, was manning a key position when enemy soldiers wounded him and killed four Marines around him. Propping himself against his M-60, he unleashed a deadly accurate stream of fire into the shadowy ranks of the Viet Cong. Though wounded again and again, he repelled two attempts to overrun his position. During the third assault, a grenade explosion threw him to the ground unconscious. Convinced they had killed one more Marine, the enemy soldiers moved on down the trench line, pressing their attack against the remaining fortifications. Private Newlin soon regained consciousness, crawled back to his weapon, and brought it to bear on the rear of the enemy troops, causing havoc and confusion. When a group of enemy soldiers tried to aim a captured 106 recoilless rifle at Marine positions, Newlin shifted his fire, inflicting heavy casualties and disrupting their attempt to fire the captured weapon. When he shifted his fire back to the main enemy force, they ceased their assault on the Marine bunkers and once again concentrated their efforts on his position. He fought off two more enemy assaults until falling mortally wounded. Once again, the battlefield had been witness to an unbelievably courageous tableau of one solitary determined Marine with an M-60 machine gun turning the tide of battle. For his valiant and tenacious defense, the President of the United States awarded PFC Newlin a posthumous Medal of Honor.

Within several minutes of the attack, Lt. Col. Jackson, the battalion commander at An Hoa, ordered Echo Company to move from the western end of Antenna Valley along the river to reinforce the embattled Foxtrot Company at Nong Son. It is a mystery why the local VC Main Force or NVA commander did not employ the time-tested tactic of ambushing the relief force. While Company E was making a difficult night movement towards Nong Son, the artillery at An Hoa sprang into action and sent 75 rounds of 155mm illumination, 25 rounds of 8" high explosive, and 255 rounds of 155mm high explosive hurtling towards the target. Just to be sure the rounds were clearing the bulk of Nong Son Mountain, Major Richard "Dick" Esau, the battalion operations officer (S-3) got on the horn with a Foxtrot Company radio operator and asked him if all the rounds had

199

made it over the summit of Nong Son Mountain. The Marine's reply was reassuring...sort of...

"Major," he said, through a static-filled transmission, *"Not a one landed on top of the hill, but you could have reached up and touched them as they went over."*

Major Esau recalled years later...*"These were eight inch rounds because the 155's weren't all that accurate and I had to have something that was super accurate. It was close to midnight. It was awful dark, let's put it that way. We had no communication for a time with anyone on the hill. The recon commander on the hill across the river was Ray Taylor. I asked Ray if he could tell whether the rounds were falling on top of Nong Son Mountain and he said he didn't think so. I told him that wasn't a good enough answer, for Christ's sake. Yet he could tell that the NVA were reinforcing from the west and southwest. He could tell that, and he was tryin' to let us know. But he couldn't see a lot of what was going on at Nong Son itself. Years later at a dinner for the Order of the Purple Heart in New Jersey, a Marine came up to me and he says, 'Colonel, I just want to thank you for the artillery at Nong Son.' That was 30 some years ago and he still remembered that for Christ's sake."*

Less than half an hour after the attack began, First Lieutenant Souras rallied a squad of riflemen on the lower reaches of the hill and led them through the darkness in a counterattack towards the summit. It was nearing midnight. As he crested the top, he found the enemy had overrun several bunkers and breached the concertina in more than one place. He joined forces with a tenacious squad that had refused to be dislodged by the Vietnamese attackers and set up M-60 machine guns with advantageous fields of fire. This vigorous response forced the remaining sappers and riflemen to back off the contested ground and withdraw the way they had come. The counterattacking Marines recovered several 81mm mortar tubes and brought them into action against the retreating communist troops.

Major Esau was frantic to see the battlefield for himself...

"Colonel Jackson and I got a chopper from Marble Mountain and flew to Nong Son in the middle of the night. You have to understand

200

that we sent Foxtrot down to Nong Son more or less to lick their wounds. They had lost their company commander, Captain Jim Graham, on Operation Union II. It was a tough night landing, but it was the only thing we could do. We felt we had to do it because Foxtrot had had their fair share of problems and here Nong Son was getting overrun, at least that's the way it sounded on the radio. As Col. Jackson and I checked on the dead and wounded, I saw something there that night I will never forget if I live to be a million years old. There were two young Marines in Foxtrot Company who were machine gunners and they were inseparable—the gunner and assistant gunner, you know. One was black and the other was white. I forget their names, but they were always together. They were in a bunker together when the VC sappers climbed up over the sheer face of Nong Son Mountain that night. And the first bunker they came to was the one these two Marines were in and they threw a satchel charge into it and the two kids were trying to protect each other when the damn thing went off. I have to tell you that when we found them they were completely exsanguinated. They had no blood left. And we laid them out and one was a black man and the other was white and they looked exactly the same as far as skin color. They were blue-grey, you know. And I said to myself, Jesus Christ, if we could only see ourselves in life the way these two kids appear in death, what a wonderful world it would be.

We stayed up there a long time. Then the Assistant Division Commander, a one star, flew in with a colonel who was off to the side chipping his teeth about, 'Well you guys obviously weren't prepared up here,' and this and that and the other thing. I really didn't want to have him talkin' like that in front of the troops because it was bad for morale. And it was totally unprofessional. So I sidled up beside him as he was standing on the shear edge of that part of the hill that falls off into the coal mine and I asked him to please shut his mouth. He informed me that he was a colonel and I was a major, so I told him very simply, 'If you don't shut your fuckin' mouth, I'm going to throw you off this hill. Do you understand that?'

We got the wounded out and we got the dead out. And as we were walking around the top of the hill, we came across this VC. He couldn't have been more than fifteen years old. Some kind of round had gone right through his chest and took his heart out. He's lyin' there and I'm looking at this kid and I can see right through his chest. You could see daylight on the other side. Incredible. What a hell of a fight that was."

Shortly before 0100 4 July, Echo Company arrived at Nong Son, having completed the difficult night march from Antenna Valley without incident. They occupied the lower and middle defensive positions on the hill, allowing Foxtrot Company to consolidate the topmost bunkers and fighting holes. After evacuating the wounded and dead, Lieutenant Souras and his Marines recovered four AK-47s, 16 assault rifle magazines, a flamethrower, 12 satchel charges, 77 Chinese communist grenades, and various documents.

Second Lieutenant Bill Harvey accompanied G Company to Nong Son on 6 July to relieve F Company, which had been ordered to man the defenses at An Hoa. He was astounded an NVA sapper unit had been able to overrun the platoon at the top of the hill. In his notebook he recorded: *13 Marines and soldiers killed in action, 43 wounded in action, 39 gooks*. G Company patrols searched the battle area over the next two days and found three more enemy bodies, 14 Chicom grenades, six satchel charges, 50 bamboo canteens, and several blood soaked packs. Marines would stumble across decomposing bodies of NVA soldiers well into August.

Years later, Bill Harvey reminisced about another enemy attack that occurred well after I had rotated back to the States. Its audacity and precise execution once again stood in stark contrast to the predictability of some Marine operations. As Bill remembered it...

"It was 2 August, 1967 at An Hoa Combat Base. I was the Sparrowhawk for the battalion, which was a platoon on standby to react to any emergency that might require reinforcements. So I was supposed to be within a few minutes' call from the battalion command post. That morning they called me and told me that a squad had been ambushed. They suspected it was the mine sweep squad because they had received position reports that seemed to indicate that it was them — about 15 men from G Company, possibly Second Platoon along with some engineers. Echo Company was at Phu Loc (6) at the time. The mine sweep squad usually walked all the way to Phu Loc (6) then turned around and came back. They probably departed the wire soon after first light.

The Sparrowhawk platoon had two Amtracks right there with us ready to roll. So we jumped on the Amtracks and headed down the road. It had to be early, within a couple hours of first light. It was very sunny and hot already. The two position reports that had come into the command post were a little confusing. The squad leader or one of the other Marines had used a checkpoint as a position report in an attempt to call in fire and the other report was in coordinates. The coordinates were a thousand meters apart, so it just wasn't adding up.

We hadn't rolled that far down Liberty Road before I started getting a little concerned. I really don't know why. I got the feeling that there was something out there. I'm guessing we were halfway, or a third of the way to Phu Loc (6). So I had the Marines get off the Amtracks and deploy on the flanks of the road and move forward. I had a typical triangle with a point squad and a point fire team and the flank security out. I just barely got them organized and moving when the point called back and said, "We've got dead Marines up here, Sir." Sure enough, there they were all on one side of the road, right next to each other, spaced a foot apart. Almost like dress-right dress. They were just lying on their backs. They'd been dragged to that spot from where they had fallen and died, All except for what turned out to be Lieutenant Burtolozzi and the radio operator, who were maybe 50 feet away on the side of the road, and the point fire team, which was either three or four guys. They were a couple hundred meters farther up the road toward Phu Loc (6). Other than those five or six, the rest of the squad, eight to ten dead Marines, were lying down side-by-side. I don't think they had their helmets on. We found no weapons. One guy had his leg blown off somewhere around the knee. There were not a lot of other grievous wounds, just bullet wounds. I found the radio operator and a man lying face down. When I pulled him up and rolled him over, his face fell into his helmet. I didn't know who it was at the time, but he had glasses. That didn't mean anything to me, because I didn't know the guys from Second Platoon that well. Then minutes later Andy Johnson, who still had First Platoon, called from the battalion CP and asked me if I'd seen Burt out there. I said, 'Who?' And he said, 'Burtolozzi.' And I said, 'Why would he be out here?' He said, 'Well, they think that he was with that squad as a pay officer.' I said, 'Oh, shit. Then that's him,' because Burt wore glasses. It turned out he was the pay officer for Echo Company. He'd flown in the night before from Danang with the payroll for Echo Company, then was using the mine sweep

203

squad to get back out to pay Echo Company. It means he had a lot of MPC (military pay certificates) for the whole company: like 200 people. He had two ammo boxes full. Later somebody told me he also wanted to say goodbye to his old platoon. It seemed like it took me a long time to get back to Andy on the radio, but when I did, I just said, 'Yeah, it's him.'"

First Lieutenant Paul Charles "Burt" Bertolozzi was born in Chicago, Illinois on 20 December 1943. He received his commission as a second lieutenant in the Marine Corps in 1965 after successfully completing the ROTC program at Northern Illinois University. When Lt. Bertolozzi's platoon at Phu Lac (6) heard he had fallen, they broke out an Illinois flag that one of the Marines had brought with him from the States and signed all their names on it. Thanks to his sister Marlena Bertolozzi who still lives in Chicago, the flag now rests on display in the Command Museum at Marine Corps Recruit Depot San Diego, California. Bill Harvey continued with his sad tale...

"Then I set about trying to figure out what had happened. I was roaming around trying to reconstruct the ambush and I had been doing that for a good period of time when it suddenly occurred to me that I hadn't seen a single spent cartridge. No matter how much we crawled around on our hands and knees where the enemy was laid down in their firing positions, we found no cartridges. They'd left behind a lot of cut branches they'd been using for camouflage and things like that. Over time, I was able to reconstruct everything, but we never, ever found a single spent cartridge, either friendly or enemy. We know that there had to be some shooting going on. I mean, surprise wouldn't have been so total that nobody could even fire back. You have to assume that the Marines were able to do some firing. I'll never know why they took the time to police up all the brass, unless it was an attempt to have a psychological effect on us. Why else would they line up the bodies like they did? But on the other hand, what would they gain from a psychological impact on a platoon of Marines? That would be all they could hope for.

The VC ambush positions flanked the road. It was essentially an L-shaped ambush. There was a curve in the road, so they were able to have flanking and enfilade fire over the large area. But when they were hit, the squad was right on the curve, right in the middle. So the VC

204

were able to essentially shoot at them from two different directions even though they were mostly all on the same side of the road. Although they had that small contingent on the other side of the road, its sole function was to kill that point fire team because they were deployed forward of the main body of the ambush. Because of the distance from the point fire team to the main body, they couldn't fit them all within their L. They had to give up on something, so they decided to just handle the point fire team as if it was a separate entity. The VC, the ones that were the closest to the road were, hell—not more than 40-50 feet away from the Marines. They were right there. It was point blank. I mean, it was perfect. If you saw it, it was just perfect. That vegetation, that scrubby, bushy, grassy stuff, was perfect for camouflage. I'm sure that they'd done a good job with the vegetative camouflage over their whole bodies so they looked just like another shrub out there if anybody had looked in their direction. But the point was that I don't think that that mine sweep squad had any flank security out. And everybody was always tired. They never had a good night's sleep behind them. They'd spent the night in a hole somewhere, whether they were out on patrol or whether they were on the An Hoa lines. They probably were on the An Hoa lines the night before and they probably were running at best 33% with probably 50% holes. On a good night a Marine would be lucky to get five hours of sleep.

The clarity of hindsight over the years does nothing to resolve the questions about this ambush: was it a Soviet "Speznatz" (special operations) unit? What was the purpose of the morgue-like arrangement of the corpses? Did they police up all the brass to conceal use of a special weapon that would identify them? Bill Harvey continued with his painful reminiscence...

"At some point in time, half an hour or so after we found the bodies, a machine gunner who was an old pro—it seems like he was even a short timer who'd been there for 12 months or something like that, just ripped off his flak jacket and threw it on the ground and then threw his machine gun down and ripped off his helmet. He was acting crazy and wouldn't listen to anybody. We couldn't calm him down. He was just screaming and yelling, but not anything that made any sense. I mean, he didn't have any message to convey. He was raging at life, I guess. He just lost it. Finally, a couple Marines held him down and the corpsmen gave him a shot of morphine or sedative. Then a squad leader came up to me and said, 'Lance Corporal so and so isn't

205

acting right, Sir. He doesn't respond and he's got glassy eyes and he won't do what I tell him to and he doesn't seem to care.' I went to see him and he was right, so I threw him on the same helicopter that came in to bring the other guy out.

After I'd pretty much organized everything, the medivacs had gone, the dead were out of there, and we'd policed up the area, I took two squads and lit out after the VC ambush unit. In the process of analyzing the ambush area earlier, I had discovered a rendezvous point that wasn't that far away. From there, they'd left a very defined trail through the waist-high grassy scrub, so their trail was obvious. I took off after them as fast as the Marines would go; we actually double-timed some of the way. Soon we came across a couple of cans of M-60 ammunition and a couple ammo cans, one of which was opened with the MPC spilling out of it. Those were the ones they took from Lieutenant Bertolozzi. I would think they realized they couldn't use them, so they chucked them. But we never caught the bastards."

STONE

Early afternoon of 15 February we found him on the grassy flanks of a ridge near Alligator Lake lying in a shallow ditch partly covered by a camouflaged cape. He was a good-looking dude, obviously well fed, muscular. He had a high and tight haircut like most of the Marines in my platoon. On a web belt around his waist he carried three Chicom grenades. The pockets in his black shorts disgorged a wallet, papers, razor blades, food. I reached over and took a ruby-colored enameled pin off his shirt—a bust of Ho Chi Minh—and put it in my pocket. One of his buddies lay nearby, dead. The others had gotten away over the hill before we arrived.

Someone circling overhead in a Bird Dog observation aircraft had taken his group under fire with an M-16 then radioed the location to us. A round struck him at a high angle in the left hip. Then, as 5.56mm rounds will do, augured its way all the way down his leg to the calf. He was gravely wounded and slipping into shock so we called for a medevac. While the chopper was inbound, we learned through our Chieu Hoi that this was yen Sau, service number HT21.342, 24 years old and a squad leader of the 3rd Squad, 3rd Platoon, R-20 Doc Lap main force VC Battalion, our old nemesis. According to Sau, Foxtrot Company 2/5 had pounded his unit during Operation Tuscaloosa in late January, killing 20 and wounding 20 more. He told us the R20 Battalion had been in Loc Qui four days ago and his squad was now located in the hills to the south of us. His mission was to reconnoiter the area and inform the parent unit about Marine positions and movements. When the Huey flared out, flattening the grass with its rotor wash, we loaded him into the bay. Then he disappeared in a whirlwind of sweet exhaust and grass and dust. We began working our way off the ridge and north towards the road.

For G Company, Operation Stone had begun at 1500 hours 11 February at the An Hoa airstrip when we boarded CH-46 Sea Knight helicopters in 15 man teams. The operations order called for choppers to fly us north across the Thu Bon River to Dai Loc, where we would come under the operational control of 2nd Battalion 4th Marine Regiment. Tanks from C Company 1st Tank Battalion were to move south at 0330 the next day toward the ferry along the banks of the Song Thu Bon. At 0500, Companies E and F from 2/4 and amphibious tractors from A Company 1st Amtrack Battalion would depart, arriving at the line of departure at 0700. G Company and the 2/5 H & S Company would load into tractors at 0615. The concept was a classic "hammer and anvil"; G company would move into a blocking position several kilometers east of Phu Lac (6) while the 2/4 companies (the "hammer) would move towards them, trapping enemy units in between. Having been promoted to Company Executive Officer in January, I would be moving with the Command Group. Years later Lieutenant (now Colonel, USMCR retired) Marc Glasgow remembered Stone as his first operation as company commander, Captain Gruner having returned home two weeks prior…

"This was my first operation as G company commander, so I wanted it to go right," Glasgow told me during an interview. *"We flew to a planning session at the old French fort near Dai Loc, a structure that was kind of low slung, with bunkers at each corner — pretty massive bunkers. When they told us what the mission of G Company was going to be, I was stunned: load Marines aboard a company of M-48 tanks*

208

and charge hell for leather through the darkness south to the banks of the Thu Bon River where we would board Mike boats or amtracks. Then we would cross the river, turn east on the road next to Phu Lac (6) and proceed to a position just south of Go Noi Island where we would set up a blocking force. All this before daylight. I was stunned. Who had thought this up? They wanted us to load the troops, 10 or so to each tank, then barrel down the road at 20 miles an hour in the middle of the night until we reached the banks of the Song Thu Bon. I was very skeptical. After we set the blocking force in across the river from Go Noi Island, 2/4 would sweep south and trap any enemy units that happened to be between us. We were supposed to be in position before daylight. Needless to say, it didn't work out that way."

The river crossing on 12 February was like something out of the movie, " *The Longest Day."* Mike boats carrying M-48 tanks churned across the Song Thu Bon, throwing up impressive bow waves. Marc Glasgow remembers a glitch that developed early on...

"They offloaded the first tank from a Mike boat without any problem, then the second one overbalanced the ramp, tipping the stern of the Mike boat up in the air. You could see the propeller whirling away. That jammed up the rest of the tanks behind it, so we only had one tank with us goin' down the road past Phu Lac (6)."

Amtracks stampeded across the wide river like enraged hippos while 105 mm illumination rounds sailed overhead turning night to day, bombarding us with spent casings, and silhouetting us against the bright sand. After the casings narrowly missed several Marines, I yelled to no one in particular, "What the hell's going on? Are they trying to kill us with the casings or light us up so Charlie can finish us off like a shooting gallery at Coney Island or both?" I was skeptical of this behemoth task force; it seemed like massive overkill. Somewhere in the shadows, light infantry of the R-20 Battalion probably were maneuvering out of range or into an advantageous position.

Bill Harvey had taken command of Third Platoon in January. Stone was his first big combat operation and he was not amused at the way it was unfolding...

209

"It was a night movement to Phu Loc (6) when all hell broke loose. The sky was lit up with flares and it seemed like my platoon was totally exposed out in the middle of a rice paddy or some open area like that. I saw a tank turret sticking out of the surface of the river. Apparently that was the reason for all the flares, because a Mike boat had run aground in the middle of the river. The tank had tried to off-load, thinking it was on shore instead of the sand bar in the middle of the river, so it had just went underwater. I got on the horn and yelled at Captain Glasgow, 'Who the hell called in those flares?' and 'How come I wasn't told?' and he said, 'I called it in and it's none of your damned business!' We never had any significant contact, so it turned out to be good drill for me in night and daytime land navigation. Kind of getting the feel for the terrain and figuring out where I was."

The operation also gave Lieutenant Harvey an opportunity to hone a working relationship with his new platoon and with Staff Sergeant Wallace Carter, a senior NCO with a reputation for iron discipline, a prickly demeanor, and by-the-book operating methods. Harvey knew Carter's heroism during the ambush at Thon Bon (1) had launched a recommendation for a Silver Star. In addition to the normal trepidation a newly commissioned young officer has for a senior NCO, Harvey had to deal with this aura of battlefield audacity and professionalism that floated over Carter like the Hindenberg...

"Staff Sergeant Carter was actually my platoon sergeant for a little more than three weeks. I took over the platoon on 27 January and he transferred to the S-3 (battalion operations center) on 21 February. It was the classic case of what they tried to convey at The Basic School — the crusty old senior NCO and the snotty-nosed baby-faced lieutenant. I always had this sense that he was looking upon my leadership talents with great disdain. He'd been there so long by that point in time, whereas I would be struggling to figure out whether I was inside or outside the wire. He knew the area so well that he could call in artillery without even pulling out a map. Eventually I got to be that way, but... the troops had a great respect for him. He'd been on the drill field somewhere, MCRD San Diego, or Parris Island.

He seemed a lot taller than he probably was. He was a handsome guy—built like an Olympian—and obviously had done a good job. You have that division between officer and enlisted and I think that he didn't go out of his way to try to transfer the gauntlet of respect from him to me. I think he probably innately or consciously tried to keep it close to himself. But I can understand that. That's human nature. Like I said, I've always had the greatest respect for him, but I've got to admit that when he got transferred, I breathed a few sighs of relief."

Even though Operation Stone had a herky-jerky beginning, by 0800 we were well along the road east of Phu Lac (6) meeting light resistance in the form of sniping by small bands of VC. The tank was growling along the narrow little road, shaving off vegetation, a few banana trees, and the occasional structure from the shoulders. Suddenly firing broke out ahead, followed by the call, "corpsman up!" Trailing a banner of gray exhaust, our M-48 took off up the road to assist. I hopped up on the back of it and held on to the turret as it barreled down the narrow road past a squad of Second Platoon G Company Marines that was deployed forward. Beside the road, a Marine from Second Platoon lay on a poncho staring up at the sky with sightless eyes. The tank charged past them and they yelled, "Lieutenant! Get off that tank. There's snipers up ahead!" I jumped down and joined the squad that by now was moving in behind the tank and following in its tracks. The firing had stopped. As we moved forward, the Marines told me that VC in a trench had fired a quick burst at them, hitting the dead Marine with a lucky shot. They were making a diagonal get away move along a trench that was running more or less perpendicular to the road when one rose up, fired from the hip, dropped one of the Second Platoon Marines, and disappeared. We found the body of one VC soldier nearby.

Dan Day had seen the whole thing unfold right in front of him…

"I was on point, walkin' down the road and I saw something up ahead moving. I walked a little further then said to myself, 'I can't believe it'—four NVA sitting down. One guy had a gray shirt. One guy had his shirt off, like he was sunnin' himself. One of them kind of smiled at me. I immediately fired a burst at them. The M-14 is hard to control on full automatic, so it went kind of high. I started chasing after them and slipped in the mud, landing on my butt. Then I shot towards the bottom of the trail and hit a guy in the back. He flipped

211

backwards as a combination of the round hitting him and slipping in the mud. So I got on the side of the trail in one of two little trenches that flanked the road and returned their fire. A couple more Marines joined me and started firing down the road. I called for guns up and an M-79 grenade launcher. One of the Marines who joined us was Lance Corporal Edwards, a young black Marine from a guard unit near San Francisco, or Marine barracks somewhere and he didn't have any field experience. Sometime in the month of February Corporal Crum, our fire team leader, went on R&R to Bangkok leaving me, a PFC, as senior Marine in the squad. So they put Edwards in charge when he showed up. But he looked to me for guidance even though he outranked me because I'd been in country six or seven months.

The night before we went on the operation he said to me, 'Day, in this pack I wrote two letters: one to my girlfriend, one to my mother. If I get killed, I want you to make sure they get mailed back home.' I said, 'Look, Edwards, quit talking that way.' He was always talking morbid like he was going to get killed. So the very next day he came up to help out on this brief firefight. He didn't come up the trench line. If he would have just stayed in the trench, he probably wouldn't have got shot. But he just froze, kind of standing up. I was looking back at him when he took a round right in the heart."

Then Marc Glasgow, the new company commander, received some interesting news over the radio...

"The OE observation plane flying around south of us saw a dude on a water buffalo moving parallel to us along the ridge near Alligator Lake. Every time the company moved, he moved. When we stopped, he stopped. The OE thought it was suspicious, so I ordered the tank to take him out. The 90mm round was right on target and there wasn't much left of man or beast in the impact area. A bit later one of the Marines took a sniper shot through the head. When I got to him he was still conscious, hadn't gone into shock, even though the round had gone in his right ear and out his left. He died about ten minutes later."

Late that afternoon a short but spirited firefight broke out ahead of us. Soon after it ended, some Marines came back down the road carrying a young Vietnamese farm boy in a poncho. He couldn't have been any more than thirteen-years-old, had been hit multiple times and looked bad; he was unconscious.

The Marines told us he got caught in the crossfire. Where should we take him, they asked, obviously anguished he was so young and a non-combatant at that. Not far from where we stood, on the edge of the hamlet of Tho Son (1), was a Buddhist monastery off the side of the road—a long plaster and cement building with a tile roof and white exterior walls surrounded by well-trimmed gardens aglow in the oblique rays of the westering sun.

When we inquired at the gate, a Buddhist priest appeared, dressed in a long blue cotton robe fastened at the neck, with white trousers underneath. His head was shaved and a sparse gray beard dangled from his chin. A religious medal hung from his neck. He was sturdy looking, about 60 years old, and had hands like teakwood carvings. After one of our Chieu Hoi explained what had happened, he invited us into the courtyard, then into one of the cool dark corridors where we laid the boy gently on the floor. Although a corpsman had dressed his wounds, you could tell he was struggling to live. Pale and pierced with bullet holes, he was a heart-wrenching sight. He died twenty minutes later.

The order was passed to hunker in for the night and soon the sound of entrenching tools clattering against hard clay and the growling and crunching of the M-48 tank waddling into position like some prehistoric monster on the far side of the graveyard rang through the still air. A strip of western sky glowed peach and salmon behind dark thunderheads. The priest led our command group down a corridor to the threshold of a small room in a wing of the monastery. The doors were made of heavy hardwood and the windows were an open plaster grid design. Before allowing us to enter, he swept the hard packed dirt floor with a twig broom. Then he placed a woven straw mat on a large wooden bed, behind which sat a small red coffin filled with rice. How kind of him, I thought, to offer such relatively luxurious quarters to American military commanders. But then these pious stewards of a spiritual sanctuary rarely judged travelers; they dispensed their generosity in equal measure to one and all.

213

After the evening meal I sat on a garden wall and watched as the priest walked slowly across the carefully raked sand courtyard then up the brick steps into a corridor of the pagoda to a chest-high altar that held candles and two ceramic vases with flowers. His blue robe was soiled at the hem. A large hollow red gourd hung from an overhead beam next to a brass bell. He lit three incense sticks that burned like slender cigarettes in the crepuscular light, sending thin threads of smoke curling upward and upward. Then he lit two candles and knelt at the altar, opened a prayer book and began a slow chant accompanied by a steady rhythm on the red gourd, a rhythm punctuated by occasional beats on the bell. It struck me at that moment no matter its denomination, religion is an abiding pan-global conviction that endures even the ravages of war. Here we were, a company of heavily armed Marines, collaborating with Buddhist priests over the fate of a badly injured civilian youth. It was obvious we shared values that transcended eastern and western cultures. But my Vietnamese was not good enough to understand his words, so I followed the gaze of a benign and corpulent golden Buddha out the door past the courtyard and across the road to where Marines were camouflaging their fighting holes and setting night watch schedules.

Early the next morning the tank fired again and again from the graveyard, killing ten enemy soldiers on a nearby ridge, and blasting me out of a fitful sleep on the hard bed in the monastery. While the half moon flew through a platinum and pewter sky, I lay in the darkness thinking about the Vietnamese boy whom the war had just chewed up and spit out. As hardened as we had become as warriors to battlefield deaths, whether our own or the enemy's, innocent civilians were something else. My own brother would be thirteen in October. I could only hope that right now the twin demons of remorse and regret were circling as persistently over the VC commander as they were over me. An artillery barrage whumped a muffled rhythm somewhere in the distance, and I drifted off again.

Operation Stone ended on 16 February when all units returned to the 2/4 command post. The final tally was 28 VC firmed killed and 30 probably killed. We lost two Marines suffered nine wounded in the 5-day operation.

LIFE IN THE BAT CAVE

The day after Operation Stone ended on 20 February I was assigned to the battalion operations section (S-3) at An Hoa combat base. This was consistent with standard policy to pull people out of the field towards the end of their Vietnam tour if at all possible. By the middle of April I would have been away from the States thirteen and half months. My new job was assistant to Major Richard "Dick" Esau, the operations officer. My staff designation was S-3 Alpha. After my experience as battalion adjutant for the First Anti-Tank Battalion in Camp Pendleton, I was uneasy about the assignment. The last thing I wanted after the positive experience of serving as platoon commander in the field, then executive officer in a line company was dealing with mountains of paperwork and oceans of minutia.

I reported in to my first day on the job wearing a soft utility cover instead of a helmet—a real luxury by field standards. The Combat Operations Center (COC) was a fifteen-foot by twelve-foot sandbag pillbox sunk four feet in the ground, located pretty much in the center of gravity of An Hoa Combat Base. We soon named it "The Bat Cave" because of its dim ambiance, even at noon, and the parallels in our minds to the cartoon characters "Bat Man" and "Robin" who used such a sanctuary to hatch ingenious schemes against dark forces arrayed across the globe. "Holy search and destroy, Bat Man" became one of our favorite expressions. By sunset of that first day, my fears of becoming a glorified "Remington Raider" had dissipated like morning mist over the Song Thu Bon. Dick Esau revealed himself to be a personable, highly motivated and extremely competent operations officer. He was full of energy and positive reinforcement. Rather than driving his staff forward, he led them forward with visions of improving S-3 shop operations to the benefit of the line companies and for our replacements. He soon learned the previous stewards of S-3 had operated pretty much out of a message book, for whatever reason—probably the exigencies of combat operations on the heels of a complicated move from Con Thien in November of the previous year. He saw a need to, "Tighten up a bit, tie up loose ends and organize better" so operations against Viet Cong and NVA forces could be planned well in advance, with more success.

Soon we found ourselves pursuing Major Esau's mandates for 16 to 18 hours per day: drafting standing operating procedures (SOPs) and directives; drawing a schematic of the base complete with grid coordinates and final protective fires; planning field operations; writing the operational orders for them, and after action reports once they concluded. Soon I found myself walking the defensive perimeter, collaborating with the company commanders about integrating final protective fires, the first step in compiling a comprehensive battalion fire plan.

Having been recently assigned to the S-3 section, Staff Sergeant Wallace Carter, one of the heroes of the ambush at Thon Bon (1), grumbled occasionally. The quintessential field Marine, he reminded me of a sleek panther prowling an English garden at high tea, growling from time to time and baring his teeth. In other words, he was out of his element. That he much preferred field operations to staff work was apparent. One day when I admonished him about misspellings and grammatical errors in a report, he snapped, " I don't like anyone criticizing my English, lieutenant." Regardless of his attitude, numerical and written accuracy was an immutable precept in the S-3 shop. An error either way could cost lives. Once I plotted H & I fires too close to the location of a night ambush. Acetate overlays for the day's activities exposed the error before it could cause any harm; but the incident pounded home to me the exacting nature of the process.

It was not uncommon, especially when a new "search and destroy" operation was in the planning stages, to fall into the rack at 0200 and rise up the next morning with 0600 reveille. Despite the long hours, the days flew by in a blur of projects that covered a wide spectrum of battalion activities. Spurred on in the Bat Cave by Major Esau's enthusiasm, we improved on battalion operations planning, standardized procedures, and tightened up the defensive perimeter. From time to time, reminders we were in a war zone intruded on our relatively secure enclave.

One such intrusion occurred on 25 February 1967 while the An Hoa Combat Base was settling in for the night. Darkness crept up from the rice paddies, blurring the edges of the battalion perimeter where troops in flak jackets and helmets stood sentinel in sandbagged fighting bunkers.

"Lights out" signaled the end of the day in strong-back hootches like the one several of us officers and NCOs occupied near the airfield. I had just begun a long spiraling descent into the labyrinth of dreams, hastened by unaccustomed luxuries: a cot, blankets, wooden floor, corrugated steel roof, and mess hall chow. Then my world exploded with one tachycardic epithet: "INCOMING!"

Instinct carried me out the door barefoot, steel helmet, rifle, and flak jacket somehow in place, and catapulted me into a trench full of six other Marines. Like UFO's drifting down from the Andromeda Galaxy, magnesium flares threw swaying shadows across the landing strip in front of us, illuminating a sheaf of eighty two millimeter mortar rounds that were chewing up the Marston mats like a horizontal tornado. Dust, rocks, and twisted metal flew into the air as the row of exploding

217

rounds marched towards our pitifully shallow protection. Razor sharp shrapnel peppered the corrugated steel roof behind us, accelerating our pulses as we imagined the carnage high-explosive rounds detonating simultaneously in our trench would inflict.

Into my right field of vision, which was primed for onrushing North Vietnamese infantry, streaked a ghost-white object coming fast directly at our position from fifty yards out. Whoever it was pumped his arms and legs furiously in a good imitation of a college 880 man. Before I could scream an alarm, the lance corporal beside me yelled, "Sergeant Franklin[10]! Haul ass!"

One of my former NCOs had been in the middle of a shower when the mortar barrage began. He bolted so quickly he left his flip-flops on the ground in a running position and his towel flew off. He dove into our trench at full speed buck naked, laughing like a hyena and prompting the whole trench full of Marines to burst out in sympathetic hilarity. Then we grew silent and hunkered down, for the mortar rounds were almost upon us. We had seen the last sheaf hit the apron of the runway and knew the interval was right for the next one to score a direct hit on our trench. To our immense relief, the trajectories rose high behind us at the last moment and we heard the shells detonating deep inside the base. Then it was silent again except for a faint, sonorous rhythm like fingers thrumming a pocket comb—paddy frogs stubbornly serenading the advent of spring.

Sergeant Dale Farnham was with Second Platoon when the VC mortar crew blew up our dreams...

"We had just come back in (from patrol) that afternoon and they had given us new rubber ladies. We were so happy because we didn't have no cots in the hootches. Guys were sleepin' on the floor on C-ration cartons and like that. Fortunately, there was somebody awake in the hardback when the barrage come in. But when it did come in, we all took off like crazy. After the barrage, there wasn't a rubber lady left standing inflated. They were all punctured. Everybody was so danged mad about the rubber ladies, they were ready to go out and chop some

---

[10] Not his real name.

218

VC heads off."

As soon as it was apparent NVA infantry were not following close behind the barrage, I leaped out of the trench and took off down the row of tents, making a beeline for the COC where I knew Major Esau would be busier than the proverbial physically challenged paperhanger. Just before I reached the bunker, several 105mm artillery pieces pumped rounds out into the night. Later I learned a Marine in the observation tower had spotted the enemy mortar crew across the Thu Bon River and directed counter-battery fire right on the money. Scratch one mortar crew.

Despite having taken a direct hit at one of the entrances, the command bunker was a beehive of activity. An enlisted Marine with a quarter-sized piece of razor-sharp shrapnel sticking out of his bleeding chin staggered over. While talking to the 105 battery on one radio and the tank platoon on another, Major Esau directed him to the nearest aid station. Situation reports (sitreps) were beginning to flow in from the line. A cacophony of radio chatter filled the Bat Cave. Our primary concern was the mortar attack was prelude to a sizeable NVA or VC infantry assault. The line companies on perimeter duty were on full alert, so attention was focused on reserve forces should such an attack materialize. Fortunately it never did. A damage assessment revealed most of the casualties were in Headquarters and Service (H & S) Company. By contrast, casualties in the line companies were fewer because they instantly recognized incoming from outgoing fire and took protective measures with more alacrity. Years later, Major (now retired colonel) Esau told me while he and his staff were firing up the COC during the mortar attack, First Sergeant Johnson noticed something awry. He walked over to Esau, reached up, and turned his helmet around 180 degrees to the correct position. Then he walked over to the radios without saying a word—just another senior NCO squaring away his major. With his helmet on correctly, Dick Esau turned to the multiple tasks at hand...

"The whole idea from the Three Shop perspective was to get the counter battery fire goin' and we were doin' pretty good there. The thing I liked about the artillery kids is that they took a couple of 82mm rounds in their pits, but they never moved. They just ignored them

219

and continued with counter battery. Just one enemy round hit the entrance to the COC and collapsed it. I'm in there tryin' to find out where the rounds are coming from and whether or not the enemy is reinforcing; what are we hearing from the people on the line out there? I want to know whether this is a prelude to an attack. Some people reacted differently. For instance, Doctor Donnelly, the dentist, was bound and determined to get back to California to practice dentistry. He wasn't going to get killed in Southeast Asia. He had dug a hole next to his hootch and one of his dental corpsmen had actually built him a slide so that he could come out of his rack, get on this slide and scoot right into his trench and be safe from any barrage. He's hunkered down in there and the mortar attack is over, so about six of us went over and pissed in his trench. We said, 'Oh, we thought this was a urinal, right? Nobody would have something like this next to his hootch.' But you know, he was a good guy and an awfully good dentist. He was great on medcaps and county fairs. He would do wonderful things for people who had been chewing betel nut for years because of the pain in their mouths. Tom Beatty, the battalion surgeon, was out of this world. He was very special. He came out of the battalion aid station in the middle of the mortar attack and started treating the wounded, including the Marine with shrapnel in his chin."

RETURN TO THE WORLD

Apr1 1967 was a harbinger of brutally hot weather to come. Heat waves shimmered over the greening rice paddies while thunderheads piled high over the Que Son Mountains. Just after sunset the air cooled. Pastel hues glowed beyond the darkening ridges. That afternoon I had finished plotting the last defensive fire plans for the An Hoa perimeter, blending them into a multicolored map that included grid lines, rice paddies, buildings and a schematic of the final defensive fires that encircled the combat base. Major Esau seemed pleased with the result. I took some time off to pack my personal gear in a sea bag and a wooden chest I had bought in the Philippines. After dinner at the mess hall, I sauntered over to the "Club", a strong-back hootch that served as a gathering place and bar for officers and senior non-commissioned officers. A wide variety of alcoholic libations flowed more or less freely in an atmosphere occluded with cigarette and cigar smoke and ringing with boisterous laughter. It seemed fitting to me on the night before my departure back to The World I should spend a little time with the officers and senior staff NCOs of the battalion. About the time I ordered my third Budweiser beer, someone yelled, "Hey Lieutenant Buchanan. Outside. Someone wants to see you!" Mumbling something about why didn't they just come the hell on in, I stepped outside into the heavy night air. There reflected in the light from the open door were several enlisted Marines from 2nd Platoon Golf Company, my first infantry command. One of them said, "Sir, we heard you're leaving tomorrow and we thought we would come on over and just say goodbye and good luck and all that and wish you well." Taken aback by my emotional response to this farewell gesture, I groped around for the right words to say to warriors who had taught me a great deal about unit cohesion, courage, and professionalism under fire. We kidded back and forth for a few minutes, talked tactics, tried to guess what the future held, then a silence fell and it was time to say goodbye. I shook hands with each Marine, wished them all well, turned and walked back into the "Club." Decades later, as time and events began to circle back towards closure, this farewell gesture by Marines of Second Platoon would abide in my memory and eventually come to rest as a catalytic event in the Preface to this memoir.

Midmorning the next day I strapped myself into a CH-46 helicopter, then watched through a porthole as An Hoa Combat Base faded into a sea of rice paddies, then disappeared against the backdrop of the Que Son Mountains. Logic would dictate I landed at Danang, then boarded a flight for either Okinawa or the U.S. mainland. But to this day there is a persistent blank space in my memory that spans my departure from An Hoa to the moment my parents greeted me at San Francisco International Airport after thirteen and a half months overseas.

In January 1968 I left the Marine Corps and returned to civilian life. I spent the next few months at the home of my parents in Los Altos Hills, California. Watching yellow mustard explode across the meadows and apricot blossoms burst like popcorn on the branches of orchard trees black with rain as spring moved across the coast range, had a calming effect. It was a season for renewal and for sorting things out. I hoped my internal compass would kick in and show me the path to the next phase of my life as surely as my Silva compass had guided me through the jungles of Vietnam. Without a lot of enthusiasm, I poked about corporate America, looking for a likely niche for my talents and desires. The more I inquired, the more I realized the market for amphibious landings, night ambushes, and infantry assaults was weak. Nevertheless, I persevered. One morning I noticed an ad in the classified section of the San Jose Mercury News. It said, "Editing. Small publishing concern seeks mature, experienced editor for commercial brochures and advertising copy." Could it be my recent assignment as assistant operations officer at An Hoa Combat Base would qualify me? I put on my only sport coat and tie, shined my shoes, and drove down to Palo Alto. I found the firm on a side street off Channing Avenue: a small two-story brownstone structure. The principal of the establishment had a professorial look about him: beard, sport coat, open collar shirt. He was affable enough as we discussed the position he had advertised. As soon as we ventured into my military background, he seemed to tense up. He handed me an application and told me to fill it out in the adjacent office. His associate would be available if I had any questions. Then he disappeared down the hallway. I had just completed the top portion of the form when a thin young lady with long black hair and sharp features strode purposefully into the room. Her gray dress matched her personality perfectly. Without any introduction or prelude, she leaned down and literally hissed in my ear, "You can fill out the application all you like, but we don't hire baby killers around here!" Before I could respond, she walked out. With an ember of anger glowing in my gut, I started to follow her, but thought better of it. Soon I was walking down Channing towards University Avenue where I had parked my car.

My second attempt to re-enter the society I had left in 1966 took me to the cloistered halls of academia. For some reason I thought a graduate degree in English would serve me well in future endeavors—perhaps as a distinguished professor at a nearby university. A week after my disastrous experience at the

223

publishing firm, I drove to the Stanford University campus in Palo Alto and walked over to the English Department. Without a clue about the best person to contact, or any definite appointment, I walked upstairs to the second floor and knocked on an office door bearing a sign that read *H. Bruce Franklin — Associate Professor of English and American Literature*. The slender man who answered my knock looked affable enough and seemed to be between classes. On one wall hung a red and black etching of Ho Chi Minh that bore a remarkable resemblance to the enameled pin I had liberated from the shirt of Nguyen Sau, the VC reconnaissance soldier during Operation Stone. Scattered among books on English literature were a few tomes about revolution, the third world, Marx, Lenin, and other communist icons.

Mr. Franklin invited me in. After I explained my purpose, he motioned to a chair and we began talking about the Stanford graduate English program. Inevitably, the conversation turned to my undergraduate degree at Oregon State University and the period of time that had elapsed since graduation in 1964. At my mention of the Marine Corps and my combat assignment in Vietnam, Mr. Franklin tensed, then leaned forward in his chair and asked earnestly, "But didn't the Marines in your unit oppose the war and refuse your orders to fight the Viet Cong and North Vietnamese forces?" I assured him my experience had been exactly the opposite; the Marines I served with fought fiercely and with great military professionalism under appalling circumstances. I added with a few exceptions, the Main Force Viet Cong and NVA who were bold enough to oppose us in large units suffered horrific casualties. He seemed shaken by my remarks, but not convinced. The rest of the conversation was a polite attempt by both of us to disengage and go our separate ways. As I walked across the greensward near Hoover Tower towards my car, I chuckled at the irony of having battled communists in a foreign land 10,000 miles away only to encounter their sympathizers twice in a row in my own country.

Later that year I learned H. Bruce Franklin was a notorious rabble-rouser associated with the Revolutionary Communist Party (RCP), formerly the Revolutionary Union (RU), a Marxist-

224

Leninist organization that espoused the violent overthrow of the United States government. When he became academically and politically insufferable, Stanford University dismissed him on February 12, 1971 for inciting "occupation of the university computer center, urging defiance of a police order to disperse, and calling a nighttime rally for violent action." The cushy job and benefits Mr. Franklin had enjoyed since 1965 evaporated overnight.

Eventually I found a challenging and rewarding position with the U.S. Government, married a vivacious and sympathetic woman whose warmth and understanding have carried me through many a difficult episode, bought a house, got a bird dog, and gave up my peripatetic lifestyle. As the years rolled by, a conviction grew within me that my tour with the Marines in Vietnam had become a prism through which I viewed much of what life served up thereafter. Never again would I experience cold, hunger, exhaustion, fright, courage, depression or elation on the same scale. Nor would I know the kind of teamwork, loyalty, sense of mission, dedication or professionalism the Marines of Golf Company, 2nd Battalion 5th Marine Regiment displayed in combat. As for the fallen, those whose voices have been stilled forever, their memory is both an abiding source of inspiration and a wellspring of profound sadness.

BIOGRAPHIES

JOHN RICHARD BATES

John R. Bates was born in 1946 in Little Rock, Arkansas. He enlisted in the Marine Corps on 23 March, 1966. After graduation from Marine Corps Recruit Depot at San Diego, California, John went through Infantry Training Regiment and Basic Infantry Training School at Camp Pendleton, California. In October, he was at Marine Corps Air Station El Toro making one last phone call to his folks in Little Rock before flying to Vietnam. He could hear by the tone of his father's voice that he was concerned about his son's deployment to yet another conflict in Asia. 37 years later John would know the feeling well when he saw his only son Josh and his daughter-in-law Stacey sally forth to battle in Iraq. In the fall of 1966 John joined 2nd Battalion 5th Marines at Con Thien, then served as a rifleman in Sgt. Alvarez' squad in 2nd Platoon until sustaining a serious chest wound during a firefight near An Hoa on 17 December 1966. After an amazingly swift recovery at Charlie Med in Danang, John rejoined his platoon in late January 1967. He was wounded twice more before rotating back to the States, once by grenade fragments, once by a punji stake.

In March 1968 the Marine Corps mustered Sergeant Bates out of its ranks due to his wounds. Although devastated to see his dream of a career in the Marine Corps evaporate, John persevered. He went back to school in Arkansas, and pestered the local Marine Corps recruiting officer until he relented and

228

allowed him to apply for Officers Candidate School leading to a commission in November 1975 as an infantry officer. Since then his assignments have included among others, platoon commander for Charlie 1/7; 3rd Marine Division in Okinawa; 12th Marine Corps District; Inspector/Instructor for Echo, 2nd Bn, 23rd Marines, San Bruno, California; Marine Air Group 24; Executive Officer and acting Battalion Commander for 1st Bn, 3rd Marines in Desert Shield and Desert Storm; S-3 of The Basic School; G-3 Ground Operations Officer for Marine Forces Pacific; Commander of 2nd Bn, 3rd Marines. As a colonel, John served as Fleet Marine Officer for 2nd Fleet in Norfolk, Virginia and Force Protection Officer for 7th Fleet aboard the USS Blue Ridge out of Yokosuka, Japan. As this book was being written in the summer of 2003, Colonel Bates added, *"I owe many in Golf 2/5 for examples of courage and leadership that have kept me on what I believe to be the correct path over the years. You taught me that second only to mission accomplishment, taking care of your Marines is the most important thing you can do for them and for our Corps. Lt. Buchanan was the leadership example that I wanted, and needed, especially in a combat environment. I have passed stories of his example to many of the Marines in uniform today. "Thanks, Lt. Buchanan!"*

John's son, 1st Lt. Joshua Rustin Bates (Weapons 1/7), and his new bride 1st Lt. Stacey Lafreniere-Bates (VMU-1), are just completing Operation Iraqi Freedom. His beautiful wife Stephanie deserves special credit for putting up with his continual deployments for over 30 years and having the hardest job of all—waiting for her family to return. An amazing footnote to John's narrative about his hospitalization in the chapter titled *Nong Son* is the return of his cigarette lighter 35 years later by a civilian who bought it from a street vendor in Vietnam in 1997. Despite his war wounds, John still has a passion for running (50+ marathons and ultra-distance runs) and is an active military and civilian skydiver. And yes…he rides a Harley.

WILLIAM L. BUCHANAN

Born into a Marine family at Quantico, Virginia in 1942, the author spent his early years trekking from pillar to post, namely Massachusetts, San Clemente, Camp Lejeune, the South Coast of France, Camp Pendleton, Carlisle Army Barracks, The Pentagon, and back to Quantico. Upon graduation from Oregon State University and successful completion of The Platoon Leader's Class (PLC), the author was sworn in as a 2nd lieutenant in the USMCR December 1964. Upon graduation from The Basic School in 1965, his first field assignment was with the 1st Anti Tank Battalion in Camp Pendleton, California. After serving a few months as battalion adjutant, he became the platoon commander of 3rd Platoon B Company. He embarked from San Diego in March 1966, as part of a Special Landing Force (SLF) comprised of Battalion Landing Team 3/5. After training in the Philippines, BLT 3.5 conducted amphibious operations along the South Vietnamese coast until late July 1966 at which time it made a final landing at Chu Lai and disbanded. Lieutenant Buchanan joined G Company 2/5 as platoon commander of 2nd Platoon on 17 October 1966. He served in that billet until his promotion to company executive officer late January 1967, then battalion assistant operations officer. He left the Marine Corps in January 1968 as a captain.

From 1969 until 1996 he served as a Special Agent with the Federal Bureau of Investigation in Oklahoma City and Tulsa,

Oklahoma, Chicago, Illinois, and Monterey and San Francisco, California. His career included assignments in general criminal matters, white-collar crime, foreign (Near East/North Africa) counter-terrorism and foreign (Soviet) counter intelligence.

After retiring from the FBI in March 1996, Buchanan and his partner Rick Smith formed a firm in San Francisco called Cannon Street, Incorporated that provides investigative services to corporations and law firms. He lives in Mill Valley, California with his wife Claire and his 15-year-old bird dog Maxwell's Lost River Trailblazer. Not as frequently as he would like, he pursues his passions for backcountry skiing, land navigation, ocean kayaking, hiking, photography, rock climbing, organic gardening, astronomy and writing. During the nearly two years that it took to complete *Full Circle: A Marine Rifle Company in Vietnam* he had the privilege of becoming reacquainted with many of the men and officers of G Company and Echo Company, 2nd Battalion, 5th Marines. Without their assistance and input, the book never would have been published. Thus, it is a tribute not only to their service and sacrifice during the Vietnam War, but to their contribution to setting the record straight after all these years. For that he will be forever grateful.

RONALD W. CARBONE

Ron enlisted in the Marine Corps December 26, 1965 as a J-reservist on a two-year enlistment. His original MOS was 0100 office poggy. After he requested combat orders, his MOS changed to 0311 rifleman, a distinction that enhanced his pride in having received a marksman badge at Parris Island. Ron shipped out to Vietnam September 13, 1966 from Okinawa, arriving in Danang the same day. He immediately was assigned to 2nd Battalion, 5th Marines. A couple of weeks later he flew to Con Thien and reported in to 3rd Platoon, G Company. Ron fought as a rifleman in a number of combat operations around Con Thien and in the An Hoa TAOR until he left Vietnam October 13, 1967. He was released from active duty in the Marine Corps early November 1967.

After his Vietnam experience, Ron attended Wentworth Technical Institute, Boston Massachusetts from 1968 until he graduated with an Associate degree in mechanical engineering in 1970. Later he attended Lowell Technological Institute, Lowell Massachusetts from 1973 until 1976, graduating with a Bachelor of Science degree in mechanical engineering. Ron applied his engineering education as an employee for Pratt & Whitney (gas turbine manufacturer) in East Hartford Connecticut, from 1976 until 1991, when the company downsized. He was married June 28, 1982 and has two children: Patrick age 19, and Laura age 14.

Currently Ron works for Jacobs Vehicle Systems (diesel engine retarder manufacturer) in Bloomfield Connecticut. He keeps in shape by jogging and doing yard work. He also is a history buff.

DANIEL H. DAY

Dan graduated from St. Mary's High School in 1965, then enlisted in the Marine Corps March of 1966. After boot camp at MCRD in San Diego, he completed Basic Infantry Training School at Camp Pendleton, and then was assigned to Staging Battalion. Dan joined 2nd Battalion 5th Marines in late August 1966 at Chu Lai, Republic of Vietnam and was assigned a billet consistent with his 0311 MOS in 2nd Platoon G Company—automatic rifleman. Two weeks later, the battalion moved to Dong Ha, then to the combat base at Con Thien to engage North Vietnamese forces in Operation Prairie I. Dan participated in combat operations against Viet Cong and North Vietnamese units in the An Hoa TAOR from late November 1966 until he and approximately 32 other Marines were wounded when an amtrack hit a command-detonated land mine on 10 April 1967. A Lance Corporal at the time, Dan spent two months recuperating from wounds at a hospital in Yokosuka, Japan. Then he was transferred to Okinawa. In September 1967 he was assigned to 5th Military Police Battalion at Camp Pendleton, California. He received an honorable discharge from the Marine Corps in March 1969. He especially remembers the following Marines from his service in Vietnam: Joe Madruga, Vernon Horn, Kelly Crum, Bill Gavin, Bobby Dale Draper (KIA 2 August 1967), Sergeant Wayne Eugene Dawson (KIA 19 December, 1966), Corporal A.D. Stout, Sgt. Sherman Crebbs, and Lance Corporal Lamb.

In August 1969, Dan joined the St. Louis Metropolitan Police Department. In 1976 he was awarded a B.S.in Legal Justice / Political Science from Maryville College. In October 1976 he entered on duty as an inspector with Internal Revenue Service Inspection, then transferred laterally to the Bureau of Alcohol, Tobacco, and Firearms (ATF), retiring after 21 years of service. In January 1996, he retired from the U.S. Army Reserves with the rank of CWO-3 Criminal Investigator. For the past two years he has been an investigator for the St. Charles County Prosecuting Attorney's Office in St. Charles, Missouri. He and his wife Betty have five children. His outside interests are golfing, pistol shooting and fishing.

DALE W. FARNHAM

Dale enlisted in the Marine Corps 9 August 1961 at Albany, New York. After Boot Camp at Parris Island, then Infantry Training Regiment at Camp LeJeune, he was assigned to Headquarters and Service Company Draft pending government air transportation to San Diego California in January 1962. He then boarded the USS Mann in San Diego for deployment to Naha, Okinawa where he was assigned to 3rd Reconnaissance Battalion. A promotion to Lance Corporal followed. From Okinawa, he deployed for four months to the Republic of South Vietnam, then returned to CONUS in late April 1963 enroute to a Military Police Company at Fleet Marine Force Atlantic in Norfolk, Virginia. There he received a promotion to corporal. In August 1965 Dale reenlisted for NAD McAllister Oklahoma security duty. He was promoted to sergeant and placed in charge of the Port Section of the Guard. After less than a year on station, orders arrived to report to Staging Battalion, Camp Pendleton, California in July 1966 for further transfer to 1st Marine Division and the Republic of South Vietnam. In the fall of 1966 he joined 2nd Platoon G Company, 2nd Battalion, 5th Marine Regiment and remained with that unit until May 1967 when he was medivaced to Japan for 35 days for further surgery and treatment. After medical recovery, he was sent to Fitzsimons US Army Hospital in Denver Colorado where he was attached to I&I staff, 15th Self Propelled 155 Gun Battery from June 1967 until May 1968. He received his Staff Sergeant chevrons in April 1968. In August 1968 he joined Staging Battalion at Camp Pendleton as permanent staff processing personnel who were deploying to Vietnam. In November 1970 Dale transferred to Marine Barracks NNSY Portsmouth, Virginia as the Personnel Chief and received a promotion to Gunnery Sergeant. In November 1974 he was transferred to Headquarters III MAF in Okinawa and joined the Commanding General's staff as Administrative Assistant. During that assignment, he was involved with Frequent Wind, Eagle Pull and the Mayaguez incident.

In December 1975 Dale was assigned to Headquarters Marine Corps for duty as Admin Chief to Gen Louis H. Wilson Jr, 26th Commandant of the Marine Corps. In December 1978 he was transferred to U.S. Naval Force, Korea for duty as Administrative Assistant to the C-5 Combined Forces Command, U.S. Forces, Seoul Korea. There he received a promotion to Master Sergeant. August of 1982, Dale reported to Marine Corps Base Camp Pendleton for duty with Schools Battalion as Personnel Officer and NCOIC of the Administrative School. He was promoted to Master Gunnery Sergeant, then reassigned to Base Inspector's Office in 1987 as Duty Base Inspector until he retired in September 1991. Dale considers his Marine Corps career as, "Lots of fun and an education that money could not buy."

After his retirement, he accepted a position in the security department at SCE Nuclear Power Plant in San Onofre, California. After a reduction in force there in 1995, Dale worked for a private security company in Oceanside California. In 1998 he became the proud owner and operator (with his lovely wife Carole) of the Sunny Deli in San Diego California. He works there every day and enjoys it tremendously. He has two sons, a daughter, and four grandchildren.

WILLIAM FRANCIS GAVIN

In 1964 after graduating from high school in St. Louis, Missouri, Bill enlisted in the "Platoon Leader's Class" at a local college. The PLC is a Marine Corps program for college students that leads to a commission as a 2nd lieutenant upon graduation. After the Marines landed at Danang in 1965, Bill thought he might miss the war, so he "flunked out" of college, triggering an automatic enlistment as a private. Five months later, he had attained the rank of PFC and was a 0311 rifleman with Third Squad, Third Platoon G Company, 2nd Battalion, 5th Marines.

In his own words he says, *"All I ever wanted to be was a Marine, have the honor of serving in combat and make the Corps my career. In Vietnam, the marines of Third Platoon became my new family and to this day they still are my family. We shared danger, death, mud, blood and everything else day and night, month after month in the jungles of Vietnam. The bond that we formed in combat was incredible and doesn't fade with time. Those marines are my brothers and those Marines who died over there will always remain alive in my memory as long as I live."*

On 8 May 1967 while walking point during Operation Union I in Antenna Valley, an enemy bullet blew out four inches of the femur in Gavin's right leg. It was a life-threatening arterial wound that Gavin survived partly due to the field medicine that Navy corpsman "Doc" Thacker applied before evacuation by helicopter. On 21 March 1968, the Marine Corps gave 21 year-old Corporal Bill Gavin a medical retirement. Years later, Bill Harvey, Third Platoon Commander, had this to say about Gavin's breed of warrior:

"He brought to the battlefield a special level of intellect which only complemented his innate skills as hunter and marksman. He was convinced he was good and sought to become better each day. He's a special guy, Bill. Anyone who would overlook a lifetime of medical neglect and still love the Marine Corps unconditionally has a personal constitution that puts him in a different league. He is a mountain of a man who was never given the gratitude he deserves."

His dream of a Marine Corps career shattered by an AK-47 bullet, Bill found work in St. Louis as a bank guard then a sporting goods salesman. But neither job satisfied his hunger for challenge and service. Restless and enervated by the city, Bill married his childhood sweetheart Mary Jo in June 1970. Two months later they drove his truck to Alaska to start a new life as a professional hunting guide. The years rolled on and Alaska's wilderness beauty infused in him a sense of inner peace that somehow he'd lost along the way. Summers were filled with salmon and trout fishing and the spring and fall with grizzly hunting. After an adverse inner ear reaction to an antibiotic in 1995 affected his balance, he gave up the guide business. These days he lives in semi-retirement in Soldotna, Alaska with his second wife Fay and his bulldog Ace.

MARC GLASGOW

Marc entered the Marine Corps through the Officer Candidate School (OCS) program in March 1964. He received his commission as a second lieutenant, then attended The Basic School (TBS) at Quantico, Virginia for six months. While at TBS he played center for the Marine football team. His designation as MOS 1310 (heavy equipment engineer) led to his first assignment after TBS with an engineer platoon in 2nd Bn 22nd Marines. He then was selected to attend combat engineer school at Camp Lejeune, where he continued his football career. During the Dominican Republic crisis in 1965, Marc's assignment as base prosecutor of wayward Marines convinced him he wanted nothing to do with lawyering. He received his orders to 9th Engineers at Camp Pendleton in the Fall of 1965. His unit mounted out for Vietnam in late May or early June of 1966 then took 22 days to float across the Pacific from San Diego to Chu Lai, Republic of South Vietnam. Almost immediately, he received orders for a special mission with 7th Engineers in Danang: building the main supply route (MSR) south from Danang, through Dai Loc and An Hoa, to the coal mine at Nong Son. In October 1966 he volunteered for an infantry unit and soon found himself working for Captain John Gruner at Con Thien as platoon commander of 3rd Platoon G Company. After Operation Mississippi he became executive officer, then commanding officer of G Company. A short assignment in the "Bat Cave" with Major Esau carried him to his departure for "The World" in April 1967. He left active duty with the Corps on April 27, 1967 and four months later joined 3rd Bn 23rd Marines, a reserve unit in Cleveland. He remained with this outfit for 16 years. In 1981 he joined a mobilization training unit (MTU) where he received a promotion to Colonel. In 1984 he became OIC 4th District, MCRSC. His duties regularly took him to Twenty Nine Palms to train on mechanized task force operations. His retirement at the rank of Colonel in March 2001 marked a total service time of 36 years, 11 months, 18 days.

For the last 36 years Marc has been the co-owner (Vice President) of Stein, Inc., a steel mill slag contractor in Broadview Heights, Ohio. He is president of the Broadview Heights Council and the Brecksville-Broadview Heights Schools Foundation. He also is trustee of Easter Seals of Northeast Ohio. Marc lives in Brecksville, Ohio with his wife Gail. His daughter Erin will attain a degree in business in one year, then plans to attend Marshall Law School at Cleveland State. When autumn rolls around, Marc sallies forth into the crisp and colorful hardwood forests of New York, Ohio, Pennsylvania, and Alabama armed with a long gun or a hunting bow, stalking turkeys and deer. To his great relief, so far none of these critters has returned fire.

CHARLES GUTIERREZ

Charles enlisted in the Marine Corps March 29, 1964, went through boot camp at MCRD San Diego, then soon thereafter found himself floating across the Atlantic towards the Mediterranean Sea with Delta 1/8. A B-52 crash off the coast of Spain involving a nuclear weapon altered the mission. The squadron turned around and returned to Camp Lejeune. Preferring combat to yet another training phase at Camp Lejeune, Charles volunteered for Vietnam. He joined 2nd Platoon G Company 2/5 in March 1966 while it was deployed on Hill 65 at Chu Lai. Not long after the battalion moved to Con Thien, he contracted a bad case of malaria and was evacuated to the hospital ship Repose for a month. There he received a number of transfusions and lost 30 to 40 pounds of body weight. December 1, 1966 he had recovered sufficiently for reassignment to G Company, which at the time was conducting combat operations in the An Hoa TAOR. Charles was one of the first Marines to fall wounded in the ambush at Thon Bon (1). While recovering in the hospital at Danang, Chris Noel visited his ward Christmas morning wearing a mini skirt and singing carols. Following close on her heels, (perhaps to redeem their recently perverted souls) was the reverend Billy Graham. Charles has especially fond memories of Craig Valness, who was at his side during the ambush at Thon Bon (1), and Corporal Crum from Twin Forks, Kentucky who got wounded in December near Phu Lac (6). Since Crum was 26 years old, the Marines of 2nd Platoon called him "Pop." Charles' serious wounds required a medical transfer to Japan, then Travis Air Force Base, and finally to Balboa Hospital in San Diego. An infection in his leg required hospitalization until the end of 1967.

After leaving the Marine Corps in January 1968 as a Sergeant, Charles attended San Jose City College and received a AA degree. Then he transferred to San Jose State University and obtained a medical technician degree and a BS in microbiology. As if those academic credentials weren't prestigious enough, he went on to obtain a masters degree in microbiology at East Tennessee State University. He then attended medical school at Quillen College of Medicine, Johnson City, Tennessee. For 22 years he has been supervisor of the microbiology department at James Quillen VA Medical Center (Mountain Home) Tennessee.

In his spare time, Charles volunteers as a scientific advisor to a group that helps veterans who are suffering from Persian Gulf syndrome. His collection of 45s & LPs has reached 7000 records. Charles is the proud father of five children.

WILLIAM FRANCIS HARVEY

Bill was born in Rochester, Vermont, home of the Green Mountain Boys of Revolutionary War fame. After successfully passing the gantlets of elementary school and high school, he enrolled in the University of Vermont, (then Castleton State College) and entered the PLC program. He was commissioned a 2nd Lieutenant and began a six months course that ended in December 1966. By January of the following year he found himself  leading Third Platoon G Company, 2/5 in combat operations in the An Hoa TAOR. From November 1967 until January 1968 he served as S-3a of 2nd Battalion 5th Marines, then from February until May of that year as company commander of Hotel and Golf Companies. Bill's exploits during the battle for Hue are mentioned on page 221 in the book *Battle for Hue* by Keith William Nolan. After returning Stateside in 1968, Bill served as platoon commander and S-3 of the 2nd Force Reconnaissance Company at Camp Lejeune, North Carolina from July 1968 until December 1969. From January until September 1970 he attended Amphibious Warfare School at Quantico, then was Company Commander of Kilo Company 3/5 from October to December of 1970 during a second tour in Vietnam. In January 1971 he became commander of Kilo Company 3/1. June of 1971 he returned to the States and was assigned as the Inspector-Instructor of Company D, 4th Reconnaissance Battalion in Albuquerque, New Mexico where he remained until August of 1974. From September 1974 until July 1977 he lent his considerable combat experience to students as Staff Platoon Commander (twice) and Company Commander (twice), at The Basic School, Quantico, Virginia. From 1977 until his retirement from the Marine Corps in 1987, Bill filled a variety of billets in different locations including Camp Smith, Hawaii, Quantico, Virginia, Okinawa, Japan, Camp Pendleton, California and Headquarters Marine Corps in Washington, D.C.

244

For three years after his retirement Bill managed a landscaping company in Bethesda, Maryland. For the next three years (until 1994) he managed an engineering company in Baltimore. From that time until the present he has worked as a stonemason in his hometown of Rochester, Vermont, specializing in Vermont fieldstone walls, flagstone patios and, occasionally, water features. By his calculation, he has built over two miles of stone walls and over two acres of patios. He is married to his high school sweetheart, Judy Pierce, with whom he spends most of his free time gardening, cross-country skiing and mountain biking. His two sons, Sean and Brit, live in Albuquerque, New Mexico. This past winter Brit and his wife Dusti, gave Bill and Judy their first grandson, Chance Harvey. He has three stepchildren: Doug, Sarah and Dan. Dan was a Marine for six years. Doug is still a Marine and, at the time of this writing, is an infantry platoon sergeant deployed in Operation Iraqi Freedom.

CHARLES F. MOHNEY

"Chip" Mohney joined the Marine Corps in August 1964. After boot camp and Infantry Training Regiment he served from December 1964 until April 1966 in Kilo Company, 3rd Bn. 8th Marines as an M-60 machine gun ammo carrier, then gunner, and team leader. Shortly after his promotion to Cpl Squad Leader, he received orders for Vietnam. A month at Staging Battalion Camp Pendleton led to an assignment in G 2/5 as the Third Squad leader, 3d Platoon. In March 1967 he became Section Leader of M60 machineguns. Mohney spent 2.5 months on the hospital ship U.S.S. Sanctuary recovering from wounds he sustained during operations around the An Hoa Combat Base in April 1967. Upon his return to G 2/5, he received his Sergeant's stripes. In July 1967 he rotated back to the States and was assigned to C Company 1st Bn. 2nd Marines as an M60 machinegun squad leader. After a Mediterranean cruise, he was transferred to Camp Geiger as a weapons instructor at Infantry Training Regiment. Aug 1968 Chip was discharged from the Marine Corps. His patriotism got the better of him and in October 1969 he reenlisted for a second tour in Viet Nam. This time he was assigned to Hotel Company, 2nd Bn. 26th Marines and served as the platoon guide and acting platoon sergeant. When the 26th Marines returned to the states Mohney was transferred to Mike Company, 3rd Bn. 7th Marines, which occupied LZ Baldy. After 8 months back in country, he received orders for the 9th Marines in Okinawa. Upon his return to the states he was assigned to 1st Marine Division at Camp Pendleton.

Upon his promotion to Staff Sergeant in 1971, he was transferred to State Department duty, and consequently served as NCOIC Prague Czechoslovakia and then The Hague, Holland. He thoroughly enjoyed this "pre-terrorist" embassy duty. While in Prague, Chip met and married a Northern Irish girl to whom he still is married after 28 years. After State Department duty he was transferred to Mike Company, 3rd Bn. 4th Marines in Okinawa where he served as platoon sergeant. When he made Gunnery Sergeant, he served as the Company Gunny. Upon returning to the States he was assigned to 2nd FSSG Motor Transport Battalion as S-3 Operations Chief. He then received orders for drill instructor duty at Parris Island. Following graduation from DI School he joined the 3rd Recruit Training Battalion, then served as an instructor at Drill Instructor School where he received a promotion to 1st Sgt. After plum duty at Marine Barracks in Washington DC, it became his turn to serve the dreaded one-year unaccompanied tour in Okinawa. Later he spent most of a tour in Korea building hardbacks and doing roadwork with 9th Engineers Support Battalion: a real education for a grunt. After Korea he found himself assigned to OCS for the summer Platoon Leaders Class in Quantico Virginia. Then he was 1st Sgt of a military police company. He retired from the Marine Corps in December 1985.

Since retiring he has tried his hand at several occupations, including a stained glass studio that made custom stained glass windows, offered classes and sold supplies. He worked in construction in Canada for six years, but eventually patriotism lured him back to "the good old US of A." After several years of driving 18-wheelers and cement trucks, Chip works for a concrete and block-making plant. He is an accomplished amateur photographer specializing in birds. His work can be seen at www.birdhelpers.com.

JOHN PRESTON PETERSON

John grew up near the California Central Valley town of Stockton. After one semester of college, John enlisted in the Marine Corps for a period of two years. The recruiter told him he had a 99% chance of going to the infantry. In March 1966, John went off to boot camp in San Diego. After eight weeks of boot camp and another three months of infantry training, he got orders to the Second Marine Division at Camp Lejeune, North Carolina. However, things were heating up in South Vietnam and after a week, John found himself headed back to Camp Pendleton with orders to the Republic of South Vietnam. He arrived there in mid-September assigned to Echo Company, Second Battalion, Fifth Marine Regiment of the First Marine Division. After a number of combat operations in the An Hoa TAOR, John was wounded in the hip by a sniper's bullet on March 1, 1967. By early June he had recovered sufficiently to rejoin E Company and finish his tour in mid-October.

John was released from active duty with the Marine Corps in March of 1968. He decided to continue his education and started classes at the local community college in Stockton. He was interested in a career in law enforcement and, following the advice of one of his instructors, got a job in the Sacramento office of the FBI. While working as a clerical employee at the FBI office, he continued his education at Sacramento State College. In 1972, John was awarded a Bachelor's degree and was hired as an FBI agent pending successful completion of the FBI Academy located on the Marine Corps Base, Quantico, Virginia. During the next twenty-six years, John worked on numerous investigations in West Texas, Northern Virginia, and the San Francisco Bay Area. He had a leading role during the yearlong investigation of Soviet spy and former U.S. Navy warrant officer, John Walker in the mid-1980s. John finished a rewarding career with the FBI in 1998. He currently works in Carson City, Nevada, as a criminal investigator for the state Department of Public Safety. He has two grown daughters; one of whom is a U.S. Marine and the other is studying to go into the field of law enforcement.

Richard Allen Wilhite

A native of Kirksville, Missouri, Richard enlisted in the Marine Corps in August 1965 at the age of 17. He survived boot camp at MCRD in San Diego with Platoon 165, then advanced infantry training, then radio school. After graduation on December 20, 1965 as a 2531 radio operator, he received a promotion to Private First Class and was given boot leave for Christmas. He was such a gung ho Marine that he flew back to Camp Pendleton from his home several days early and reported in to the 2nd Battalion, 5th Marines, First Marine Division. Thirty days later he found himself in Okinawa training for combat in Vietnam. After Okinawa, Wilhite hit the beach at Danang, Republic of South Vietnam, then later was assigned as the battalion radio operator for Captain John Gruner, commanding officer of Golf Company. Wilhite, who was at Captain Gruner's side 24 hours a day for several months and several operations, still remembers Captain Gruner as a quiet man who kept to himself, but never panicked or lost control under adverse circumstances. In February 1967 Wilhite's combat tour ended and he rotated back to "The World."

After 30 days of home leave stateside, he reported back to Camp Pendleton and was assigned to Golf Battery 3/13 as a forward observer radio operator. A year of stateside duty, two promotions and the Tet offensive prompted him to volunteer

250

for another combat tour in Vietnam. That time he flew over with the 27th Marines. From February 1968 till August 30,1968 he called in artillery support fire missions for the grunts. One operation that stands out in his mind is operation Allen Brook where a lot of good Marines were lost. September of that year, Wilhite was assigned to the 12th Marine Regiment at Dong Ha, near the DMZ where he served as a radio operator until March 1969 when he returned to the States. Within a week of his return, he became a civilian and was on his way back home.

After his service in the Marines, Wilhite moved to Tulsa, Oklahoma and attended Spartan School of Aeronautics. He obtained an aircraft mechanic's license and began work on his pilot's license. He then attended Northeast Missouri University for a short time, got married and moved with his new wife Carolyn to Woodward, Oklahoma where he accepted a job with Sears, Roebuck and Company. For 18 years he worked as a catalog store manager, then owner for Sears Roebuck. He now works as a manager for an auto parts store in Liberal, Kansas. Two wonderful children have given him and his wife Carolyn four grandchildren, who fill every weekend these days. Richard's favorite pastime is working in the yard and landscaping.

IN MEMORIAM

These are representations of rubbings taken from the Vietnam War Memorial of brave G Company Marines who died in Vietnam.

PATRICK F CAMPBELL ◆
10-8-66

REGIS P DEBOLD ◆
10-12-66

LARRY J COX ◆
10-13-66

CARROLL J HEBERT ◆
11-29-66

DAVID M MILLS ◆
12-15-66

WAYNE E DAWSON ◆
12-19-66

ROGER W EDWARDS ◆
2-17-67

PHILIP J KIMPEL ◆
3-11-67

WAYNE T MILLER ◆

3-19-67

WILLIAM J O'BRIEN ◆

3-28-67

MICHAEL J HARE ◆

6-17-67

RUSSELL R ROULIER ◆

6-21-67

RAYMOND L ABBOTT ◆

8-2-67

PAUL C BERTOLOZZI ◆

8-2-67

ROBERT D DRAPER ◆

8-2-67

PATRICK B HOPPE ◆

8-2-67

JOHN K JOHNSON ◆

8-2-67

JAMES R MAJORS ◆

8-2-67

LARRY G SALISBERRY ◆

8-2-67

MICHAEL L TROMBLEY ◆

8-2-67

GENE H ELLIS JR ◆

8-14-67

GEORGE E PARTIN ◆

8-14-67

GLOSSARY

A-4 Skyhawk   A lightweight, single engine light attack and ground support aircraft. Nicknamed "scooter" by admiring pilots.

Air strike   Attack on a ground target by aircraft

AK-47   Soviet or Chinese assault rifle invented by Andre Kalashnikov

Amtrack   An armored amphibious tractor used to deliver troops from ships to the beach.

Arty   Short for artillery

ARVN   Army of the Republic of Vietnam (South Vietnamese army)

Bandolier   A canvas or cloth strap with pockets for clips of ammunition usually worn across the chest.

Battalion   A combat unit comprised of four rifle companies and a headquarters company: usually around 1000 personnel.

Bird Dog   A light aircraft used for aerial observation, usually a Cessna.

C-4   A white, putty-like explosive

C Rations   Canned combat rations for field operations. Also called C-Rats.

Capt.   Abbreviation for the rank of captain.

Charles, Charlie   American military slang for Viet Cong (military radio code Victor Charlie)

Chieu Hoi	A program administered jointly by the Americans and South Vietnamese military to encourage defections from communist units. Chieu Hois then worked as scouts for infantry units.
Chicom	Short for Chinese communist
Chinook	Boeing model CH-47 helicopter.
Chopper	Slang for helicopter
Click	Slang for kilometer
CO	Commanding Officer.
Col.	Abbreviation for the rank of colonel. Usually the commander of a regiment.
Concertina	Rolls of barbed wire used around fixed defensive positions.
Contact	Exchanging fire with enemy forces.
CP	Command Post.
Dike	Raised earthen boundary of a rice paddy, usually with a trail on the top.
Division	A military unit with three regiments, usually consisting of a total of 10,000 men.
DMZ	Demilitarized Zone.
Doc	Navy corpsman.
Enfilade fire	Fire directed down the long axis of a combat formation of soldiers.

F-4 (Phantom) A fighter-bomber used for bombing missions over North Vietnam as well as close air support for infantry units.

FAC   Forward Air Controller

Firefight   An exchange of gunfire with an enemy force.

Fire mission   A request for indirect large caliber support.

Fire Team   The smallest organized infantry unit in the Marine Corps—four Marines, one with an automatic weapon. Each squad contained three fire teams.

FO   Forward Observer.

Force Recon   Reconnaissance units attached under operational control of the division.

G-2   Intelligence unit at division or larger level.

G-3   Operations unit at division or larger level.

Grazing fire   Small arms fire that is low to the ground.

Grid Square   Vertical and horizontal navigation markings on a map comprising one kilometer by one kilometer.

Gunship   A helicopter fitted with attack armament.

H-34   Sikorsky UH-34 helicopter with a single main rotor.

H & I   Harassing and interdicting artillery or naval gunfire directed at suspected enemy positions.

Hamlet	A small cluster of homes in rural Vietnam comprising a village. Thus, the sixth hamlet in Phu Lac village would be called Phu Lac (6).
HE	High explosive.
Helipad	A solid landing surface for helicopters.
Ho Chi Minh Trail	A web of roads and trails constructed by the North Vietnamese Army to funnel troops and supplies to combat zones in the south. It extended from North Vietnam along the Laos and Cambodian borders all the way to Saigon.
Hootch	Slang for living quarters, whether bamboo or canvas.
HQ	Headquarters
I Corps	The northernmost of 4 U.S. military zones in South Vietnam.
Immersion foot	A foot condition characterized by sloughing off of skin, raw spots, and bleeding caused by prolonged exposure to moisture. Also known as trench foot.
Incoming	Enemy fire (usually indirect) directed at your position.
Jolly Green Giant	A large helicopter used in Vietnam for rescue operations.
KIA	Killed In Action.
K-Bar	A standard issue combat knife.
KC-130	Lockheed Hercules four engine cargo aircraft.
LAAW	Light anti-tank assault weapon. Shoulder-fired rocket launcher used against light armored

vehicles and bunkers.

LMG	Light machine gun.
LP	Listening post. A position manned by one or two Marines outside the perimeter wire to provide early warning of an enemy approach
LPH	Landing platform helicopter. A ship designed to accommodate combat helicopter operations
Lt.	Lieutenant
LZ	Landing zone
M-1	A 30-caliber carbine used by the U.S. military in World War II.
M-14	7.62mm combat rifle used by field Marines until the M-16 replaced it.
M-48	"Patton" medium tank used primarily in the Korean War.
M-60	7.62mm light machine gun
M-79	Single shot 40mm grenade launcher.
MACV	Military Assistance Command Vietnam. Headquarters for all military operations in Vietnam.
Main force	Well trained and well-equipped full-time Viet Cong units as opposed to local "du kich" or guerillas.
Maj.	Major
Medevac	Medical evacuation

MIA	Missing in action
MOS	Military occupational specialty
MP	Military police
Napalm	Jellied gasoline dropped in canisters from allied aircraft.
NCO	Non-commissioned officer. A rank awarded to senior enlisted personnel starting with sergeant.
Number one	Vietnamese slang for "the best"
Number ten	Vietnamese slang for "the worst"
NVA	North Vietnamese Army
O-1 Bird Dog	A light observation aircraft
OP	Observation post, usually established on high ground to observe enemy activity.
Op	Short for "operation"
PFC	Private first class
Point	The man at the front of the formation in a combat patrol
POW	Prisoner of War
PRC-25	"Prick twenty-five" or combat radio.
Punji stakes	Sharpened wooden or bamboo stakes placed at the bottom of a camouflaged hole to cause foot injuries.
Purple Heart	A U.S. medal awarded to military personnel who were wounded in combat.

PX   Post Exchange.

R & R   Rest and Relaxation. Any official furlough away from the combat zone.

RDP   Soviet light machine gun

Saddle up   An informal order to grab your gear and prepare to move out.

Sappers   Enemy soldiers specially trained in penetration of defensive positions and application of explosives to destroy bunkers, firing positions, personnel and equipment prior to a main infantry assault.

Satchel charge   An explosive charge carried in a bag or satchel by sappers.

Search and destroy   Combat operations by infantry units to locate and annihilate enemy units.

Sgt.   Sergeant

Short rounds   Large caliber shells that fall short of their target.

Short timer   Someone with less than a month left on his overseas tour.

Sitrep   Situation Report

SKS   A communist bloc 7.62mm standard infantry-issue automatic rifle

Smoke   A canister containing colored smoke used for marking ground positions for aircraft or other visual signaling purposes.

Spider hole   A concealed one-man fighting hole often used by the VC and NVA troops.

Spooky   AC-47 or AC 119 aircraft outfitted with Gatling guns and illumination flares used to support ground troops.

Spotter round A single artillery round fired to mark a position or determine target coverage for the artillery forward observer.

SSgt.   Staff sergeant

TAOR   Tactical Area of Responsibility.

TDY   Temporary Duty

Top   Slang for first sergeant.

VC   Viet Cong or communist guerilla.

WIA   Wounded in Action

WP or Willy Peter   White phosphorous grenade, mortar, or artillery round.

ORDER FORM

If you enjoyed this book and would like to purchase additional copies, please visit the web site www.baylaurelpress.com or fax this form to (415) 383-1812 for credit card orders. For payment by check, mail this form with your check or money order to the address listed below..

Name: _____

Street Address: _____

City: _____ State: _____ Zip: _____

Telephone Number: _____

Email (please print): _____

Payment by: Check ☐ Credit Card ☐

Credit Card Number: _____

Expiration Date: _____

Credit Card Type: Mastercard ☐ Visa ☐ Discover ☐ American Express ☐

Full Circle: A Marine Rifle Company in Vietnam
_____ Copies @ $16.95   Subtotal _____
California Residents Please Add $1.23 Per Book Sales Tax   _____
Shipping: USPS Priority Mail $5.00/first copy*,   _____
$3.50 each additional copy;
USPS Media Rate $2.00 first copy,
$0.75 each additional copy.

Total Enclosed (or charge my credit card above   _____

_____
Signature for Credit Card Purchase

Send completed order form and your check or money order to:

Baylaurel Press
775 E. Blithedale Ave. #251
Mill Valley, CA 94941
(415) 383-1812 fax
www.baylaurelpress.com
books@baylaurelpress.com

* International shipping is extra. Please contact us for the shipping rates to your location.